WINNING: *The Psychology of Competition*

Books by Stuart H. Walker

The Techniques of Small Boat Racing (ed.)
The Tactics of Small Boat Racing
Performance Advances in Small Boat Racing (ed.)
Wind and Strategy
Advanced Racing Tactics
Winning: The Psychology of Competition

WINNING: The Psychology of Competition

Stuart H. Walker

Illustrations by Thomas C. Price

W. W. Norton & Company • NEW YORK • LONDON

Copyright © 1980 by Stuart H. Walker
Published simultaneously in Canada
by George J. McLeod Limited,
Toronto. Printed in the United States of America.
All Rights Reserved
First Edition

Library of Congress Cataloging in Publication Data

Walker, Stuart H
    Winning, the psychology of competition.

    Bibliography: p.
    1. Competition (Psychology) I. Title.
BF637.C47W34   1980   158'.1   79–27032
ISBN 0–393–03255–8

Designed by Mary A. Brown

1 2 3 4 5 6 7 8 9 0

To Frances Walker

The Best Wife a Competitor Could Have
            and

To Nathan Schnaper

The Best Friend a Competitor Could Have

Contents

Preface

I HAVE WRITTEN THIS BOOK FOR THE SAME REASON THAT I WROTE each of my previous books—I recognized a major factor in the attainment of competence that has hitherto not been adequately understood. An extensive study of techniques, tactics, and strategy has only served to convince me that something else is more important, that the outcome of competition cannot be explained or determined by an understanding of these elements alone. Psychological factors, what competition means to the competitor, seem to be far more significant.

My interest in psychology derives in part from my professional activities. As a teacher of medicine, I am aware, and attempt to make my students aware, of the psychological determinants of behavior. I have been involved in the psychiatric treatment of many psychological disturbances. I have read and consulted extensively with my psychiatric colleagues in regard to the psychological observations I have made. I believe that my understanding of the inexact science of psychology is consistent with that of my colleagues who are more expert in the field and that my observations extend the ability of psychology to explain the behavior of competitors.

The book is designed to explain why winners win, why losers lose—and why everyone else finishes in the same position time after time. It demonstrates that psychological factors are the major determinants of success and failure. I hope that winners will be as fascinated by this exposition as losers—but I doubt that they will. Winners are infrequently concerned with books or with beliefs, and in part because they are already winning, they are not interested in why they are doing so. The book is an explanation of what exists, but it will be read largely by those who wish to alter what exists, who wish to win instead of lose.

In addition to observations deriving from my personal experience, many anecdotes recounted in magazines, newspapers, and books are included. In some instances I have had to rely upon interpretations made by others, or upon limited information, in explaining the behavior described, but usually its origin is obvious. I have utilized examples from both professional and amateur competition. My experience with professional athletes makes me doubt that they differ greatly from amateurs. I believe their greater concern for outcome and the money that depends upon outcome merely adds to the extraneous pressure perceived by all competitors, and does not constitute a qualitative difference.

Some years ago, by means of a questionnaire, I made a survey of the motivation of my sailing competitors. The questionnaire was designed to evaluate the significance of nine major factors in determining competence: aggressiveness, self-control, realistic appraisal, self-confidence, trusting, determination, conscientiousness, high-goal setting, and leadership. I discovered that there was little difference between world-class and local competitors in how they perceived themselves. The differences that did exist were only in intensity, and there was much overlapping of the results for the two groups. The scores of the successful sailors tended to be high over the entire range of tested attributes but were seldom extremely high for any particular one. This result is probably consistent with the wide range of skill and understanding required for successful sailboat racing. World-class competitors may be characterized as well rounded and not burdened by any extreme motivation. The insight provided by the survey is discussed in the text where pertinent.

According to the principle of the conservation of psychic energy, every action is used for multiple psychological purposes. Therefore, my explanation for a given element of behavior is clearly only one (though usually the most important) of many possible explanations. In a few instances, I have used the same anecdote to reveal two different motivations. The particular behavior discussed may in addition illustrate a response to some other psychological influence of which I am unaware.

To achieve a coherent and understandable presentation of competitive behavior, I have had to organize the book into obviously artificial segments. It is not possible to isolate the particular elements of behavior completely, so that one of them is, say, an example of a loss of control of impulsivity, while another is an example of intellectualization. I hope that despite the categorization the reader will recognize that the explanation given is not necessarily the only valid one.

The organization I have used is partly adapted from Eric Berne's concept of the psyche as including a Child, an internalized Parent, and an Adult. The Child represents what survives of the impulsive, assertive, power-seeking, but fearful and threatened infant. The Parent represents the internalization of the restrictive, guilt-engendering parental behavior observed during early life. The Adult represents the ego functions, acquired during development toward maturity, which are necessary to autonomous existence. The book is divided into sections. The first discusses general psychological concepts as they relate to competition. Three major sections discuss behavior derived chiefly from the Child, the Parent, and the Adult. The discussion of Adult behavior is further divided in accordance with the ego functions pertinent to competition: control of the Child and the Parent; appraisal of external reality; self-appraisal; memory, attention, and conception; and the management of intrapersonal relationships. The use of defenses to protect the ego from unacceptable pain (anxiety or guilt) and the attainment of courage and mastery are discussed in the final two sections.

Each section includes a presentation of both the benefits and the detriments resulting from the presence, disturbance, or absence of particular attributes. I have tried to avoid indicating what should or should not be done. But since most competitors are seeking to enhance their competence, I have indicated which attitudes and responses will help them in that respect and which will be detrimental. Since enjoyment should result from efforts to attain competence, and competence from feelings of enjoyment, I have treated the motivations toward these two as synonymous. I have avoided indicating that a given behavior will directly increase the likelihood of winning or of losing, for attainment of the one and avoidance of the other is adversely affected by any direct concern with either. If competence is attained, winning will follow.

The book has been written for competitors and is intended to help them better to understand themselves and better to enjoy what they are doing. Competition is an important part of their lives and should be a source of greater satisfaction than they often allow it to be. To the extent that they understand themselves and improve their control of themselves, they will attain competence (control of their game), and competence leads to courage, creativity, and fun. Lack of understanding and lack of control lead to fear, depression, and incompetence—and no fun. Competition is too good to waste.

WINNING: *The Psychology of Competition*

Part One

Competitive Behavior

1 / Competing

It is courage the world needs, not infallibility
. . . courage is always the surest wisdom.
—WILFRED GRENFELL

COMPETENT GAME PLAYING LEAVES NO LASTING MONUMENTS, NO AR-
tistic treasures, no musical compositions. Yet the display of excellence in competition, though ephemeral, is no less important and
no less satisfying to the creator and the observer than it is in the other
arts. A player enters a world of challenge, risk, and uncertainty and
for a few moments re-creates it in accordance with his own design. He
displays a unique statement of his presence, influences the course and
outcome of an untold story, and alters the behavior of his fellow competitors.

In few activities other than competition can a participant find a
similar opportunity to assert his unique significance and simultaneously attain approval from the people he most respects. For his
competitors become the people who mean the most to him. Their
shared respect for the game and for the significance of involvement in
it make them the most valued judges of his accomplishments. He

3

wants both the opportunity they provide him to display his competence and their approval.

Competition at its best is the greatest of the performing arts. At its worst it is mere grubbing about for the approval of the mob. For most of us, competitors and spectators alike, it is something in between, intermittently joyous and exhilarating but often demanding, tension-producing, and distressing. We enter competition to please ourselves and end up struggling to please others.

Most competitors think of themselves as being primarily motivated to develop, demonstrate, and enjoy competence. Many, however, are also concerned with the demonstration of power, courage, and aggressiveness. They use competition to overcome feelings of dependence, helplessness, and loss of individuality. Others are more concerned with being approved, appreciated, and admired. They use competition to overcome feelings of being separated, abandoned, and unloved. Competition permits the demonstration of individual significance which gratifies desires for both assertiveness and approval. The key word is "demonstration." Competitors perform in public; they assert themselves in the presence of others—of their competitors at the very least.

Winning is the object of the game, so competitors attempt to win. They want to impress their competitors, to be admired for their success in meeting the requirements set for them. They are pleased with themselves when they "look good"—when they win—and they feel disappointed, distressed, when they fail to do so. But though they profess (and often believe) that winning is all important, and though the "how-to" literature is filled with recommendations on ways of doing so, winning is not the main concern of most competitors. Few actually win; few would compete if winning were their primary motivation. (Indeed, one could make a far stronger case for losing as a primary motivation.) Even winners—perhaps winners in particular—are characterized by a desire to demonstrate competence; winning is a by-product, satisfying because it fulfills both the need to demonstrate competence and the need to be approved.

Competition is characterized by a variety of paradoxes which derive from the difficulty of satisfying at once a wish to demonstrate aggressive individuality and a wish to be approved and protected. Many psychological needs are served by a single action, and each response to a stimulus represents the sum of myriad desires. Often simultaneously, and at least alternately, the competitor seeks opposing goals. He wants to have his cake and eat it too. He wants to be daring, and he wants to be careful. He wants to expose himself, and he wants to hide. He delights in risk and uncertainty—early in the race—and resents it later on. He desires victory and feels undeserving if he achieves it. He wants to fight *and* to flee, to charge *and* to escape.

He seeks freedom, unrestrained opportunity for assertiveness, *and* structured restriction in accordance with the rules of the game—to satisfy both the Child and the Parent within him. He wishes for certainty, preparing himself so as to assure a victory, *and* for uncertainty, delighting in surprises. He desires to learn, to gain from each experience, *and* also to be fully knowledgeable, to be an expert. He wants to win, to attain success, but also to perpetuate the joy of striving toward that success. He wants to display courage *and* to reduce risk and hedge against the possibility of loss. Alternately or simultaneously he wants to conquer his enemies *and* please his friends. He wants to deserve his victory, to win with difficulty, *and* to win with certainty, with ease. He professes always to wish to win, but he often wishes to lose.

Because the competitor's motivation is mixed, because he attempts to prove the opposite of what exists or to attain the opposite of what he seems to desire, his responses are often paradoxical and confusing even to him. Some competitors are angered by success, complacent in defeat. Some feel satisfaction in depression, anxiety in elation. Guilt is aroused by victory, allayed by disaster. The outcome achieved is often the reverse of that consciously intended: the need to win diminishes the chances for succes; the effort to concentrate obstructs concentration; the desire to be consistent leads to inconsistency. Hence it is not surprising that understanding the competitor's behavior is so difficult for the observer—and is often clearly impossible for the competitor himself.

Essentially, the competitor seeks action for its own sake regardless of the outcome. He wishes to be distinguishable—whether as a winner or as a loser. He feels the urge to cause, to stimulate, to create. He seeks situations that will affect him and that he will affect, that provide the opportunity for a response, whether beneficial or detrimental. He delights in risk, in uncertainty, in challenge, in surprise. He wishes to sense life, preferring pain to lack of sensation and failure to lack of trial. He is courageous; he accepts the risk, even the probability, of failure in order to realize the possibility of the perfect performance.

Each of us desires to assert his individuality, to establish himself as distinctive, to be recognized as special, to expose his true self. But at the same time each of us feels the opposing desire to be secure, protected, loved, hidden. Otto Rank characterizes these feelings as "death fear" and "life fear." "Death fear" is the fear of losing one's self, one's distinctiveness, one's independence—of complying, of accepting the world as it is without leaving a mark upon it. "Life fear" is the fear of being separate, abandoned, unloved—of risking a change. All of us oscillate between these extremes, usually remaining far from either end of the spectrum.

The infant, dependent upon those who care for him, discovers at an early age that his aggressiveness is threatening, and by age three, to avoid the anxiety this behavior precipitates, markedly limits it. Thereafter, he develops a pattern of controlled, less assertive behavior which he feels will be acceptable to his parents. He acquires guilt, an uncomfortable feeling that appears whenever his aggressiveness *or* his passivity is in excess of that in his ideal pattern. (Guilt, the awareness of sin, is probably not innate, but rather acquired at a very early age.) One consequence, for most of us, is that whenever we are particularly aggressive we feel some guilt. According to Rollo May, many people have a sense that creativity "offends the gods"; they experience an inexplicable guilt when they are creative. Creators may be yearning for immortality, competitors only for victory, but they share an awareness of guilt when they succeed.

During competition, the participant exposes his talent, skill, and intellect to his competitors and/or the spectators for their applause or ridicule. He feels tense, anxious, fearful at the prospect of the exposure, and breathes a sigh of relief as he escapes into hiding at its completion. If he fails, he employs some defensive technique to avoid additional exposure; if he wins, he maintains the exposure, often flaunting his success. Australian Soling sailor David Forbes, after a poor showing at the 1976 Olympics, told me, "We'll have to do better before we can show ourselves in the bar!" The elation of victory is due in part to the joy of escape from the exposed condition and the satisfaction that one dared the exposure and "got away with it."

Assertiveness is often counterphobic; it represents a need to observe oneself being assertive and exposed, thus denying the need to be protected, dependent, hidden. Competitive exposure is daring, often frightening. The competitor risks loss of approval, abandonment, if he fails. But success is also threatening, for to attempt the godlike behavior required for winning revives old fears that originated in power struggles with parents. Competition is a means of denying that one is affected by such fears of abandonment or exposure. But many an individual protests too much, taking on any competition, in any condition, again and again. And *some are never satisfied*—never able to convince themselves that their fears do not exist.

Only in games are some competitors able to act out their counterphobia, to dare exposure of their aggressiveness or to risk revealing their unacceptable need for protection. When the game is used to solve real-world problems, the boundaries between reality and fantasy often disappear. The daring competitor says, "Come and watch me. If I look good, I hope you'll think this performance represents the real me. If I look bad, I know you'll recognize, as I do, that it's only a game!"

Competition serves one additional purpose. It appeals to the Parent within, the Parent that tells us we should get what we deserve. The structure of competition serves this end. Those who work hard, develop their skills, spend their money, should win (and usually do); and those who don't, should lose (and usually do). Losing frequently provides an opportunity for self-punishment—which is *always* felt to be deserved. And winning provides an opportunity for guilt—which is *always* felt to be deserved. The winner reacts like the survivor of the almost annihilated platoon or the shipwreck: "Why me? Poor them. (How guilty I feel; how undeserved was my salvation.)" Competition permits the aggressive not only to display their aggressiveness but to atone for it as well!

Satisfaction in competition is achieved either by displaying individual excellence (as competence or courage) *or* by gaining approval. The competitor wishes to fulfill both his need to be special and distinctive and his need to be accepted and secure. An excellent performance reassures him concerning his significance; victory reassures him concerning his security. If he gains both, he is joyous. However, only performance is under the control of the individual competitor; winning is not. If winning is required for satisfaction, the competitor will often be disappointed. Performance can be improved and competence can be gained; satisfaction, during both the striving for excellence and the demonstration of it, will necessarily follow. The acquisition of competence provides both the expectation of future success and the strength to withstand the disappointments which inevitably arise from poor performance and from losing. When competence is acquired, winning will follow sooner or later—and the ultimate but fortunately unattainable goal, the perfect performance combined with the impossible victory, becomes conceivable.

2 / Personality Development

You have to love a sport to play it well and love grows out of enjoyment.

—JACK NICKLAUS

A PERSON WHO ACTS SOLELY IN HIS OWN INTEREST IS CONSIDERED SELF-ish or childish; one who, at the other extreme, acts solely in the interest of others is considered inhibited or submissive. A mature adult achieves an appropriate balance between these needs, acting in his own best interests without infringing upon the rights of others. He accepts responsibilities and limitations without anger or resentment and seeks personal satisfaction without experiencing guilt.

Many psychologists represent the conflict between the need to please oneself and the need to please others as occurring between a Child that persists within the adult personality and a Parent that has been internalized. The degree to which the Child in the personality continues to be manifest depends upon the parental behavior to which the person was exposed as a child. A submissive, indulgent parent may permit the continued expression of impulsive, inconsistent behavior, while an overbearing, punitive parent may inhibit the expression of selfish, "childish" wishes. Dominance by the Child is manifested by persistence of the fears of early childhood—fears of being helpless in the face of threatening, all-powerful beings—and persistence of the need to assert independence, distinction, and significance in opposition to that threat of helplessness. Dominance by the Parent is manifested by persistence of the fears of later childhood—fears of being abandoned, unloved, and unacceptable—and persistence of the need to be compliant, appreciated, and approved so as to counteract the guilt that failure arouses.

Every infant demands to be fed, held, and satisfied. In most instances and in most cultures, during the early months of his life, his demands are fully and immediately met. Ultimately, however (usually by the end of his first year), his parents cease to comply with his every wish and the baby finds that, increasingly and frighteningly, he is in conflict with his erstwhile servants. In the second and third years of life, the struggle for power is open and unremitting. The child refuses to comply with parental demands (his typical response is "no"); he is enraged (has a "temper tantrum") when he is directly thwarted; and he resorts to a variety of "neurotic" techniques (ritualism, compulsion) related to feeding, sleeping, toilet training, and the like. This behavior is designed to avoid recognition of his relative helplessness and to ward off the overwhelming fright that accompanies this recognition. With the internalization of the Parent into the child's personality, beginning at about age three, self-imposed limitation, self-discipline, appears. Thereafter, the child attempts to please his parents, particularly the parent of the opposite sex, by patterning his behavior after the behavior he perceives in the parent of the same sex. The power struggle is no longer overt, a matter of "me against the world"; it is transformed into a covert attempt to displace one parent by gaining the exclusive love and attention of the other.

The child gradually adopts a pattern of behavior that he believes will be pleasing to this parent and to others. He expects that to the extent that he follows this pattern, he will be sheltered from direct conflicts, which he has learned he is bound to lose, and hence be protected against the fear that awareness of conflict arouses. He obtains reassurance that he is loved (safe) and that he remains powerful (able to determine his actions and control his environment). The pattern of behavior that is internalized (the Parent) is largely copied from his parent's actual behavior as observed during childhood and adolescence (although the parent's teachings may also be internalized). The child henceforth demonstrates a desire to please, a wish to be approved, awareness of a standard of right and wrong, a conscience: he must hereafter either behave in a manner that is socially acceptable or suffer feelings of guilt. During the early teen years, the assertive Child again becomes dominant, but the Parent persists, and assumes at least equivalent, often dominant, stature in maturity.

In early adolescence an Adult begins to form within the psyche. The Adult is an internalization of the behavior observed in adult models, modified by the recognition of the significance of cause and effect in interpersonal relationships. It replaces impulsivity and fear with reason. It conceptualizes and stimulates behavior in the long-term best interests of the individual.

Mediation of acceptable compromises in struggles for control between Child, internalized Parent, and Adult depend upon the development of the ego. The ego senses the desires of the Child, the requirements of the Parent, and the intentions of the Adult and determines the behavior, the responses, the actions most appropriate to these mixed perceptions. The ego remembers feelings engendered in the past and organizes perceptions and remembrances into unified, realistic attitudes. It deals with basic questions involving behavior: Will it be better to act in accordance with innate desires—get what's in it for me?—or to avoid infringing upon the rights of others? Will the contemplated action cause me subsequently to feel guilty, or am I forgoing it unnecessarily because of a fear of that guilt? The ego becomes a computer that organizes, evaluates, and judges internal feelings and chooses appropriate responses.

The feelings and drives of the Child and the Parent persist into adult life in all of us. We all continue to be assertive and to wish to be approved. In some individuals, however, these feelings and drives find expression as compelling needs. The Child fear of helplessness and dependence may be seen in a compelling need to be assertive, an obligation to demonstrate dominance. This may mean that, to avoid overt anxiety, whenever the individual is opposed he will be obliged to behave in the manner typical of a two-year-old, to engage in a battle. The Parental requirement that one behave in an approved manner may be seen in a compelling need to be approved, to abide scrupulously by parental dictates, to be deserving. When an individual with this need faces the risk of failure or fails to behave in accordance with parental standards, he feels guilt. If the Child or the Parent retains excessive dominance of the adult personality, the ego is handicapped by recurring anxiety or guilt.

How well the developing ego resolves the struggle of the child to assert his individuality, his independence, his power, how well it enables him to handle his desire to displace one parent and gain the exclusive attention and/or affection of the other, determines how he will behave in interpersonal relationships in the future. If his ego attains an appropriate degree of control over Child and Parent and enhances the development of the Adult, he will be able to retain a feeling of self-respect, of personal significance, while accepting the need to limit his behavior so as not to infringe upon the rights of others. Unfortunately, few reach this state of maturity, of mental toughness. When in later life conflict with another person develops, old fears concerning loss of omnipotence or displacement of "father" may be reawakened. Most adults, either because their childhood power struggles could not be resolved or because their internalized Parent restricts their ability to deal with conflicts, recurrently display inappropriate responses in interpersonal relationships.

Every adult personality reflects, to varying degrees, each of the three states—Child, Parent, and Adult. A varied, satisfying, and successful life is possible only if all three are expressed. But the Adult—a realistic computer—should be in over-all command. To obviate the necessity of analyzing every trivial action, the Adult should delegate authority to the Parent to manage routine, automatic, traditional matters. The Child should be freed to feel—to experience joy, fun, gratitude, appreciation, tenderness, love, accomplishment, victory, as well as pain, sadness, fear, and loneliness—and to act spontaneously. In the Child reside creativity, intuition, aggressiveness, determination, and natural responsiveness.

Because much of modern life is routine, requiring automatic responses, and this day-to-day activity is managed by the Parent, the beliefs and positions of the internalized Parent become increasingly ingrained. Constant preoccupation with Parental concerns tends to restrict the expression of the Child, so that even in play during which the Child should be released, the Parent often remains in charge, inhibiting, restricting, censuring. Spontaneity, awareness, and enjoyment may be lost or markedly diminished.

The stages in the evolution of game playing parallel those in the development of an individual. At first the participants join in the game for fun, to play together. The Child "don't know no better," so competition can be undertaken without tension, without concern for the outcome. In time, however, the competitors begin to restrict themselves, censure themselves, inhibit themselves—to assure victory, a finish ahead of their usual position. For example, instead of being an all-out fling, with joy in the risk and the uncertainty, the start of a sailboat race will be "conservative," with the participants attempting to cover and to plan for each leg. Development should continue beyond this stage: in a game it is appropriate for the Child to be in the ascendance; The attainment of autonomy, the ultimate state of ego development, should permit the full play of the Child, under the protective supervision of the Adult. Once the fundamentals have been learned (in accordance with Parental restrictions), security and confidence develop. Thereafter, as the personality is liberated from excessive intervention, improvisation and creativity become possible. Successful and satisfying performance requires mental toughness—control by the Adult when decisions are required, release by the Adult of the Child when sensitivity and spontaneity are appropriate, and delegation of authority by the Adult to the Parent when, but only when, automatic responsiveness is sufficient. High levels of performance require both the Child *and* the Parent, both a fearless sweep down a planing reach *and* a carefully managed series of tacks utilizing every shift on the weather leg, both a smashing serve *and* a top-spin lob.

3 / Defenses and the Playing of Ulterior "Games"

Minds are like parachutes. They only function when they are open.

—THOMAS ROBERT DEWAR

THE PSYCHE (THE PERSONALITY AS A WHOLE) IS CHARACTERIZED BY A system of checks and balances, techniques to diminish or negate painful feelings. Actions and the contemplation of actions that have survival value—eating, sleeping, manifestations of creativity, mastery, or courage—are pleasing and result in elation. Actions and the contemplation of actions that are presumed to diminish the chances of survival—aggression in the face of overwhelming opposition, noncompliance with Parental demands, socially unacceptable behavior—are frightening and result in depression. Except for short periods, pain, fear, a sense of being threatened, and depression are unacceptable to the ego. Because such feelings are distracting and preoccupying, they would in themselves, if allowed to persist, diminish chances for survival. The psyche therefore resorts to defenses against them. The result is the restoration of attention to external reality and of control of behavior at the expense of specific deficiencies in the appraisal of reality and in internal control.

13

The defenses by which the ego is protected might be described as various kinds of magic. They deny reality—assign responsibility for an action to someone other than its actual originator, attribute observed phenomena to godlike intervention or "luck." They may require that the individual act in opposition to his true long-term interests, perhaps actually causing him to surrender, run away, or defeat himself without being aware that he is doing so. They may cause him to rationalize and intellectualize or, as we shall see, to create a "game" with which to be preoccupied so that he will be unable to recognize the threatening aspects of the real world around him. The magic usually works. The psyche feels at ease, relaxed, free of pain, anxiety, or guilt—at the cost, however, of an unawareness, an irrationality, that impairs some aspects of performance, competitive or otherwise.

From early life our Parent forces us to take up certain positions, to present ourselves in accordance with certain predetermined patterns. Adoption of these positions is one means of avoiding the perception of a threat or the initiation of an action that would be frightening. We work very hard to stabilize these positions, perfecting our required roles. The role Nice Guy, for example, is played assiduously by the person who feels that to be accepted one must be attentive, concerned, and forgiving. Many competitors, are more involved in playing Nice Guy than they are in performing well. To maintain such positions requires certain rituals, in this instance open, candid efforts to demonstrate Nice Guy-ness and elicit stroking from others who appreciate Nice Guy-ness.

Sometimes we may find that our positions are difficult to stabilize, fail to provide the requisite protection, or are inconsistent with other psychic needs. Then, according to Eric Berne, in *Games People Play,* we resort to the playing of "games"—that is, we repetitiously undertake certain standardized transactions with one or more other people for an ulterior purpose and with the expectation of a pay-off.

Just as a confidence "game" requires the co-operation of a victim, so these "games" require a co-operating partner. Because psychic needs are so variable, there is almost always someone available whose own "game" makes him willing to act in this capacity. From early childhood each of us selects playmates, companions, spouses, business associates, who have a readiness to play our "game." We gravitate to activities in which suitable partners will be found. For example, people interested in playing one role or the other in "Winners and Losers" tend to enter into competition. It should be noted, by the way, that in this instance the Winner is not necessarily the actual winner of the race, since the "game" may be played between any of the competitors, with victory determined by their relative position at the finish.

"Games" played by competitors may be regarded as appropriate if their pay-off is consistent with enhanced performance and winning, and as inappropriate if their pay-off requires diminished performance or losing. But playing any "game" detracts from playing *the* game, diminishes awareness of the pleasure of participation and the determinants of success, and often requires behavior inimical to the real interests of the player.

One common "game" played by competitors—a derivative of the pastime "Look Ma No Hands" described by Eric Berne—illustrates the characteristics of "games" in general. It is appropriate—that is, its pay-off is consistent with winning. The pay-off is protection against the fear of losing. As is typical in "games," however, the need to play this one frequently blocks victory in the actual game. One advantage of "Look Ma No Hands" is the avoidance of defeat: "They didn't beat me, I wasn't competing in their game. Instead of playing *the* game, I was playing my game." There is the appearance of mastery: "I was not defeated. I determined the outcome." Another advantage is reassurance about self-control, self-determination, and stature. The "game" also protects against fears concerning the assumption of responsibility: "Even if I win, I didn't intend to; you [the Parent] can't blame me for usurping your position." Another advantage is the implication of superiority: "I'm uncommitted to this trivial activity." And there is the guarantee of winning regardless of the actual outcome: "If I win I have achieved an extraordinary victory inasmuch as I really wasn't trying; if I lose, I've demonstrated my superiority, as I wasn't committed anyway."

In the fact that they play "games" competitors are no different from anyone else. However, the "games" they choose tend to be different from those chosen by noncompetitors, and more obviously detrimental. An individual sport such as sailboat racing attracts "game" players because the disguise of their ulterior intents is facilitated by the imprecision, the indeterminate nature, of the sport. However, although the "game" itself may go undetected, its effect is always evident. The purpose of competing is to demonstrate competence and to win. The purpose of "game" playing is to attain an unrelated pay-off, and to the extent that such a pay-off is sought, performance suffers.

A strong ego—one in which a strong Adult is in control—maintains an awareness of its own internal workings that precludes the playing of ulterior "games"; the Child and Parent are under sufficient control so that "games" are neither attempted nor needed. An ego of lesser strength, too severely threatened by the fear of helplessness or abandonment and unable to face the overt pain of anxiety or guilt, may erect a protective defense, a manipulation of reality, such as the creation of a "game." Though the competitor's performance may suffer less than it would if he were harassed by overt anxiety, defenses are nonetheless detrimental. They require a denial of reality, behavior that conforms to the protective intention regardless of whether or not such behavior is appropriate to the attainment of competence or success.

4 / The Attainment of Competence

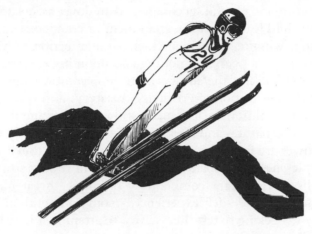

Success is simply the extension and utilization of an entire series of failures.

—BRUCE C. OGILVIE

JACK NICKLAUS SAYS THAT AT ABOUT THE AGE OF TEN HE DISCOVERED that "hitting a ball well was a lot more fun than hitting it badly, which made me want to get better at it as quickly as possible." This desire to perform better must be a fundamental human feeling. The attainment of competence, at least in primitive societies, is a prerequisite to survival. It is not surprising that we find both the striving toward competence and the demonstration of it enjoyable—and that once we attain it we cannot refrain from demonstrating it again and again.

Nicklaus also says, "Whichever way you choose to guide a child, be sure to impart a sense of fun. At first, that will almost certainly lie simply in hitting—or hitting at—a golf ball. Once it begins to fly upward and forward, the child who doesn't want to compete with his new skill is rare indeed." The pleasure associated with the attainment of competence, and the drive that is thereby engendered, lead directly to competition. Competition is the most direct route to competence.

Everyone competes. Infants compete with everything outside

themselves for the attention of their parents and the control of their world. Children compete with one parent for the affection of the other. Older children compete with one another for the approval of their teachers. Each child competes with his peers for admiration, praise, appreciation. In most families and most childhood situations, this competition is playful, accompanied by love, associated with respect. The child learns that the attainment of competence is fun in itself and that winning is incidental, that the affection of his parents, the approval of his peers, do not depend upon his success or failure. For such a child, and the adult whom he becomes, competition is a satisfying demonstration of creativity, mastery, and courage.

But some children are less successful in recognizing that competitive behavior is natural and pleasing. They may find early that struggles for power are frightening and that failure leaves them with a feeling of helplessness and isolation. Thereafter, in similar situations, the same feelings reappear; competition becomes threatening. Many adults who have had such experiences avoid competition; others are enticed by it, seeking to test themselves, to attempt at long last a satisfying resolution of the frightening relationship.

Within the adult personality of some competitors, the feelings and fears of the Child persist and demand reassurance concerning independence and significance, evidence of power, proof of safety. Competition may then be used to obtain reassurance or to demonstrate power. Or it may be used for the reliving of childhood struggles with authority, with rivals, with leaders, or of childhood campaigns to gain approval, recognition, and affection. Some of us seem to be forced, willy-nilly, to retrace our previous course when a similar situation appears ("symbolically") in later life. Such "acting out" unfortunately never succeeds in providing a new solution. It results, instead, merely in a repetition of what happened before, with the same unsatisfactory, anxiety-provoking outcome. The symbolic situation is recognized (unconsciously), pain or fear is aroused, a response—attack, surrender, escape, paralysis—occurs, and for minutes or hours afterward, preoccupation with the incident persists. The advertent or inadvertent utilization of competitive activity for such purposes diminishes the overt satisfaction it supplies and detracts from the attainment of competence.

Just as many individuals enter into competition for ulterior Child purposes, so many enter because of (or in defiance of) ulterior Parental demands. Their internalized Parent requires that their behavior conform to standards, established in childhood, which have become increasingly stabilized, confirmed, and structured. They may need to compete in order to demonstrate, in the face of Parental skepticism, their competence, or to gain the approval they never received as children. If Parental restrictions are not honored meticulously, old fears of disapproval and loss of affection are aroused. Because of the belittling of their Parent they may feel undeserving, and to atone for their undeserved victories they are sometimes forced to lose. Needing to be approved first, to become competent second, some have a greater need to please their competitors than to beat them. Others, resenting the obligation to win, lose deliberately.

Mike Flanagan, the Oriole pitcher, has described how, in an eleven-inning high-school game, he struck out thirty-one batters and walked but one. "I thought my Dad would finally tell me how well I had done. But no. What he said was, 'How come you walked that guy?' "

Perfectionism in a parent often stimulates competitiveness (but sometimes markedly suppresses it). Obtaining parental approval and, later, self-approval may require assiduous preparation, continuous progress, and perfect performance, and hence the effort may greatly enhance the attainment of competence. The success of many competitors can be attributed to the high level of achievement demanded during childhood and to the consequent internalization of a perfectionistic Parent. However, this demand for perfection is commonly distorted into an excessive need to win. The result is diminished satisfaction from the attainment of competence and from participation and a preoccupation with extraneous needs to behave in an approved fashion. Such competitors are often winners, but they tend to be inconsistent, have difficulty staying at the top, and are likely to "blow the big ones."

Tim Gallwey, author of *The Inner Game of Tennis*, has emphasized the interference of "Self I" (Parent) with "Self II" (Child) in athletic performance. He coaches his tennis pupils to release themselves from the inhibitions, the restrictions, the censures, of the Parent. "Just have fun," he says. "Don't try to do it right. Don't be concerned with the effect of a particular action on the outcome of the game." In other words, his advice is to play, be a child, release oneself into Child behavior. Playing a game *is* Child behavior and is socially accepted as Child behavior. It need not be restricted by Parental requirements, Parental positions, Parental concern with outcome. Participation in sport means playing a game for *me;* there should be no concern for *thee.* Obvious as this may seem, few are able to play as if they believe it.

Sandy Van Zandt came by a few weeks ago and we reminisced about the "good old days" when we both sailed International 14's with a small group of enthusiastic and unsophisticated East Coast sailors. How much fun we had; there has not been a time since when we have sailed with such unalloyed joy. We looked forward excitedly to each 14 weekend, never worrying about the possibility of losing, delighting in the expectation of new challenges, new surprises. Sandy pointed out how little we "knew" in those days—we certainly gave no thought to aerodynamics or inversions—but how well we sailed. As we became more knowledgeable the fun began to diminish. The more we learned about how the sailing "should" be done, the less we enjoyed it. And our performance began to suffer. We may have become better able to predict a persistent shift or to rig our masts to reduce windage, but we became less and less able to plane a 14 in 25 knots without fear of capsize, or to feather her to windward in a gusty northwesterly. The more we let our Parent into the act, the less capable our Child became of feeling the joy inherent in sailing and of responding to the unpredictable elements that matter in racing.

There now exists a whole world of sailing in Lasers and catamarans, at schools and off beaches, that is characterized by pure fun, Child behavior, and the absence of Parental intrusion. Among the participating sailors are many who are highly talented—who can flip a Laser without getting their feet wet, plane dead downwind without a broach, tack without losing a tenth of a knot in speed. These talents are not learned; they are innate, instinctive, Child responses to unconscious perceptions. Such awareness cannot be described, let alone taught. Alas, as these sailors progress, as they learn—about strategy, tactics, and boat speed—they may lose much of this awareness. As they become concerned with the outcome of what they are doing, the need to win this race (so as to qualify for the next), they dull those unconscious perceptions, inhibit those responses, diminish those talents. Perhaps this loss is a "natural" consequence of aging, and perhaps the shift from International 14 to Cal 25 is part of a "natural" evolution. But "natural" or not, it is associated with greater and greater preoccupation with outcome and significance, and less and less sensitivity to the moment, the fun, the spontaneity.

The compromise between the need for personal gratification and the need for social acceptance that is appropriate to most life situations is inappropriate to competitive sport. The only limitation on behavior in a competitor's own best interest should be the rules of the game. The competitor need not—indeed, should not—feel guilty about or try to avoid, infringements upon the feelings of others. Few are able to achieve such freedom, however. Most are unable to be fully spontaneous, to release themselves from the fears that Child behavior arouses or to escape from extraneous concerns for the approval of others. And worse, for many individuals there is no escape from competing. They cannot step aside, out of the contest, and say, "So much for participation!" Their Child, demanding an appropriate resolution to some early conflict, sends them back into the fray again and again to repeat the same old inappropriate response. Or their Parent requires that they return to the frightening experience, to prove to themselves that they are not vulnerable, not weak, that they are tough enough to take it "like a man."

During competition, when situations arise that demand impulsive responses, previously unrecognized anxieties, sources of guilt, and ulterior needs for being in competition become evident. Competition not only reveals these fears and needs but permits their fullest expression. The Adult is nowhere more threatened than in competitive activity. Many, indeed, select competitive activity because it provides an ideal realm for the counterphobic demonstration of daring.

The reasons for entering competition are, consequently, a mixture of the appropriate and the inappropriate: the desire to develop and demonstrate competence—creativity, mastery, and courage—to feel the joy associated with performing well, to realize the satisfaction attendant upon winning, combined with the desire to relive an inadequately resolved experience of childhood or to comply with an extraneous Parental demand. We seek to enhance our skill because enjoyment is directly proportional to the degree of competence achieved. And we feel thwarted when we recognize how often our own psyche interferes with our progress. If our ego development was impaired, if the Child or the Parent preoccupies the Adult with an excessive awareness of its fears and demands, defenses are required and our competitive performance suffers. The individual's own personality is the major obstacle to the attainment of competence and the enjoyment of its demonstration. No ego is so effective that it always acts in its own best, long-term interest. But almost all of us could do better and, with insight, would do better.

What is desired from competition
1. To assert independence, significance, and power—to satisfy the Child
2. To accomplish this assertion within a structure (the rules of the game) and in accordance with an internalized standard—to satisfy the Parent
3. To develop and demonstrate competence—creativity, mastery, and courage—as a means of satisfying both Child and Parent, of being assertive and being approved
4. To enjoy the development and demonstration of competence—to play. Joy is a direct consequence of both the striving to develop competence and the demonstration of its attainment, and accounts for the desire to compete repeatedly.
5. To win—through the attainment of competence

What is necessary to the development and demonstration of competence
1. The presence of a functionally effective ego
   a) Control of the Child without inappropriate limitation of:
      Joy
      Creativity
      Determination
      Aggressiveness
      Courage
   b) Control of the Parent without inappropriate submission to the need for:
      Approval
      Acceptance
      A sense that one is deserving
   c) Realistic appraisal of external reality
   d) Realistic self-appraisal
   e) Realistic remembrance, attention, and conception
   f) Trust and respect for one's competitors
   g) Freedom from the need to utilize defenses to protect the ego

What interferes with the development and demonstration of competence
1. Inadequate control of the Child
   a) Persistent awareness of threats to independence, significance, and power ("death fear")—leading to anxiety
   b) Behavior designed to protect against such threats—defenses, including "game" playing, and counterphobic daring

    c) Persistent need to demonstrate aggressiveness, power, and independence

2. Inadequate control of the Parent

    a) Persistent awareness of threats to being secure, loved, and approved ("life fear")—leading to anxiety and guilt

    b) Behavior designed to protect against such threats—defenses, including "game" playing, and counterphobic hostility or submission

    c) Persistent need to be approved, to win

    d) Behavior designed to atone for guilt associated with future or past failure—leading to depression and self-punishment

Part Two

Motivation: The Child

5 / Playing the Racing Game

The world has nothing to bestow;
From our own selves our joys must flow.
—NATHANIEL COTTON

SOME SAY THAT RACING ISN'T FUN, WINNING IS. BUT SINCE SO FEW are winners, winning cannot be the prime attraction. For most of us, the game's the thing—the uncertainty, the risk, the challenge, the potential for adventure. Game playing is the release of the Child. It provides an opportunity to discharge our psychic and physical energy in *a manner of our own selection*, free of the contraints of the real world. The selection of sailboat racing for this purpose permits the individual to design an adventure in which his choice is unrestricted and in which success or failure is not predetermined. The game is large enough to require total involvement and great enough to involve others whom we respect. To be so involved in an experience which we create for ourselves is to play.

Every category of behavior may be either play or work. When we seek adventure for its own sake, we are playing; when we seek an outcome for its own sake, we are working. Dennis Conner at the 1976 Olympics made the revealing comment that if his life-style depended

27

upon it, he would have gone about his preparation differently. (He would have "worked at" it.) Since he was presumably seeking an adventure rather than a specific outcome, he was playing. To be involved in play is to experience a story, a "happening," whose course and outcome are unknown. To play is to relish uncertainty, to delight in surprise. To require a specific outcome, to attempt to predetermine a result is to work. To know that you will win, to predetermine that you will win, to require that you will win is not fun.

Play is usually considered to be unimportant, frivolous. According to a common ethic, it may be desirable only if it is useful: if it aids us in mastery over our bodies or minds, if it serves to relax and release us from our usual tension, and thus facilitates later work. But to the extent that it is so used, "play" turns into work, an activity in which the outcome is more important than the experience. And when a specific outcome becomes important, failure to achieve that outcome may be frightening, embarrassing, or depressing. Actually, however play can be the most satisfying aspect of our lives. It is important in itself. It should not be perverted into work, and it requires no apology.

The instinctive play of animals and of children typifies the best play of adults. When animals play, conflict is always present, but is precisely controlled by rules of behavior. The rules seem to give evidence of a mutual respect among the participants, as they limit the weapons (perhaps claws, or teeth), the manner in which the weapons are to be used, the sites of attack, the positions when attacking. There is a beginning (the approach) and an end (the withdrawal). The participants do not appear to be concerned with the outcome. The play of children takes the form of a more fully developed story. Again there is a beginning, an end, and action in between—a plot. Participation is what matters. The child acquires an identity, is involved in meaningful activity in accordance with his own design. Again there is little evidence of interest in or concern for the outcome. The play transports the participants into another world, where real time and real concerns are of no significance. Conflict is entirely external; the child (and the Child in the adult) is at ease with himself and the situation he creates.

Adults and older children convert this primitive play into games by adding two new features—skill and chance. One of the greatest attractions of games is that they create a situation of equality which is denied the players in ordinary life. Games are always organized so that all players are even at the beginning. Skill and chance determine the plot and the outcome. The player who best utilizes his skill and the chances available is the winner.

A game has rules and boundaries to assure this situation. The rules guarantee that the activity of each player will have equal weight. They delineate the conditions which outline the plot. No one and nothing from the outside world may intrude within the boundaries of the game. The rules are intended to release the player from his own psychic needs; conflict should reside in the game, outside the player. And a game is organized so as to permit play in isolation, in a separate world.

A game is taken seriously by the players. The game itself is at stake. To paraphrase Charlie Brown, Failure is not in losing, but in no longer believing that winning is worth while. To play fully is to believe in the significance of the game—to ignore the risks, enjoy the chances, accept the outcome. One plays to win because winning is the object of the game, not for the sake of winning. To seek to win at all costs, to attempt to predetermine the outcome, is to destroy the game.

To the extent that chance is a significant determinant of outcome, the game becomes more exciting, more encompassing, more intriguing. Because of chance both the plot and the outcome are uncertain, surprises will occur, the game will be an adventure. When a pecking order based on skill is established, when the outcome is predictable, the game is no longer an adventure and ceases to be fun. The athlete giving a demonstration of skill may be excited, but he is not transported into another world as he would be during a game involving chance, such as football. What adventure is there for the player who can predict his finishing position as he enters?

Sailboat racing exemplifies a game in which chance outweighs skill. Entry into competition can be joyous because even for the least skilled there is a possibility of success. A neophyte *can* race against Buddy Melges and *may* beat him. That skill does still matter, so that the likelihood of success for the poorly skilled is relatively small, merely makes the chance of victory more alluring. The more unlikely the desired outcome, the greater the adventure and the greater the joy in victory.

Integral to the playing of a game is the delight that accompanies the taking of a risk. To release the Child, to play the game, to be game, is to take a risk. In motor racing the risk may be of losing one's life. In most games it is merely of losing one's sense of satisfaction, one's joy in displaying skill, courage, or fortitude. But to take the risk is to enter into adventure. To delight in the chance of success is to sense the excitement of surprise, the tension of uncertainty. Robert Neale (in *In Praise of Play*) says that to be dead certain is to be dead. To feel uncertainty, doubt, surprise, to permit spontaneity, is to be alive. Without a full acceptance of the unexpected, a game is not played. Frank Shorter after losing the 1976 Olympic marathon in the rain was asked if he would not have done better in different conditions. He replied that the question was not relevant, that competitors had practiced for four years and come from all over the world to race at that place, at that time, and in whatever conditions were present. Richie Stearns, who won the final race at SPORT 1975, looked back in astonishment as we whooped and hollered in our delight at finishing second. We had had so many adventures en route, had survived so many near disasters, had come back from far behind so often, that the surprise of gaining second place brought a tremendous satisfaction. To expect to lose periodically, to accept the risk of loss, makes victory all the more delightful.

6 / The Fun of It

Happiness is not a station you arrive at, but a manner of traveling.

—MARGARET LEE RUNBECK

PATSY NEAL, IN WRITING ABOUT WOMEN IN SPORTS, DESCRIBES THE state of most amateurs in competitive activity:

> Until recently, women have always been spontaneous in their play . . . and have possessed a certain child-like innocence in their sports activities. They played for the fun of it. . . . Rather than pure, simple fun, it is now work. One no longer plays because of the sense of "being" it gives to the individual. One no longer practices for hours on end because of the pure pursuit of excellence and the sense of rapture it brings. . . . What in the world has happened to the split basketballs, the dusty soft-ball diamonds and the mismatched uniforms worn by sweaty, active, laughing, fun-loving participants who organized their own games and played until body and soul could take the exhilaration no longer?

Well, Patsy, some of these people are still to be found in sailing. Efforts to gain monetary support, to succeed in the pre-trials so as to be eligible for the final trials, or to win selection as an Olympic representative preoccupy many, but the rest of us still enjoy the game.

Most sailors feel a sense of harmony, a simple joy, as they push off in their boat and respond to the first heeling gust. Many racing sailors find satisfaction, as did Patsy Neal, in "the pure pursuit of excellence." We play the racing game because we delight in the peace that accompanies separation from the "real world," the excitement of the unexpected, the surprises we know are in store. We are exhilarated by victory, which always seems possible, and by the camaraderie which binds us to our competitors. We are intrigued by the love–hate, teammate–opponent, friend–foe relationships that characterize racing and are revealed in our contrasting behavior afloat and ashore.

When Paul Henderson, Canada's bareheaded boy with cheek, acquired a new 14 in the spring of 1969, he named her *Crocus*. He had spent the previous two years in bondage to the Olympic effort and felt that his return to 14'ing was the reappearance of spring, the restoration of joy to a world of tension and drudgery.

In many fleets racing has become less enjoyable because of the presence of a few who make winning their work, who attempt to replace the game of chance with a game of skill. Fortunately, they haven't succeeded and are unlikely to do so. Sailing is a game of chance and nothing can alter that.

To succeed, and to receive the approval that accompanies success, is fun. I never felt better, was never more pleased with life, than when I leaped overboard to celebrate winning the Prince of Wales Cup for International 14's; I was the first American to do so. I was little less exhilarated as I accepted the trophy that had been the be-all and end-all of so many sailors for so many years and explained how I had "done it." Nine years later, on the same occasion, Jeremy Pudney announced that there was "not a person here who would not be happy to die having won on Thursday [Prince of Wales Cup day]." "Speak for yourself" came from the back of the room.

A victory against the odds is fun because it is a surprise. A victory that is expected is dull and pointless. My teammates and I were delighted when we beat Canada to win the Emerson Trophy in 1961, the first time the United States had won it in thirty-eight years. But when, as the first visiting helmsman in the West Coast Championship, I won the six-foot-high William Randolph Hearst Trophy, I was merely embarrassed. Jerry Pangborn, winner of Class C in the 14's at the LSSA Regatta, seemed equally embarrassed when he walked away from the trophy table with an armload of sterling trophies—the residue of the glorious past of the LSSA.

Winning is fun for the winner, who feels with Uffa Fox "pleased that he has won as he sailed extremely well and better than the rest." All the world *does* love a winner, at least for the moment, and winning *is* the object of the game. I enjoy memories of my victories and am pleased with the admiring glances of my colleagues as they survey my trophy room. (My estimate of my own significance was only slightly diminished when I overheard a cousin who hadn't visited me in twenty years ask, "Why would anyone buy so many pewter mugs?")

Fame, like winning, is relative—not only to the accomplishment but to the degree to which others are aware of the accomplishment. Dick Vine, after one of the races of the 1961 CDA Regatta, remarked that he "now knew what it was like to be a hundred yards to windward of God." He was speaking of Stewart Morris, British Olympian and thirteen-time winner of the Prince of Wales Cup. The same Stewart Morris, managing a schoolboy regatta at his home club at Itchenor, required that in the strong winds all boats be reefed to the first batten. Subsequently, he overheard a youngster remark, "What does that old fool know about sailing dinghies in a breeze?"

One of the junior sailors at our club, who had known me for many years as a 14 and Soling sailor, was surprised to see me attending to my daughter's injured foot. Then light dawned and he exclaimed, "That's why they call you Doctor Walker!" At the 1969 International Team Match at Kingston, I became aware of a stranger making his way through the dinghy park toward me. After introducing himself and indicating that he'd "always wanted to meet" me, he looked perplexed. In response to my inquiry, he admitted, "Somehow I always thought you'd be taller!" It's fun to be the center of attention, but one has to recognize that much of fame derives from accidents of communication and the farther it spreads the less likely it is to be based in reality. Then too, there are those who look for an opportunity to put down the famous. "How are you going to write this one up, Stu?" (Explain this disaster!)

Much of the fun of racing is in the camaraderie, the sharing of common experiences with old friends. In most classes the regatta circuit is like a perpetual college reunion. We meet the same old gang year after year at the same regattas, to swap yarns about the vicissitudes of the preceding year. This behavior is clearly not limited to the tail-enders, who might be accused of attending just for the parties. Sailboat racing becomes a bond that cuts across our diverse backgrounds, permitting a lawyer to communicate with a guitar player, and isolates us from the uninterested rest of the world. Because of their desire to maintain this rapport, this feeling of making contact, being open, sharing with friends, most sailors settle down in a particular class at a particular level in the regatta circuit, local or international. Even (particularly?) wives may be shut out of this camaraderie, which as the price of admission requires its devotees to have sailed the race. Winning is fun in part because it grants the recipient a front-row seat at the party that follows; there would be less satisfaction in winning if there were no subsequent get-together to attend.

Some of the fun is designed to indicate the affection and esteem of the group for a particular member. Before Glen Foster and his newly acquired bride appeared at Bermuda Race Week, we decorated his 14 *Crescendo* with paper ribbons and water colors and renamed her *Honeymoon Hotel*. After an article by George O'Day stated that multihulls were the wave of the future and single-hulled boats should henceforward be used as flower boxes, we filled his 14 with dirt and planted it with oleanders. We once presented him with a rubber rudder so he'd have more time to make up his mind.

Part of the camaraderie is in the way we talk about ourselves—usually deprecatingly. We don't wish to be isolated from the group. The fun is in the togetherness. If we win, we were "lucky." Stewart Morris, after winning the Hayling Hull: "We got a little behind so had to hurry." If we lose, we have an explanation or we disappear. George O'Day told the group that he had promised his wife Miriam that the Douglas Trophy (best two out of three, match-race series, United States against Canada) would be won in two races so he could return from Canada on Saturday night. The Douglas was won in two races, all right, but by Canadian Paul McLaughlin (and George did go home Saturday night).

The boasts that are made (and remembered) are clearly in jest. They are carefully spelled out to ensure that no one is repelled by them. The fun is in pleasing, in being accepted, being approved, by our competitors. When Tom Marston acquired as crew, for the first time, a big 202-pounder, he announced that together they constituted a triple threat: "If we hit you, we'll go clean through. If we miss you, our wake will sink you. If you're coming at us, I'll throw him over with a line on him, and everyone knows you can't foul a moored vessel!" Peter Hunter, who for a long time crewed for Stewart Morris, had his favorite, which he claimed he used whenever he saw a port-tacker on a collision course. "At forty yards I see another face in another window; I wave. At thirty yards I see another face looking around another jib, worried; I smile and quietly say, 'Starboard.' At twenty yards I recite the little memory poem 'Boom on the right, keep out of the light.' At ten yards I raise my voice, 'Starboard' again. At five yards, 'Which half do you want to sail home in?'"

The game is fun—if it is played without excessive concern for the outcome. The acquisition and display of competence is fun. (We become addicted to doing what we do well!) Winning is fun—even when one recognizes its significance. And being a part of the group, a member of the fraternity, is fun.

7 / The Joy of Victory

A person is never happy except at the price of some ignorance.

—ANATOLE FRANCE

ONE WEEKEND IN CHICAGO IN 1976 WE (THE EAST COAST) BEAT THREE-boat Soling teams from the Midwest, the South, and Canada. The regatta, conducted in borrowed boats, had been billed as "fun." The Canadians came with blood in their eyes, however, and were sorely distressed when we won the match by beating them in the final race. The team which placed last in the series was the only team to beat us—which meant that everyone concerned perceived themselves as winners! My crew's perception was that their frozen hands had been used more effectively than anyone else's and that they deserved to win. The Canadians felt that they had been robbed; if a jib sheet hadn't disappeared, they wouldn't have lost the winning combination which they held at the beginning of the second round of the final race. I was elated because we had beaten a team that seemed unduly intent on winning, but my elation was considerably diminished by my awareness that we had really only been floundering about in borrowed boats, with pick-up crews, and with many of the top Soling competitors absent.

Winning is always "better than a sharp stick in the eye," but as the outcome of this regatta shows, the satisfaction attendant upon winning is by no means absolute. It is markedly modified by one's perception of the significance of the accomplishment, and this perception is dependent upon the caliber and attitude of the opposition as well as on the skill, intellect, and effort required. An easy victory over a weak opponent provides little satisfaction. In sailing, success is measured in terms of movement in the pecking order; a second is satisfying when a third was expected. In a different regatta against a different fleet, a different outcome would be satisfying. Winning is a one-time event; it means only that at a particular time and place a particular player performed better than the others who were present.

The exultation I felt when I won the Prince of Wales Cup may last me a lifetime. It may have to, since such unalloyed satisfaction—victory against seemingly impossible odds—is unlikely to come my way again. No American had ever won this premier trophy of the class, and on my first attempt I had beaten eighty-four of England's best. I had planned the race thoroughly. I had the speed, the strategy, and the skill appropriate to the moment and led from start to finish. There was no way I could minimize the significance of the victory. It contained all the ingredients necessary for satisfaction.

But we racing sailors are rarely satisfied. Winning doesn't satisfy us—we need to do it again, and again. The taste of success seems merely to whet the appetite for more. When we lose, the compulsion to seek future success is overpowering; the need to get out on the course the following weekend is irresistible. We cannot quit when we are ahead, after we've won, and we certainly cannot quit when we're behind, after we've lost. We are addicted.

Although exultation on the course usually allays any doubt about the significance of the victory to come, the delight is difficult to maintain. Two junior sailors in our club, the Lamb twins, Dick and Dave, were once discussing in a bull session how they'd like to depart this earth. One of them announced that if he had to die, he'd like to do so as he crossed the final finish line to win the Mallory Cup. The other said he thought he'd prefer to wait until after the trophy presentation! They may have been wiser than I thought them at the time. They may have recognized that if they were to stay around to evaluate their accomplishment, they would be considerably less satisfied with it.

The illusion that winning is everything, inherent in the joy of anticipation, usually fades in a realistic appraisal of the accomplishment. "On any given day in the National Football League . . ." any given team can win. A corresponding hope is characteristic of racing sailors. *Any*one can win—not just the gods. But if anyone can win, how significant is winning? Sometimes it merely takes luck or a poor performance by the opposition. There is almost always the probability that someone else, who happened to be somewhere else, could have done better—would have won had he been present. Valerie Foster, on her honeymoon during the Princess Elizabeth Series in Bermuda, said, "If Glen loses, it will look bad for him; if he wins, it will look bad for me!" Winning is not done alone; someone else always has to make a mistake.

If you never win, the illusion persists that you could some day through your own efforts. If you do win, the illusion is gone and the reality that the victory was at least partially a gift is all too evident. Following a great emotional investment, the realistic appraisal that winning depended upon the failure of others may have a devastating effect. The great Australian long-distance runner Ron Clarke said, "The best of all possible results, a world record, made me miserable. The excitement had been in the training and the race itself." If the goal is achievable, it isn't significant. Mark Spitz described his mood after his return from winning his seven gold medals at Munich: "I became sick of myself. I never knew how far down someone could drop, especially after being up so high." In advance of the event, it is easy to maintain the illusion that winning will demonstrate both the significance and the stature of the winner. Afterward, the need to realistically evaluate the accomplishment always results in a lower appraisal.

Those who win regularly sometimes find themselves in the twin bind of feeling little satisfaction unless they do win and fearing they will lose their "reputation" if they don't. The fear is, of course, illusory, since the one thing competitors are able to evaluate realistically is the competence of their opponents. One win does not impress them—nor does one loss.

The game exists; winning is its object. Sailors take to racing because they want to play, to compete, to win. The desire to win is intrinsic. Any competitor who does not desire to win, who does not take the game seriously, is not game. To doubt the significance of winning is to demean one's competitors. And winning is fun; it feels good.

There is no reason to disparage the desirability of winning. What is necessary, however, is to recognize that although winning is the object of the game, it is not the object of playing the game. To the extent that winning becomes the only object, to the extent that the Parent becomes dominant and the Child subjugated, the satisfaction to be gained in playing is diminished. Mental toughness, which permits a realistic appraisal of the game, supports the Child in producing the exultation that accompanies winning and blocks the Parent from producing the depression that accompanies losing.

8 / How to Win without Really Trying

To travel hopefully is a better thing than to arrive.
—ROBERT LOUIS STEVENSON

When the One Great Scorer comes to write
against your name—
He marks—not that you won or lost—but
how you played the game.

Grantland Rice wrote this famous couplet to accompany the Baron de Coubertin's statement that participation rather than winning is what matters in the Olympic games. Most competitors give such opinions lip service only. They do not regard the fun of playing as a substitute for winning. For although winning may not be everything, and often isn't very much of anything, it is always more satisfying than losing. The pleasure that accompanies the playing of the game and the joy that accompanies an excellent performance are diminished by losing, enhanced by winning. Fortunately, we do not have to give up one satisfaction to attain the other. The more the competitor enjoys and attributes significance to the play itself, the more likely he is to win. The essence of winning behavior is relaxed enjoyment, playing the game.

(I find that I'm often tempted, as was Grantland Rice, to tell the reader what he "should" do—to win, to enjoy, to relax, to benefit from reading this book! "Should" is, however, not the point. We don't race because we "should." I am attempting to describe a rational approach to competition, not a moral one.)

Those who enjoy playing the game, who relax in competition, are able to concentrate on their performance, on the game, and thus on the object of the game—winning. Those who fear to fail, who cannot relax, who are continually concerned with the effect each move will have upon the outcome, are unable to play. They blow the start of a race, they make the big mistakes, they are unable to sail two good races in a row. They lose because they are unable to concentrate on what matters—the proper management of each individual element.

Jack Nicklaus was asked how he felt when he made the putt that won the 1975 Masters. "That's why I'm here," he replied, "to be in a position to make a putt that means that much." The attitude is a relaxed acceptance of the situation as it is; the feeling is exultation at the magnitude of the risk. Steve Kelly, the U.S. Olympic kayaking representative, says that the greatest satisfaction is in competing against the best, because doing so means that you are one of the best. Jethro Pugh, the Dallas Cowboy lineman, says that you never know how good you are until you play against the best. Earl Bell, a top U.S. pole vaulter, lent his own pole to competitor Dave Roberts when the latter broke his in the 1976 Olympic trials. Dave Curtis, who may have the most appropriate attitude of any racing sailor I know, says about recent Soling fleets, "Everyone is fast." Of Jan Merrill, the U.S. Olympic runner, her coach says, "See how's she's enjoying it. That's all I ever tell her to do in a race. Just have fun!" All of these champions find joy in the competition itself, and their joy is proportional to the excellence of their competitors. Instead of fearing the opponents' excellence as a threat to their own success, they delight in it because it enhances the significance of the match. They believe in the importance of the game, the importance of playing.

Becoming involved in play for its own sake is relaxing. So also is becoming involved in the anticipation of adventures ahead, as distinguished from concern with the accomplishment of the moment. Jack Nicklaus says that he is fighting the future, that his challenge is to excel for all time. "My goal is to win as many major championships as possible. You can always find goals. As long as I can continue to improve, as long as I can keep the desire to work toward those goals,

I'll play." He is at ease with his stature, doesn't fear the risk of losing, takes satisfaction in anticipating the accomplishments to come. Similarly, many sailors find more pleasure in mounting a new fitting on Tuesday or driving to a regatta on Friday, than they do in racing on Saturday. Others are able to view each event as training for the next, for some more important competition in the future. Steve Kelly won a major preliminary regatta prior to the 1976 trials. He was exultant: "Oh my God, what a feeling!" He was anticipating the trials and the Olympics to come, not merely exulting in the accomplishment itself.

Those who strive toward future goals—possibly unreachable— are better able to make a realistic appraisal of present success or failure. Each event is treated as a learning and testing experience rather than as an end in itself. The outcome of a particular event is unimportant except as a demonstration of the need for further improvement in a particular skill or of the attainment of a particular level of competence. This attitude, essential to the development of skill, is also relaxing. Since the goal is to improve individual elements of performance, satisfaction is attainable without winning, and winning is treated appropriately as an unexpected, unrequired, additional joy. And with attention paid to performance and to progressive improvement in performance, winning becomes more likely.

We return to racing again and again because racing is an adventure—always new, always surprising—characterized, as Robert Neale has observed, by peace, freedom, delight, and illusion.

The peace of the adventure is in the state of being unthreatened. Such peace derives from knowing that the undertaking *is* an adventure, not a test of stature or worth.

The freedom of the adventure is provided in racing by the rules of the game. No player is obligated to another; he is required only to play in accordance with the rules. Each player has the same standing as every other; no player seeks or expects special privileges; no player resents being (temporarily) defeated.

Delight is inherent in the risk, the excitement of the action, the uncertainty of the outcome. Success is a gift; failure is to be expected: it is the rule, not the exception. Where competitors are of equal ability, each should expect to win an equal number of times— and to lose at all other times.

The illusion of the adventure of racing is that the game is everything. Each competitor reinforces the illusion for the others, and all experience the charm and enchantment of acting in another world.

Gone are the tribulations of the real world. Present is the awareness of the wind, the waves, and the sky.

Competition can be fun, and the very circumstance (playing against superior competition) which reduces the likelihood of a successful outcome may actually increase the fun. Anticipation, learning, the acquisition of skill, can be fun. Competition can be an exciting, fulfilling adventure. Winning *isn't* everything, and it certainly isn't necessary. On the other hand, winning is fun, and attitudes and behavior which increase its likelihood are appropriate. If preoccupation with the outcome made victory more likely, it might be justified. In fact, it does not; the tension engendered diminishes both the pleasure of competition and the likelihood of winning.

John McMurty, a professor of philosophy at Guelph University, says, "The pursuit of victory works to reduce the chance for excellence in the true performance by rendering it subservient to emerging victorious." The pursuit of improvement in performance leads to victory, but the pursuit of victory leads to deterioration in performance.

Whatever the mechanism by which it is achieved, relaxation is essential to successful performance. Joint studies by Thomas Tutko and Bruce Ogilvie reveal that the trait "relaxed to athletic achievement" reinforces self-control so as to benefit almost all aspects of athletic performance. Successful competitors exhibit lower levels of tension than unsuccessful competitors (licensed sports-car drivers being the least tense). Competitors who rate poorly for this trait are susceptible to annoyance, are less confident in unfamiliar situations, tend to be cynical, and are easily frustrated. Techniques which reduce pre-event tension and enhance relaxation have been demonstrated to affect performance favorably.

Realistic evaluation of the significance of an event and its outcome aids relaxation. Robert Ringer, in *Winning Through Intimidation*, his book about real estate and life, proposes the Ice Ball Theory: In fifty billion years the sun will burn out and the earth will turn into a ball of ice—regardless of what happens today! Since all activity, and indeed life itself, is so relatively meaningless, why not have some fun and try to win?

Ringer says that he always approaches a real-estate deal with the expectation that it won't work. Because he doesn't expect to win, he doesn't become emotionally committed. Instead, he is able to preserve a realistic, analytic approach to the evolving problem. Hartley

Watlington, one of the outstanding sailors of the 14 class in the 1950's, raced at Annapolis one fall. When his crew lowered the spinnaker through the jib sheets, under the bow and over the pole, ever-relaxed Hartley calmly suggested, "While you're about it, would you fix me a cup of tea?"

Tim Gallwey stresses the importance of relaxation in tennis. "Try loving the ball," he says. "Judge these shots on your fun-meter." He tells his students, "I don't care if your shots go in or out, hit the net or hit the ceiling. The object is simply to have fun." And he recommends, "Ride across the net with the ball; experience the wind and feel the gravity pull you down to earth." In other words, they are to relax, pay no attention to the effect of the shot on the game, have fun. And his students perform better after a few minutes than those who are conventionally instructed after six weeks. They are so involved in the play, in the individual elements of performance, that they have no thought for the outcome. They are as relaxed as they would be if they were indifferent to the outcome.

Of course, the competitor who was in truth indifferent to the outcome would derive no satisfaction from improved performance or victory. And if he were indifferent he would be unable to acquire sufficient skill to play effectively. What is required is relaxation in the presence of a desire to win.

Not everyone can find adventure in every race; most of us feel threatened, at least while we are being beaten. We become preoccupied, fearful, depressed. We make mistakes. We lose races—in part, at least—because we lose our sense of adventure, the freedom to perform at our best. The conclusion is simple. Relax, be a Child, enjoy the adventure, play the game—and increase the likelihood of success. Fight, seek only to win, struggle to avoid defeat—and decrease the likelihood of success.

9 / "Nice Guys Finish Last"

I would rather men should ask why no statue has been erected in my honor, than why one was.
—MARCUS PORCIUS CATO

THERE WE WERE, HERMAN WHITON AND I, ALL BY OURSELVES (IN SIXTH or seventh place) in the middle of the second beat at CORK—and Herman was on starboard and on a collision course. I hated to tack right on his lee bow, but I wasn't sure I could cross. I called to him, "Do you want me to tack or to cross?" There was some sort of reply, I couldn't tell what, and suddenly I had to make up my own mind. I tacked—when I should have flicked my stern around his bow—and immediately thereafter recognized that I had done so too close. I dropped out of the race and sailed for the beach, railing bitterly against the fates, Herman Whiton, and my own good intentions. If I hadn't worried about him, if I had just ignored his problems, I would have decided well in advance what to do, and would have done it, and there would have been no trouble. "No more Mister Nice Guy," I swore (and my wife hung a plaque on the kitchen wall to remind me of my oath forevermore).

Conrad Dobler, who is one of the most effective linemen in the

45

National Football League, says, "I'll do anything I can get away with to protect my quarterback. . . . Tell me I can't do it and that's all I need. When I started out, no one gave a damn who I was. I had to prove to everyone that they had a fight on their hands. All the bad mouthing I get is just fuel. If a guy says he doesn't respect me, he just makes my job that much easier." Many believe that the hostility of a Conrad Dobler is beneficial. The hostile player receives at least grudging respect and often intimidates his competitors so that they permit him to take advantage of them. Is hostility indeed necessary? Do nice guys finish last?

The aggressive person feels free to show anger; he will not allow others to take advantage of him, and asserts his strength when opportunities to do so appear. The submissive person is unable to show anger; he allows others to take advantage of him, and avoids asserting his strength. Because the aggressive person functions at the expense of the submissive one, many people decry aggressiveness. It seems counter to the Christian ethic; nice guys shouldn't be aggressive. Some believe that the only justification for aggressiveness in games is that it provides an outlet for energy whose release in the real world would be antisocial. However, as we shall see, aggressiveness is of real value in games, enhancing enjoyment as well as contributing to a successful outcome. Hostility, is something else, and is unnecessary and undesirable. Winning requires aggressiveness, not hostility, but some players find it hard to recognize the distinction.

Appropriate ("instrumental") aggressiveness is beneficial to a player in that it permits him to feel no concern for the opinions and feelings of others and to demonstrate his strength whenever such a demonstration is useful. The ability to display aggressiveness represents a freedom from guilt regarding power, and indicates the presence of a brave Child, an approving Parent, and a controlling, realistic Adult. Dobler's remarks demonstrate that an associated attribute may be a disregard for the rules and a disrespect for competitors—that is, hostility. This "reactive" aggressiveness derives from a lack of self-control, a failure of realistic appraisal, and a confusion on the part of the internalized Parent concerning power.

The lack of concern for the feelings of competitors is useful because it eliminates one distraction. If you don't care what the other fellow thinks, you can tack on him whenever you wish. If you do care, you may be limited to tacking on him only during the latter part of the last beat. During the remainder of the race you must be careful to tack far enough to leeward or to windward so that he is not adversely affected, and you will therefore give up, to some degree, the ideal strategic position. In oscillating winds, for example, every time you fail to tack precisely where you should, you lose. Is it reasonable to lose deliberately in oscillating winds? Or at any other time?

George O'Day, never too mindful of the limitations of class rules, was finally required to repeat the annual buoyancy test for the 14 class. After he passed, I asked him how it felt to be legal at last. "Somehow," George replied, "it takes all the fun out of it." A similar lack of concern for his competitor's opinion characterized Sam Merrick's response to my comment that his coming out of nowhere to pass me on the final beat of the last race of the 1978 Atlantic Coast Championship had cost me second place: "You don't know how sorry I am!"

This is not a lack of compassion like Conrad Dobler's; concern for the other guy is simply put out of the game, relegated to the real world. Mercy is appropriate—it makes the game more fun—but no one expects to be given a break, and no one should relinquish an advantage, or fail to seize one, out of concern for a competitor. The rules of the game, not the rules of society, limit a participant's behavior. He need pay no attention to what is deserved nor feel any obligation to give up his place to someone more deserving.

Syd Corser told me a fascinating story about how he and Noel Robins once reached an essential tie the day before the final race for the Australian 14-footer title. This was Noel's first season back in 14's after he had been almost completely paralyzed in an automobile accident, and Syd, one of his closest friends, was all too aware of how much this championship would mean to Noel. He thought of letting up a little to give Noel a better chance and then realized how foolish that would be. Noel was testing himself; he wasn't interested in collecting gifts. The best thing Syd could do for Noel (and himself) was to play the game as hard as possible. How little the title would mean to Noel (and he did win it) if it were given to him! We should not deprive our competitors of their "good fight." Competition is not Christmas.

The aggressive competitor is also characterized by his willingness, even his active desire, to demonstrate his superiority. I am reminded of Paul Elvstrom's jibes in heavy weather off the launching ramps at Melbourne as most competitors huddled ashore awaiting the diminution of the gale, and of Dennis Conner's ferrying competitors on his Tempest among the moored boats at the 1976 trials. Strahan

Soames describes Edward Heath's assertiveness: "He gives an impression of strength, of single-mindedness and of purpose that is almost intimidating. He is strong and he knows it." At Hyères in early 1976, David Howlett told the race committee exactly what he thought of their competence (for which he was subsequently banned from the final race). He seemed to feel no internal qualms over this conflict with authority as he proceeded to win the regatta, without sailing that race!

Garry Hoyt says, "The first thing to get straight about close cover is that, to make it work right, you have to turn on an active desire for malicious mischief. After all, that sonafabitch is trying to pass you, which is an enormous personal insult. In righteous indignation you are going to crap upon him, in the sincere hope that from this he will acquire new and proper respect." The aggressive individual wants you to respect him, not to love him. He does not want to please you; he wants to impress you. Tom Turral, the Storm King, describing the "good old days" in 14 racing, says, "Whoever arrived at a mark first, rounded first. This resulted in a great deal of pushing and pulling when a fleet of forty dinghies barged down on the windward starting mark. Norman Gooderham, perennial commodore of the Royal Canadian Yacht Club, is credited with being the first to bring along a broom handle to crack the knuckles of anyone who pushed his boat!" When I interviewed Dennis Conner before the start of the Kingston Olympic regatta, he told me that he believed in the existence of a pecking order and that it was important to establish the order early. He mused that John Albrechtson (who—ironically—subsequently won) remembered the 1971 Star World Championship, where Conner was first and Albrechtson third.

The pattern of assertiveness is a spectrum. At one end are the people who delight in conflict, who seek opportunities to demonstrate their superiority. At the other end are those who prefer to avoid confrontation at all cost. Of any two competitors, one will lie nearer to one end of the spectrum than the other; one will be more assertive, the other more submissive. In a conflict, between these two, the former will win, the latter will lose. There is more to winning games and races than beating one's immediate neighbor, but the winner of such a match is taking a step forward, the loser a step backward.

To be aggressive is appropriate; it serves the purpose of the game: to perform better than the opposition—to win. Those who are submissive will not be pleased at being beaten, but pleasing the submissive is not the purpose of the game. Being aggressive is not being un-nice; it is both respectable and respectful. Being hostile *is* being un-nice; it is unnecessary and disrespectful. The aggressive player is self-controlled, able to restrain his concern for others, to overcome his need to be deserving. The hostile player is uncontrolled, unable to re-strain his anger, his resentment, his need to retaliate or to vindicate himself. His lack of concern for others, his assertion of strength, is in-tended not to demonstrate competence, but to injure or punish.

While playing, animals limit their aggression. Only certain weapons, certain moves, are permitted, and as soon as the vanquished submits, the conqueror restrains his attack. The aggressive competitor uses his strength appropriately, carefully. The competitor under the influence of anger or fear loses control, lashes out without regard to the rules; aggression then becomes unrestrained, hostile. There are those who push to the head of the line at the hoist, who demand special treatment, who throw their weight around, who become ob-noxious.

Hostility out of control serves no purpose. Even in football, the Conrad Doblers impair their performance when they lose control. They may intimidate, but they are all the more easily trapped by a controlled opponent, all the more likely to be detected in their infrac-tions and penalized for violating the rules.

Being a nice guy does not contribute to successful performance; it has nothing to do with it. But feeling guilty, being submissive, avoid-ing confrontation does interfere with performance. If you roll over for Mr. Big, you can't expect to win. Nice, guilty guys will not finish first. However, hostile un-nice guys also impair their performance, by their lack of control. They are as likely to finish last as the nice, guilty guys. Being nice or being mean has nothing to do with performance. Nice guys can finish first—if they are aggressive enough to "stick it" to the aggressive guys who are already there!

10 / Determination

If there is one characteristic which all winners share, it is impatience with, and intolerance for, losing.

—GARRY HOYT

DESIRE HAS TO DO WITH MOTIVATION AND OUTCOME; ONE DESIRES BE-cause one is motivated by a need for a given outcome. If the motivation is inappropriate, the desire may be detrimental. Hence, desire has moral overtones. Determination, on the other hand, is not related to outcome. It is essentially an amoral attribute; the determined individual applies his determination to whatever he undertakes. Therefore, determination results in a uniformly beneficial effect; it increases the likelihood of satisfaction and success in every endeavor. In particular, it increases the likelihood of developing competence and therefore of gaining satisfaction from the demonstration of competence. It may also be associated with satisfaction from striving alone. Determination is characteristic of a strong controlling Adult that permits appropriate expression of the Child. It is oriented to the self, rather than to others; it does not involve guilt; and it is associated with satisfaction regardless of outcome. It is a truly desirable attribute that characterizes successful performers.

A number of different terms have been used to describe the attributes which stimulate an effort to excel. *Drive* means initiative, an innate motivating tendency that prompts activity. Like determination, it is essentially independent of purpose and outcome, Child-motivated but adapted to Adult purposes. *Desire* is drive directed at a particular goal. It is synonymous with "wanting." *Need* implies a compulsion, derived from the internalized Parent, to achieve the outcome desired. *Conscientiousness* is guilt-proneness which results in the individual's working scrupulously so as to deserve the desired outcome. Like desire and need, it is outcome-oriented and Parent-determined. *Expectation* is not synonymous with desire; it concerns the outcome believed in, not the outcome wanted.

In a 1964 list of British International 14's, the following sequence appears:

K745	Frivolity	J. S. Wigmore	Chase S.C.
K746	Hilarity	H. Binyon	Itchenor S.C.
K753	Despair	I. W. D. Cox	Itchenor S.C.

After *Frivolity* and *Hilarity*, should there be *Despair?* A good reason, involving a mother-in-law, underlies that choice of name, but unlike most mother-in-law stories, this one has no satisfying sequel (or at least none has been revealed to me). One of the prettiest 14's ever created, according to those who saw her, was *Delight* (not in the 1964 list), which Ian Cox built with his own hands during untold, lonely hours of work in the back of his two-car garage. The boat was ready for the sixteenth and final coat of varnish when his mother-in-law, driving a large, unfamiliar, automatic automobile, went straight through the garage, the boat, and the back wall and dumped the lot— now all in small pieces—into the fishpond. Nothing salvageable remained of *Delight*. Cox then went ahead and constructed a second boat (behind a stone wall, I trust), which he named *Despair*. That's determination.

The determined person responds positively to challenges. Difficulties, obstacles, setbacks, seem only to incite him to further effort. The more unlikely success appears, the more the determined person strives to succeed. The sports world is filled with stories of youngsters who, told they would never walk again, surmounted the odds to attain championship performance. Of course, these examples are exceptional, but the sequence seen in them is not coincidental. Those who have the talent and the determination to be great performers are stimulated by disaster to even greater effort—effort beyond that which would have been otherwise invested. Ian Cox proudly demonstrating to himself that he could do a better job the second time around, and satirically naming the effort *Despair*, exemplifies the way the determined rise to a challenge. Determination is more than endurance and perseverance, more than the enjoyment of training and conditioning, more than continuous maximal exertion; it is characterized by the exertion of an even greater effort in response to difficulty. Tell the determined person that he can't do something, show him that it is impossible, and watch him succeed.

Determination is a major element in preparation to compete. Paul Elvstrom is an archetype of determination. He dedicated twelve years of his life to winning four gold medals, spending hours each day on his hiking platform, sailing throughout the winter in Denmark's Sound, jibing time after time in the strongest possible winds. John Albrechtson has described Paul's preparation of his "new" Star (purchased from Albrechtson) for the Star World Championship at Kiel: "I noticed how extraordinarily painstaking Paul was in looking after the boat before and between the races. He was always the first to and the last from *Scandale* and there was always something to be done."

In *Sports Psyching*, by Thomas Tutko and Umberto Tosi, the behavior of the determined athlete is described. He has extremely high endurance; he enjoys prolonged and repetitive practice sessions; he keeps himself in top physical condition; he never gives up and can always be counted upon to exert every ounce of available effort.

Buddy Melges, in a letter to me, described his preparation for his gold medal winning performance at the 1972 Olympics:

> I suppose the mental attitude is the one big thing in yacht racing—to be able to get yourself and the crew up when it really counts. We accomplished this by sailing alone at Lake Geneva. We practiced tacking and jibing—what I consider the blocking and tackling of sailing—to maintain boat speed on smooth tacks, to maintain composure on high wind jibes and, finally, we just sailed ourselves into condition. Oftentimes too much sailing is done boat on boat. Although it does improve the steering, you lose the most important thing—boat handling. Sail triangles, windwards, leewards (on a one hundred yard per leg course) until it gets really boring. When sail trim and boat handling have been improved, the resultant performance seems to equal that of the guy who sails straight away for boat speed. It's nice to have both, but if I had my choice, I'd take the boat handling in class racing.

Bill Abbott, visiting Melges at Zenda, recalls that these practice sessions were conducted in early morning and late afternoon, day in and day out, until the ice covered the lake in the fall and as soon as it had cleared away in the spring.

Determination continues beyond preparation into performance. Again, setbacks and frustration increase the effort of the determined competitor. Handicaps tend to have beneficial effects. In 1965 Bud Easter, after demanding a place for a West Coast boat on the U.S. International 14 team, failed to qualify. Following this defeat, he returned to win the U.S. National Regatta by a huge margin and beat every boat on every one of the international teams! Buddy Melges broke his mast (as did many others) during the second race of the 1972 Soling Olympic trials. He spent the following night meticulously transferring the essential elements of the old rig to a new mast and then, with a fifth and a DNF (Did Not Finish) behind him, proceeded to win the trials 2–1–1–1–2. By contrast, in 1976, when he should have won with ease, without a handicap, he finished third.

The Russians and the East Germans seem to thrive on adversity. Indeed, they seem determined to continue, to put forth their absolutely best effort, whether far ahead or hopelessly behind. Such determination is often extremely useful, as it was in the notorious fifth race of the 1976 Olympics, when Russian Boris Budnikov and East German Dieter Below finished at the head of a confused and harried Soling fleet.

Paul Elvstrom sails as if he believes the old saw that the race is never over until the line is crossed and that nothing should be left undone that will possibly help. At the 1966 World Championship, he went faster after moving his Star mast a little forward, but still finished second to Lowell North. He then spent almost the entire night moving the mast another two inches forward, and went on to win the series. At Zeebrugge he capsized his Finn in a gale before the start. He swam the boat to the mole, lifted the bow to drain most of the water, bailed with his hands until the boat was sufficiently dry, and then sailed to an eighth-place finish. He won the series by a single point, counting the eighth place finish. I remember finishing a race at Essex, without a mast. I had broken it during a wild plane while leading on the penultimate leg. The final leg was to windward, but the weather-going current carried us across the line in second place—the minimum position required to win the season's championship!

Roger Bannister, speaking of potential advances in running performance, says that all physiological factors may ultimately be secondary to the "capacity for mental excitement—which brings with it the capacity to ignore or overcome the discomfort and pain." Tom Landry, perennial coach of the Dallas Cowboys, has produced a statement entitled "Willpower":

> Intellect tires, the will never,
> The brain needs sleep, the will none,
> The whole body is nothing but objectified will,
> The whole nervous system contributes the antennae of the will,
> Every action of the body is nothing but the act of the will objectified.

The handicaps which the determined must overcome are physical (pain, exhaustion, weakness) and psychological (fear, depression, feelings of inadequacy). I remember how I have felt on many nights before the final race—the race that will determine whether I have won or lost the regatta. The night before the last race of the 1965 team trials I wandered around Cape Cod telling myself that anyone as stupid as I didn't deserve to win. I finally recognized that the result was up to me, that I had merely to make up my mind that I wanted to win and determine to do it. The same doubts were cured by the same awareness before I won the Swiss Championship and the Great Lakes Championship. Determination is demonstrated when a person responds to fear and a sense of inadequacy by disregarding them, recognizing that each individual controls the quality of his own performance.

Part Three

Preparation: The Parent

11 / Should the Best Man Win?

It may be that the race is not always to the swift, nor the battle to the strong—but that's the way to bet.

—DAMON RUNYON

IS THE DRIVE TO ATTAIN OLYMPIC STATURE DIMINISHED OR ENHANCED BY attitudes and policies which govern selection at present? Does the pressure to win exerted by the Olympic selection system decrease the pleasure of competition? Does it have an adverse effect upon performance? Should skill in developing boat speed and in boat handling determine the outcome in sailboat races? To what extent do we wish chance to affect the outcome? Is performance in a regatta the only way to judge racing sailors? Should the "best man," the most skilled man, win? Do techniques which result in the selection of the most skilled produce higher Olympic placings? To what extent do selection policies, which emphasize the selection of the "best man," have a beneficial effect, or an adverse effect, upon subsequent performance?

In many nations selection as an Olympic representative may be open only to those willing and able to spend all their time preparing. Along with this progression toward full-time involvement has come an increasing emphasis upon winning. Competitors reflect the attitudes of the world around them, the pressures of family and peer groups, the implications of the communications media. The philosophy they hear announced is that the game's the thing, participation is what matters. But the questions they hear asked are, Who beat whom? Who got the medals? How many medals did they get? Who got the gold? The modern competitor feels that to be approved, admired, respected, he must win. The major recent change in yachting has been the appearance of individuals who are willing to spend the time and effort necessary to develop their skills fully and who expect that by so doing they will become unbeatable.

Only a small percentage of all U.S. sailors are involved in the tough, driving, high-caliber competition characteristic of the Olympic classes, and fewer still are willing to devote their full time to preparation for such racing. If Olympic participation is the ultimate level of the game, one would expect more sailors to be intrigued by it. The emphasis upon winning and the necessity of nearly full-time preparation seem to have turned off large numbers of racing sailors.

The course and the outcome of games such as sailboat racing depend upon both skill and chance. Games of chance are characterized by uncertainty and adventure. Games of skill are characterized by certainty and predictability. The result of a game of pure skill can be determined in advance. The most skillful will be first, and the least skillful will be last. The competitor who is concerned with outcome prefers a game of skill. The competitor who is concerned with participation prefers a game involving chance. Competitors who have devoted much time and effort to developing their skills sometimes seek to reduce the element of chance in the games they play. They prefer a game in which the most skilled is sure to succeed, in which "the best man wins."

The fundamental question is thus whether we wish to reward skill or chance, or some proportion of each. Inherent in the belief that winning is what matters is the belief that the "best man," the most skilled man, *should* win. (Ask either the "best man" or the winner!) The defect in this thesis is that actually few of us wish the "best man" to win: few of us wish to take chance out of competition, to predetermine that the most skilled will always come in first.

Sailboat racing—in most fleets in most countries during the past four decades—has been largely a game of chance. Anyone can win. To be sure, there is a pecking order based upon previously demonstrated skill; everyone knows what to expect. But each competitor enters the regatta, starts the race, with the belief that he can win. And this is the way we like it. This has been the charm of sailboat racing: because it is a game of chance, everyone has a chance. By contrast, golf and tennis (the only other sports played by a large part of the population of all ages and both sexes) are games of skill. The average golfer would not be allowed on the same course with Jack Nicklaus; the average tennis player could scarcely win a point against Jimmy Connors. Sailboat racing is so complex, there are so many unpredictable variables, there are so many competitors in the game simultaneously, situations which determine the outcome are so rarely repetitive, that the effect of skill on the outcome is less significant.

Let's assume for a moment that the "best" in a sailboat race could be infallibly selected. Theoretically a computer program could be developed which would take into account—for each member of each competing crew—previous experience, previous accomplishments, drive, determination, mental toughness, intelligence, and so on, and would also take into account—for each boat—hull shape, condition, and weight, mast flexibility, sail design and construction, sail-control layouts, instrumentation, and so on. Each factor having been appropriately weighted, the computer would determine which competitor was "best". Developing such a program would, of course, be difficult, since no one really knows how to weigh the variables, and some may exist of which we are unaware. For example, what value would be given for winning the East Coast Championship as opposed to the West Coast Championship, one of which was conducted in light air, the other in current, and in one of which the second-place boat had a breakdown? No matter, let's just assume it could be done.

If we had these means to select the "best," would we want to use them? Would we want to decide the winner of the Tuesday evening race off the dock in this manner? The club champion, then? Well, how about our fleet representative to the Nationals? Our district representative to the World Championship? If we have such an ideal technique for selecting the "best" representatives, are we then going to rely upon a regatta to determine who is the world champion? The conditions might be wrong, there might be light air (or heavy), there might be a big wind shift in one race, someone might have a breakdown, there might be a collision and the protest committee might disqualify the wrong boat (or the right one), someone might be sick, one competitor might be more adversely affected than another by the rain, the appearance of the sea breeze, or the behavior of his wife. Surely, if it would be better to select the "best" representative by the computer, then the outcome of the regatta itself should be determined by the computer.

How obviously ridiculous this is. We want to race, not select "best men." Even if a computer could determine rank order, we don't want the results of the summer series posted on the board in the spring. The whole point of sailboat racing is to experience the risks, the uncertainties, the surprises of a race, to discover the winner—not to select the "best man."

Some will object that this philosophy, applied to the choice of representatives to the Olympics, would result in fewer medals—that if East Germany is going to select the "best man," we should too; that the original Olympic concept that participation is what matters is no longer viable. The concept that all countries should send representatives in all sports has long been ignored. Many, perhaps most, refrained from sending entrants for one or more yachting classes in 1976 because they felt that their prospective representatives could not win medals. The national authorities are interested in providing their representatives with an opportunity to experience the joy of participation. They want to avoid embarrassment; they want winners. Fortunately, despite these organized efforts to turn the Olympics into tests of pure skill, there is no evidence that in yachting events "best man" selection techniques result in superior performance or in the collection of more medals.

Even in sports whose outcome is usually determined by skill alone, the "best man" may not win. In the 1976 Olympics, high jumper Dwight Stones and pole vaulter Dave Roberts, holders of world's records, were thwarted by rain and had to settle for bronze medals. Frank Shorter, thwarted in the same manner, saw the big picture, saying, in effect: "This was the day, these were the conditions in which we raced in the 1976 Olympics; I was second." Yachting medals were won in 1976 by West Germany (two golds, one bronze), the U.S. (two silvers, one bronze), England (one gold, one silver), East Germany (one gold, one bronze), Russia (two silver), Australia (two bronze), Sweden (one gold), Denmark (one gold), Spain (one silver), and Brazil (one bronze). Ten out of forty nations won medals. West Germany and the U.S. each won three; the "professional" Eastern Europeans won four. The gold medals were shared by five nations. There is no evidence that one nation's selection techniques were conspicuously better than another's, or that the highly organized team support provided to French, Swiss, Italian, and Austrian competitors during major regattas yielded greater rewards than the laissez-faire policies of the U.S. and Australia. Certainly, the selection policies of the Eastern European countries did not guarantee success.

Previous Olympic success, which should be a significant determinant of the "best man," had little effect upon the outcome. In the Soling class, none of the five previous gold medalists who were participating won medals in 1976. In the other classes two previous gold medalists (Valentin Mankin and Rodney Pattison) did win silver medals. No other previous medalists were close to the top. Prior Olympic performance does not correlate with present Olympic performance. Sailing at the Olympic level remains a game of chance.

There was a fair amount of grumbling (but none from Buddy Melges) that John Kolius was not the best Soling representative the U.S. could have selected in 1976. After all Buddy had won the gold medal in 1972, had won almost everything he entered since, and had dominated the big fleets racing in the south during the early part of the year; before the trials, John had never beaten him in a big regatta. Buddy had been to the Olympics twice before, he could handle the pressure, his self-assurance made him the ideal representative. He was the "best man"—and he hadn't been selected. The system was wrong, it was felt; there had to be a way of assuring the selection of the "best man." When John got off to a disappointing start in the Olympics, there were more grumblings and I-told-you-so's. John was embarrassed, preoccupied with the belief that Buddy would have done better—no one could convince him otherwise—and his performance showed it. Buddy had worked with him between the trials and the Olympics and had helped him improve his performance in heavy air. But John, believing (at least unconsciously) that Buddy was the "best man," believing that he had usurped Buddy's place, was ready to atone for his sins—ready to lose to reassure his benefactor that he was appreciated. Fortunately, he recovered from his misapprehensions before the end of the series and came on strong to win the silver medal.

John had clearly been the "best man" at the trials (that regatta *had* selected the "best man" in those circumstances), but burdened by misconceptions concerning the appropriateness of his selection, he did not perform at his best for much of the series. Misconceptions related to belonging or not belonging, deserving or not deserving, being the "best man" or not, undoubtedly underlie many first-time Olympic failures. It is to John's great credit that he was able to overcome these concerns and win the silver medal. Many other competitors, surprised suddenly to find themselves as Olympic representatives, have quickly demonstrated that they were not pretending to be the "best man." They would undoubtedly have performed better if someone had only assured them that having won the trials, they deserved to be at the Olympics, they belonged there, and being, or not being, the "best man" was completely irrelevant.

12 / The Need to Win

*If you win one game, you'd want to win an-
other and then another! Soon you'd want to win
every ball game you played!*

—LUCY (in *Peanuts*)

FOREKNOWLEDGE THAT WINNING IS NOT AN ESSENTIAL PART OF THE EX-
perience (when success in a series is beyond reach, when we are racing
against vastly superior competitors, when there is no need to win)
brings out our best performance. John Kolius commenced the final
race of the 1976 U.S. Olympic Soling trials with a lead that could not
be overcome unless Buddy Melges won the race *and* Kolius finished
fourth or below. He rounded the first mark next to last and then—
recognizing (unconsciously?) that his performance was no longer relevant, that the only thing that mattered was whether Buddy could
finish first—he roared through the fleet, every move strategically and
tactically correct, to round the second weather mark in the lead (and
finish third). Buddy, preoccupied with the overwhelming need to win
this most important of all races, finished sixth.

I remember a 14 regatta in the Chesapeake in which I fouled out
as I tacked to port just after the start. My intention had been to sail to
the right into the expected but not yet evident sea breeze. Knowing I

was out of the race, I decided to continue as I had planned while keeping away from the other competitors. I soon found myself in the lead, and with no pressure, completely at ease, I sailed farther and farther ahead on leg after leg. When I ducked to the wrong side of the committee boat, I led by over a mile.

I was equally relaxed when I was the captain of the East Coast team in a Soling regatta in Chicago. I was participating purely for the camaraderie, for the fun of it. As we were using whatever crews were available and borrowed boats, I didn't expect my team to do well and felt no pressure to demonstrate my own ability. In my boat there were no compasses, no hiking aids. In winds of 15–18 knots and big seas, at least one of us fell into the lee bilge every time we tacked. With nothing to prove and no need to win, I sailed well. I made the best start in every race, carefully controlled my selected opponents, and was fully aware of the tactical and strategic requirements at every moment. I finished first twice and in the other race returned to luff an opponent so as to move my teammate into a winning combination. I can remember few regattas in which I was so continuously alert to what mattered.

Most competitors delight in the emotional release, euphoria, and elation that accompany successful performance and winning. Many dread the depression, the feelings of isolation and inadequacy, that accompany poor performance and losing. The anxiety that appropriately accompanies the uncertainties and risks of the race itself stimulates and enhances performance. But when there is an extraneous need to win, a need to satisfy some unconscious obligation, the player may be distracted, confused, frightened, unable to pay attention to the things that matter. Instead of concentrating on his performance, he becomes preoccupied with the unconscious obligation to look good, be impressive, be a winner. The anxiety that is aroused by the fear of failing, the belief that losing is a disgrace, stifles performance and diminishes the chances for success.

The internalized Parent is the usual source of this extraneous need to win. The child senses what is approved, what is received with affection, what is distressing, what provokes anxiety. Through the patterns of reward and punishment, of approval and disapproval, he perceives what his parent and other adults really want—and he internalizes this pattern of expectations. For some whose parents were difficult to satisfy, competitive behavior is intended to gain approval. They compete not for the fun of participation and the joy of demonstrating competence, but to prove to their doubting Parent that they are competent, that they can win. In part because they never quite succeed in erasing the doubts, they try again and again, with more and more intensity—and consequently often appear as "winners." However, their constantly felt need to excel, to win, to satisfy the demands of their Parent, often interferes with their performance. Preoccupied with their fear of failure or distracted by their need to be approved, they are unable to release their Child, to pay attention to the game, to demonstrate competence. Whenever a competitive situation appears, they may feel forced to demonstrate superiority, whether or not the demonstration contributes to ultimate success.

Underlying the need to win is the feeling that something more is involved than success in the game at hand. Losing is regarded not as evidence that another player performed better on a particular occasion, but as a revelation of what was suspected all along—the loser's inferiority. The greater the fear that one's assertiveness is unequal to the task, that one's demand for recognition is inappropriate, the greater is the need to prove the fear unjustified—that is, to win. A tennis player once described this state of mind as an inability to recognize that one is merely hitting a ball. Fernando Lamas, asked by Johnny Carson if it bothered him to be beaten at tennis, said that his virility was not at the end of his racket. How few seem to recognize this obvious truth! Sailboat racing is a game in which one or more people in one boat attempt to cross a finish line ahead of other people in other boats. That's all. Stature, virility, social (and maternal) acceptability, are not at stake.

Artie Donovan, the former lineman, commented upon a preseason Colt–Bear game (which the Colts were losing), "The Bears think this is the Super Bowl. To the Colts it's only another preseason game." He may have been mistaken about the Colts' feelings at this particular time, but the attitude he described is a common one: when losing becomes imminent, the competitor to whom winning is all-important must deny his need to win. This attitude negates the purpose of play—participation in a game—and makes both playing and winning meaningless. At least two players must be game or there is no game. Being game means being involved in the intrinsic determinants of the competition—trying to outperform the opponents, preparing for and responding to the uncertainties, accepting the variations in luck.

The standards of professional athletes, the iron men who ignore pain, the elements, and the competition, who "always" win, may be adopted by the internalized Parent of an amateur, who will then castigate himself when he fails to meet those standards. Ron Clarke derides the emphasis in Australia on winning. There, he says, children are taught that losing is a disgrace; Clarke feels that the real disgrace is not trying, and that Australian children often avoid competition because they are afraid they may lose. The resultant feelings of inadequacy impair both the mental toughness necessary to withstand setbacks and the satisfaction associated with success.

Many competitors behave as if they believe that the winner is the "best man," that his victory demonstrates that he is a superior person. Supporters of athletes and spectators of athletic contests reinforce this belief by their adulation of the victor. (Vic Braden provides a more realistic appraisal: "One player beats himself or the other guy loses.") Social attitudes that imply that the man who wins is the best also imply that the loser is somehow defective. An internalized Parent may tell the ego the same thing, and an ego told that it is defective functions poorly.

A person who fears failure avoids situations in which failure, if it occurs, will be unmistakable. He shuns direct conflicts with his opponents—starts at the favored end, prolonged side-by-side contests on the windward leg. Thus, the competitor who desperately needs to win misses opportunities to make gains, deliberately handicaps himself, and fails to acquire much-needed experience in tight situations. As he fails more and more often, the tension becomes intolerable; ultimately, he may surrender and give up the race, the class, or even the sport.

Some competitors are partially paralyzed by their fear of failure. Before a contest they are unable to eat; after a contest they have no idea of the score. During a contest they become preoccupied—not with the situation of the moment but with analyzing the cause of their anxiety, determining how to remove it, or remembering previous cases of similar anxiety. Some resort to fatalism, taking the view that it doesn't matter what they do—they have no control over the outcome. I once sailed in a major event with a skipper who prior to the racing was unwilling to purchase any mementos related to the venue because they might remind him of his possible (expected?) defeat. His focus was entirely on the outcome. The effect was to paralyze major elements of his performance.

The relaxation essential to peak performance cannot be achieved in a state of tension and fear. To the extent that extrinsic pressures are allowed to intrude, both the pleasure and the likelihood of success diminish. To feel with University of Minnesota coach Bill Musselman that "defeat is worse than death because you have to live with defeat" imposes a ridiculous concern that must detract from performance.

Competitors always have dual needs—to assert themselves, to show their true competence, and simultaneously to be accepted and approved, to feel deserving. It is never possible to satisfy both these needs, and to the extent that the latter (the need to please others) is dominant, the first will be unsatisfied. The mental toughness necessary for successful performance is inconsistent with a Parent-dominated ego. The need to be assertive, to improve performance, increases the likelihood of winning. But the need to be approved, to win (that is, preoccupation with the avoidance of guilt), interferes with rational analysis and decision making and distracts attention from the game; it diminishes the likelihood of improving performance, and thus the likelihood of winning.

13 / Conscientiousness

The best-laid schemes o' mice an' men
Gang aft agley,
An' lea'e us naught but grief an' pain
For promised joy.

—ROBERT BURNS

CARL ROBIE, THE 200-METER BUTTERFLY-STROKE SWIMMER, DESCRIBES
his Olympic career as follows:

> I didn't want to be just an Olympic gold medalist, but in the inimitable words
> of Jesse Owens, I wanted to be "Olympic Champion." Then came defeats at
> Tokyo [he won the silver medal] with teeth that tore hearts to little pieces, forc-
> ing one to adjust a loyal opinion of oneself. . . . Defeat meant for me the
> treasure about which I had dreamed was lost forever. For the next four years I
> learned to walk again, but in walking along the way to Mexico, somehow I
> learned it was fun to run. I was not just competing to be ahead of the world but
> to be a part of it, never more, never less. Competition became the end unto it-
> self, not world beating. This attitude of "struggle" for its own sake brought me
> a victory in Mexico, however late, more meaningful than a golden dream that
> was then four years old, only because it was something I wanted to do and I did
> it. It was the "doing" that was pleasurable. The pleasure wasn't in something
> that had been "done" to which many people ascribe an (incalculable) value.

Outcome is the realm of the Parent. Winning, losing, finishing—
results, accomplishments, credits—are in the past and in the future.

The Child is concerned with joy in the present, the Parent with achievements in the past, goals in the future. The Child looks for pleasure, the Parent for approval. The Parent determines the value of past accomplishments and prejudges the significance of future goals. Standards are established: you should win this one, you may be third in that one. The Parent leaves no room for surprises. This outcome is acceptable, that is guilt-provoking. There is a need to comply with expectations.

Carl Robie was devastated when he found that despite his conscientiousness he had failed to achieve an outcome consistent with his expectation. The Parent gives no credit for performing well; only the results determine approval or disapproval. Paul Elvstrom has said, in reference to a trip to South Africa, that whenever he was invited to compete somewhere he always felt particularly obliged to win.

The Parent sets up standards, deciding what is good, what is bad, what is right, what is wrong. The Parent determines when one is deserving, when undeserving, and is the arbiter of justice, the judge of fairness. Conscientiousness is the investment of self in achieving an outcome that conforms to the expectation—the value judgment—of the Parent. To achieve less is to fail, and results in a feeling of guilt. For the conscientious there may be little satisfaction in success; the achievement was after all expected. The pleasure is only in the cessation of guilt. Conscientiousness is guilt-proneness.

In America most parents transmit a belief in the Protestant work ethic. You get what you deserve. Conscientiousness—compliance with the expectations of the internalized Parent—means working hard enough to "deserve" a desired outcome, not hoping to get something for nothing. David Thorpe used to win the last three races of each 14 regatta but never arrived in time to make the start of the first. No one worried about his over-all finishing position; he deserved no better if he couldn't arrive on time! One competitor commented, "Don't anybody give that fellow a watch; if he were able to tell time, we'd all be in trouble!"

Bruce Ogilvie uses the trait conscientiousness as being synonymous with the presence of a strong superego (internalized Parent). He says that "this personality attribute has received more social comment than any other athletic trait in that every appeal to youth, every address at an awards banquet, and every philosophy of physical education holds this trait out as a primary goal." There is little evidence that conscientiousness is developed by competitive activity, but there is suggestive evidence that it contributes to persistence, to the individual's readiness to stick to a training program despite setbacks. At the opposite pole, according to Raymond Cattell, the person lacking conscientiousness is a quitter, and is fickle, frivolous, immature, relaxed, indolent, neglectful of social chores, changeable. Competitive success would seem to require conscientiousness—and so all coaches and banquet speakers evidently believe. But even Cattell would agree that the conscientious may be unable to relax, may be less able to enjoy their competition.

The major value of conscientiousness is in training and preparation. It assures the investment of every possible ounce of energy and moment of time in the development of necessary skills and capacities. During a performance it facilitates endurance, perseverance, and tolerance for pain. Peter Barrett recalls how Georg Bruder beat him in a Finn Gold Cup—by being in better condition for the final heavy-weather race and better able to concentrate on what mattered. The handicap of the conscientious is their preoccupation with outcome, with the ultimate significance of each element of their performance. This preoccupation increases tension, interferes with realistic appraisal, and blocks self-control.

The conscientious expects that his high investment will result in a high reward—an outcome pleasing to his Parent. Paul Elvstrom says:

> Before the Melbourne and Naples Olympics, I was really training a lot in Finns and I had the feeling that the more I was sailing and the more I was in training, in particular turning marks, tacking, and beating, the better I became. But I never went out training just for the fun of sailing. I went out to try and see if I could do something better. When it was blowing very hard, I went out and practiced jibing, and when it was blowing so hard that I couldn't get forward to grab the mainsheet or anything, I was training to jibe without touching the sheets. Of course, there is also physical fitness and so we did training in the gymnasium, because if you become tired, your brain doesn't work any more. The week before every important meeting—Gold Cup and the Olympic games—I was on the water eight hours every day, so that it was the boat and me working together as one smooth thing. My advice is that you have got to spend all your time at it if you want to have a chance to win.

The unspoken corollary is, If you spend the amount of time, effort, and energy that I did, you are guaranteed success.

And the converse is; If you do not spend a significant amount of time, effort, and energy, you must expect to perform poorly and lose. Concerning his preparation for the Olympics at Acapulco, Elvstrom says, "I think a few years ago when I was very hard training in Finns, I always covered every possibility, but this time I was not going to the Olympics to win. I was going to the Olympics to enjoy myself, too scared to be too prepared in case I got my old nerves back." He came in fourth. But he also recognized that conscientiousness might work to one's disadvantage. Of the night before the last race of his first Olympics, at Torquay, he observed, "I was concentrating on everything that might happen and that's really, I should say, a disadvantage. At that time, I wanted very much to win and I concentrated too hard by thinking out what could happen so that I should be prepared for everything. Preparing like this can make a man too nervous."

The conscientious often lack a sense of humor or even a sense of reality. Some act as if they believe that their investment of self should guarantee success on every occasion. They become angry and resentful when they don't win. They seem to feel that it is unjust for someone who has trained less assiduously to beat them, and they cry out bitterly at the injustice.

However—contrary to the expectations and intentions of the conscientious—a low investment may occasionally result in a high reward. Most of those so rewarded refer deprecatingly to their "luck." Intimidated by the nearly universal faith in the Protestant ethic, rather than admit to having deserved victory, they assure the conscientious of their unworthiness! A few agnostics exist, Bruce Goldsmith notable among them. Far from preparing for an event, Bruce never even arrives at the dock until the ten-minute gun has fired. He wins not in spite of his conscientious opponents, but, seemingly, to spite them. He glories in demonstrating that a blind adherence to Parental standards is not only unnecessary but inhibiting. He stands out in my analysis of world-class competitors as the only one with a low score for conscientiousness (guilt-proneness) and determination!

What Goldsmith's behavior tells us is what has clearly been forgotten by the Parent-driven, guilt-prone, conscientious worker. We are playing a game. Although the object of the game is to win, the purpose of the game is to play. The extremely conscientious demonstrate not their strength, but their weakness; they are afraid—afraid to lose, afraid of the guilt their internalized Parent will visit upon them if they lose. It is as if they doubt their ability to win in a fair competition, with everyone equally prepared (or unprepared), equally capable, accepting the risks of competition. They require an advantage, so that the competition is unfair, guaranteeing them a better chance to win than anyone else. Paul Elvstrom attained this advantage at a time when few others prepared at all. Today the conscientious individual must work even harder because he competes against many whose Parent drives them with equal vigor. And the truly conscientious person, needing to win on every occasion, will find a way to prepare better than before—so as never to be forced into competition without an advantage.

Fortunately, there has been some backlash with respect to the old Protestant ethic, perhaps led by the awakened Elvstrom himself. Now, in the midst of full-time, fully supported efforts to ward off defeat, there is a renewed enthusiasm for playing a game and for those who are game in playing. In 1977 the New York Yankees bought the greatest stars in baseball, paid them millions to play the game, and with an advantage purchased in advance, won the World Series. Few were pleased; most recognized that anyone can win who works hard enough, invests enough time, effort, or money, acquires an advantage before the competition begins. In 1978 the Los Angeles Dodgers became the heroes of baseball fans. They represented the philosophy described by their star, Reggie Smith: "We enjoy the game and we think we are more likely to win if we are having fun."

Marty Cooksey overtook the leader of the 1977 Atlanta marathon just past the crest of the last big hill and went on to win in near record time. "There is no deceit in marathoning," she said later. "It is the same for everybody. It is what burns inside and how wisely you have judged it that gets you through the last miles. I am motivated from inside. I don't even run for a club. You can get carried away with outside things, what people expect, material things. I just came to do my best. And to show that it is good enough for the Olympics."

14 / Expectations

*Waiting and hoping are the whole of life, and as
soon as a dream is realized it is destroyed.*
—GIAN-CARLO MENOTTI

MY VICTORIES IN SUCH MAJOR EVENTS AS THE PRINCESS ELIZABETH AND
Prince of Wales Cup races resulted in part, I think, from my deciding
and assuming in advance that I would win. My expectation of success
determined the effort I put into preparation, and my preparedness determined my victory. If you expect to lose, you are very likely to do
so. If you expect to win, you are more likely to do so. If you perform
worse than than you expected to, the resultant dissatisfaction is a spur
to greater effort in the future. If you perform better than you expected
to, you are satisfied and make no effort to improve. Winners are characterized by dissatisfaction with their current status, whatever it is.

Conscientiousness is connected with the Parent-determined belief that investment of self should correlate with outcome. High goal
setting is connected with the Child-determined belief that everyone is
equally "deserving" of victory regardless of investment. To set the
goal of victory is to assume that victory is "deserved." The elimination

73

of the belief that one is basically "undeserving," is a first step toward winning.

Specific goals, particularly when they are long-range, are Parent-determined; the Child wishes to do well now. The Parent wishes for success on an occasion that will be recognized, so that approval will be gained. The Adult knows that some occasions are better tests than others and wishes for success in the more exacting test, regardless of the extent to which this success is recognized by others. Adult expectations and Adult desires are realistic. The Adult is satisfied by an improvement in performance, whether or not the expected finishing position is attained. Art Ellis says he often finds that he is more critical of his performance when he wins than when he loses.

I am impressed by how regularly regattas turn out in accordance with expectations. The results of any one race may be a surprise, but by the end of a series, those who are expected (those who expect?) to be on top are on top and those who are expected to be at the bottom are at the bottom. Bruce Ogilvie's analysis of Olympic swimming medalists indicates that they are characterized by a much higher than usual need to be on top. They require the spotlight; they enjoy attention, acclaim. Their desire to do well appears to result in their doing well. My survey of the attributes of racing sailors also indicates that their expectations correlate with their performance. Rustamova says, "When the will is as taut as a bowstring, the ant can overcome the lion." When Hans Fogh came to Miami in 1973 for his first major Soling regatta, he told me he expected to win because his preparation had been so complete—and he did win. It is easy to accept the view that if you expect to win, you will.

And though in truth this conclusion may not always be valid, its reverse is certain: if you expect to lose, you will. While training for the 1976 Olympic decathlon, Bruce Jenner at one point realized that he was preparing himself to lose, attempting to reassure himself that he could handle losing, considering ways to deal with losing. As these thoughts developed, his performance deteriorated. Without the expectation of success, his determination diminished, his practice became less effective. After a discussion with his wife at three o'clock one morning, he decided, "I'm going for the gold medal. If I'm second, I'll deal with that when it happens."

"I feel the goat rising in me now," says Charlie Brown. When there are two outs in the ninth inning, he expects to strike out, and he will. How different the outcome would be if he felt the hero rising in him. The pitcher who "knows" that the final batter will hit a home run to win the game will pitch the ball down the center of the plate. There is no sense in his trying to throw for the inside corner; he might as well throw it down the middle and get it over with. Self-fulfilling prophecies are equally characteristic of winners. Expecting to win, they do everything possible to ensure success. Most of us, expecting to finish in some intermediate position, behave similarly. If our standing as we enter the final race of a series is lower than usual, we expect to do better, concentrate on doing so, and sail our best race. If our standing as we enter the final race is higher than usual, we may expect to do worse, or at best retain our unexpected position; we accept whatever we are given, take no risks, and sail our poorest race.

The mentally tough competitor recognizes that his high expectations require—and justify—a high investment of self. The more Child-like competitor, wishing to do well but unwilling to make a major investment of energy (in part because he doesn't believe he will actually do well), does poorly. My friend Bob Bearor, accompanying me while I coached at one of Steve Colgate's race weeks in the Bahamas, commented, "They don't want to learn how to be first; they want you to pick them up and put them in first!"

The competitor with high expectations based upon a realistic (Adult) appraisal of his capabilities, resists the adverse effect of a poor outcome. Being behind or losing does not discourage him. He makes no less an effort to perform well thereafter. He expects things to change for the better. If he doesn't win the North Americans this time, he knows he will the next.

Referring to his performance at Munich in winning the gold medal, Frank Shorter says, "You can't be so goal-oriented that you win and quit. Runners keep running." For "runners," read "competitors"—*real* competitors. The desired goal, the expected outcome, is improved performance. Winning is not needed. If winning is the only goal, there is nothing beyond victory. You might as well quit.

Most competitors usually achieve approximately what they expect, and are satisfied. The result is the pecking order. We expect to achieve what we "deserve." Although the opportunity to exceed our expectations is preserved, only winners take advantage of it. Most competitors settle for fulfillment of their expectations or for the first indication that these expectations have been exceeded—as is shown by the Super Bowl Syndrome.

Only two teams (after the first) have won the National Football

League Super Bowl on their first try. The contenders work with great determination all season long to attain the division championship, to survive the first play-offs, and to reach the Super Bowl. When they have won the division championship they feel they have lived up to their expectations, and when they have won the first play-off they feel that they have exceeded their expectations—nothing more should be expected of them—and they lose. The syndrome also characterizes first-time Olympic participants from nations, such as the United States, where winning the trials is both extremely difficult and unlikely. It also characterizes the day-by-day performance of most amateur competitors. They are willing to settle for any achievement beyond their expectations, and then they quit. "We were first at the weather mark"—satisfaction enough for one weekend.

The ultimate outcome of the Super Bowl Syndrome is disaster rather than elation. When the success achieved is short of the ultimate, the next round may reveal one's deficiency, and the satisfaction associated with the initial achievement will be destroyed. When the ultimate success is indeed achieved, the need for continued striving, the previous *raison d'être* for existence, is lost, and elation may turn to depression. Witness the experience of Ron Clarke, Mark Spitz, and hundreds of others who, preoccupied with outcome, with attaining a particular goal at some seemingly unreachable level, suddenly found that they had succeeded—and that there was nothing left to strive for.

Unrealistic expectations invite disappointment and discouragement. Goals should be set that require improvement step by step. Performance is enhanced one element at a time—an improvement in jibing technique, an improvement in starting technique, better organization of a race plan. Such goals can be met; such expectations can be realized. The accomplishment of such goals is encouraging; it stimulates one to make additional effort, to expect additional progress. Like desire, expectations should be focused on improved performance. Winning will follow not because it was desired or expected, but because improvements in performance were desired, expected, and achieved.

Part Four

Mental Toughness: The Adult

Control of Drives, Impulses, and Emotions

15 / Mental Toughness

For, whether the prize be a ribbon or throne,
The victor is he who can go it alone.
                    —JOHN GODFREY SAXE

BEFORE THE 1976 OLYMPIC GAMES I ASKED HANS FOGH HOW HE HAD WON the Canadian Flying Dutchman trials, how he expected to perform in the Olympics, and how he would react to losing, if he were to do so. He replied that it was his resistance to pressure that had won the trials for him, that the younger, less experienced sailors of equal capability had become unnerved. He expected to do well in the Olympics by being conservative until the leaders sorted themselves out, and by being tough, "not getting shook whether ahead or behind," thereafter. He admitted that he could lose—something could go wrong; the con ditions were difficult, one could never be certain of victory. Hans didn't win, but his remarks (and his usual performance) demonstrate the importance of having mental toughness—of being realistic, un emotional, free to concentrate on what matters. He may have said it all when he emphasized his intention to retain control of himself, his composure, "whether ahead or behind." (As much mental toughness may be needed to control the emotions aroused by being ahead as to

79

control those aroused by being behind.) Joe Garagiola says, "We need guys who can erase mistakes." We need guys who can erase everything except the factors that determine their immediate performance.

Chris Evert has been the most successful woman tennis player in the world for several years and was named Sportswoman of the Year 1976 by *Sports Illustrated.* Yet most observers agree that she is not the best stroke maker in any particular category. Others are stronger, more talented, more explosive. But, says Margaret Court, "She concentrates to the last point." She is tough; she never gives up. She "is a clear thinker in a thoughtful game," says Sarah Pileggi. She takes the game one serve at a time, stroke after stroke after stroke.

To be mentally tough is to have one's Adult in control of one's feelings and one's behavior. The mentally tough person is objective under pressure. He isn't concerned about what others think, or embarrassed by past mistakes. Not preoccupied with what has happened or what is happening elsewhere, he is free to concentrate on what should happen. He is not intimidated by his competitors, his crew, or his own limitations. He can accept criticism without being hurt, maintain composure when the pressure is high, recover readily from adversity. He can appraise situations, problems, and competitors realistically, dispassionately, without sentiment. He has a strong ego, with the Adult always in control. Ultimately, mental toughness means the ability to perceive the world and oneself realistically, to recognize the behavior that will be in one's own interest, and to act accordingly.

Mental toughness determines the effectiveness of performance and the likelihood of success. The presence of the mental attributes that contribute to preparation—assertiveness and determination from the Child, conscientiousness and desire from the Parent—results in the acquisition of skill. Individuals characterized by these traits can be expected to sail fast and skillfully. They prepare their boats to go fast, and they prepare themselves to handle their boats well. Total performance depends on far more than this, however. It is the cumulative effect of many independent actions. Boat speed and boat-handling skills get the boat from one crisis to the next. Mental toughness gets the boat through the crises. Boat speed and boat-handling skills get the boat ahead in one race. Mental toughness gets the boat ahead in the series.

I remember at the 1976 Olympic trials sailing alongside Robbie Haines on a long starboard tack. The leaders were off to the right, and the wind was gradually veering. We were slowly working ahead of him, but he was able to keep his air clear. We kept on and on, hoping the wind would back. A quarter mile from the lay line we decided to bail out (if the wind did back, we'd lay it; if the wind kept on veering, we'd lose less). Robbie, tough enough to continue on starboard while we were beating him and tough enough to recognize that the only possibility for gain lay ahead, carried on. At the lay line the wind *had* backed and was stronger. He rounded sixth, we tenth.

The elements of ego function which contribute to racing success, as illustrated by this episode, are self-control, realistic appraisal (of the external world, other competitors, one's self and previous experience), and resistance to anxiety. These attributes permit a skipper to evaluate an external situation, his feelings about it, and his recollections of previous similar situations; to decide upon an appropriate response; and to control the impulses, fears, and guilt which are aroused, so that he may act in his own best interest.

Ego maturity, like physical maturity, depends upon proper development—the proper provision of support, respect, and discipline while we are maturing. Sometimes our Child retains too much control, and we act impulsively. Sometimes our Parent gains too much control, and we act mechanically. Failure to control either Child or Parent may interfere with our ability to make realistic appraisals, reach appropriate decisions, or act in our own best interest.

Our perceptions are often faulty. Our evaluations of our inner needs are often in error. We frequently fail to remember a previous similar situation or its outcome. We feel anxiety, react impulsively, respond as a child or a parent rather than as an adult. Competitors must accept the ego functions available to them and learn to utilize them as effectively as possible. Even the most competent are incompetent at times and must resort to compromises instead of courage.

The persistence of the Child in the adult results not so much in the continuance of Child activity as in the continuance of childhood fears and feelings. A child feels helpless and threatened in a world of more powerful beings. An inadequate resolution of these concerns during an individual's early life may leave him still feeling frightened as a grownup. In consequence, he may exploit competition as a means of reassuring himself about his significance, or he may avoid direct conflicts. His underlying anxiety may be distracting or even paralyzing. In addition, the impulsiveness that characterizes childhood behavior may persist and compromise both conscious, intended behavior and the management of this fearfulness. The individual may find it necessary to protect himself against the awareness of these threats, to deny or avoid them. The use of defenses, including "game" playing, to achieve this end is but a partial solution which substitutes a diminution in realistic appraisal for a more generalized handicap of ego function. Mental toughness, control of the Child, is necessary if one is to ignore the threats, to be appropriately assertive, without resorting to defensive techniques.

Persistent control of the ego by the Parent means that the adult continues to be anxious about his acceptability and guilty about his deserving to be accepted. We all carry into a game the need to be accepted and approved. But a few individuals have such a fear of being abandoned that compliance with Parental requirements becomes an overwhelming need and failure to comply results in intolerable guilt. Most of us at least intermittently, when we fail to behave as we should, feel anxiety and guilt and resort to handicapping defenses in order to avoid the reappearance of that guilt.

Although we return to play again and again in search of the euphoria of freedom, most of us play but intermittently during our participation in games. When the going gets tough, when the pressure is on, when what we do will determine whether we win or lose, our Parent calls us to account, demanding our conformity and requiring that we behave in accordance with previously internalized patterns. We say to ourselves, "Think what this will mean; be aware of the awful consequences of failure; remember that you were insufficient the last time you attempted this action." But to get through the crisis we need a strong Adult—mental toughness—so that we can thrust aside both the guilt and the anxiety, to control both our feelings and our actions.

If the competitor is not mentally tough, if his ego is insufficient to the task, his appraisals of the situation will not be realistic and his actions may be inappropriate. The weak ego may be unable to prevent the intrusion of unconscious, irrational perceptions. The situation becomes symbolic, representing some previous experience that was inadequately resolved and left a residue of pain and anxiety. The resulting faulty appraisals are often associated with impulsive responses. No conscious analysis of the situation is undertaken. A state of total unawareness may supervene. Action is taken in response to the unconscious perception rather than to the real situation. Responses may then be stereotyped and repetitive, and in direct opposition to the competitor's interests.

To the extent that we experience joy, relaxation, acceptance, satisfaction, we seem better able to perceive realistically and to behave appropriately. To the extent that we experience pain, fear, guilt, suspicion, hostility, rejection, we are less able to perceive realistically and to behave appropriately. Success in one race usually makes us better able to perform in the next. Failure on one leg diminishes our performance on the next. Self-assurance frees our minds to concentrate on our performance; self-belittling restricts our minds to preoccupation with our incompetence. A subservient Adult may be temporarily strengthened by positive experiences, a strong Adult temporarily weakened by negative experiences. The weak, whose experiences tend to be adverse, get weaker, and the strong, whose experiences tend to be supportive, get stronger. Nothing succeeds like success.

The attributes essential to the attainment of competence characterize the strong ego (one dominated by a strong Adult); they can be classified in relation to the defective behavior patterns that result from their absence. The person possessing the listed attributes will demonstrate creativity, mastery, and courage, will enjoy competition, and will probably win. The person lacking the listed attributes will have impaired competence, will not enjoy competition, and will probably lose.

Ego Functions	*Personality Attributes*	*Defects*
CONTROL OF DRIVES, IMPULSES, AND EMOTIONS	Self control of anxiety and guilt Aggressiveness "Pride" Equanimity	Anger Depression Panic Hostility Impulsivity Tension Confusion
REALITY TESTING	Realistic appraisal	Misapprehension Acceptance of the pecking order Susceptibility to intimidation
SELF-APPRAISAL	Self-confidence Self-assurance Self-respect	Self-doubt Self-deprecation Embarrassment Self-consciousness

Ego Functions	Personality Attributes	Defects
		Secretiveness
		Cheating
		Expectation of failure
OBJECT RELATIONS	Respect for others	Suspiciousness
	Trust	Concern about a
	Teamwork	particular opponent
	Acceptance of criticism	Assigning blame
MEMORY, CON-CEPTION, AT-TENTION	Concentration	Distraction
	Consistency	Preoccupation
	Perseverance	Complacency
	Grace under pressure	
DEFENSIVE FUNC-TIONING	Relaxation	Anxiety
		Denial
		Intellectualization
		Magical thinking
		Regression
		Escape
		Surrender
		Gamesmanship
		Deliberate courtship of defeat

16 / "Pride"

The discipline of desire is the background of character.

—JOHN LOCKE

SELF-CONTROL IS THE ATTRIBUTE MOST CLEARLY ASSOCIATED WITH COMpetitive success. Embodying the presence of a supportive internalized Parent and a controllable Child, it is the chief manifestation of a mentally tough, realistic Adult; it permits realistic responses to realistically appraised circumstances. Self-control is the ability to suppress the temptation to attain short-term satisfaction, protection, or relief at the expense of long-term satisfaction—not by denying, displacing, disguising, or diminishing awareness of short-term interests, but by recognizing them and focusing on progression toward long-term goals nevertheless. Self-control does not involve ego defenses; it signifies full awareness of threats and temptations while determining rational responses.

Pride, greed, lust, envy, gluttony, anger, and sloth, the classic seven deadly sins, characterize the behavior of infants. The maturation of a strong ego depends upon the gradual acquisition of control over such behavior. However, just as we accept the impulsiveness, acquisitiveness, selfishness, and susceptibility to anger of the young infant as normal, so we should accept the occasional re-emergence of these attributes in adults.

Bruce Ogilvie equates self-control with "pride," a trait often ascribed by great competitors to other greats. This is obviously to be distinguished from the pride included among the seven deadly sins. The latter are evidence of the continuation of infantile behavior, the former is the means by which the infantile behavior is controlled. To say of a person that "he has pride" means he has a degree of will power that permits him to overcome temptations to infantile behavior. Ogilvie has demonstrated, through his psychometric devices, that self-control is highly correlated with athletic success. A survey I made of the attributes of world-class sailors indicated that they too are characterized by a high degree of self-control. The range of scores (on a scale of 10–30) was 17–30 (average 23.7) for these competitors as compared with 14–20 (average 17.8) for local sailors. Self-control and mental toughness were two among only three attributes (the third being trust) which distinguished the highly competent from the minimally competent.

Competitors who know what they should do are far more numerous than those who do what they should. This difference is consequent to variations in self-control. "Pride" causes the competitor to forgo the temptation to give up, obtain relief from pain, take the easy way out—to be satisfied with limited success. "Pride" sets apart those who are able to do what they should despite the exigencies of the moment, the previous defeat, the present failure, the expected loss. Maintenance of the degree of self-control indicated by this conduct requires a positive attitude about oneself. The psyche must be resistant to embarrassment, depression, tension, distraction, and temptation. "He has pride" means that although the person is fully aware of the temptation to accept his present status, he does not; although he recognizes all the excuses he could use to justify not continuing his best effort, he continues. He not only knows what he should do; he does it.

Self-control is in part the ability to stifle feelings concerning an appraisal while maintaining a realistic awareness of what is being appraised. In terms of competition this means that the significance of the present action is ignored while the appropriate performance response is initiated or continued. Neither the opponent's success nor one's own failure is intimidating, disturbing, or depressing. Whether the event under appraisal is at the beginning of the game or at its end, whether it is irrelevant to the outcome or the sole determinative of it, the responsive action is the same. Except for variation in the intensity of excitement, no alteration in feeling occurs. Feelings do not preoccupy awareness, do not distract from organized appraisal, do not block rational decision making.

In sailboat racing this means that the actions and positions of other boats, instead of being regarded as threats, are utilized as indicators of wind conditions that exist elsewhere or are likely to develop. Other boats are not allowed to determine strategy. In a big lift the choice between hanging on and tacking early is based upon a realistic evaluation of whether the lift represents a persisting or an oscillating shift rather than upon the awareness that as a consequence of the change one is now far ahead or far astern. In oscillating winds a tack is continued toward the next heading shift even though the boat on the weather quarter is lifting inside. The significance of the immediate situation is ignored so one can proceed with the best long-term solution.

Continuation of a preselected course is almost always the correct strategy in light and variable air. The temptation to tack, to jibe, to deviate toward a position of presumed advantage, must be resisted. The self-controlled are able to resist. Others, fearful that the whole fleet will sail by, chase the advantage of one moment, vacating the position which will provide the advantage of the next. Or intimidated by the remembrance of their previous failure, knowing that they *should* continue their initial course, instead of making a slight alteration they plod along in a hole and are overrun. In either case the response is impulsive, based not upon careful analysis, but upon fear of expected adversity. The self-controlled select the course which is most likely to be advantageous; the intimidated select a course which is unlikely to be disastrous.

The panic-stricken shouters are too preoccupied with their feelings (fright, anger, despair) to make realistic appraisals or rational responses. Calmness is an indication of self-control and of the likelihood of rational behavior. Don Barnes describes his skipper as emerging from the cabin, in the midst of a broach to leeward in a 40-footer, to ask whether Don "would mind returning this yacht to its proper course." Remember, too, Hartley Watlington's request, during a disastrous spinnaker douse: "While you're about it, would you fix me a cup of tea?"

The American pentathlete Jane Frederick implies that self-control must be developed. "The body and mind are actually a lot alike," she says. "The more you condition them, the better they respond." Enid Rubin describes her preparation for her examination for a blue belt in karate: "Relax, go after it, let it happen, make it happen. I come to class heady, almost drunk with the intoxication of fear and change. Once inside, I put on a glove of calm. I understand what I need most is a sense of calm and a firm grounding. At first I feel all the eyes on me and then they melt into the technique." Jack Knights says of sailors involved in the fifth race of the Kingston Olympics, "Team managers have a duty to instill into their sailors a calmer attitude to haphazard winds. Instructions must be given that arms should not be thrown up in horror, floorboards must not be kicked in frustration. Instead patience must be retained and opportunities searched out and taken." Whether team managers can accomplish such effects is questionable; that the intended result is essential cannot be questioned.

Royal Robbins describes the necessity of self-control in rock climbing as follows:

> If we are keenly alert and aware of the rock and what we are doing on it, if we are honest with ourselves and our capabilities and weaknesses, if we avoid committing ourselves beyond what we know is safe, then we will climb safely. For climbing is an exercise in reality. He who sees it clearly is on safe ground, regardless of his experience or skill. But he who sees reality as he would like it to be, may have his illusions rudely stripped from his eyes when the ground comes up fast. . . .
>
> We are, of course, all mixtures of sanity and folly, of clear vision and murky romanticism. Such conflicts are a mark of the human condition. And we climb because we are human. The rock is a field of battle between our weakness and our strength. We wouldn't touch rock if we were perfectly self-controlled. And he who would climb and live must continuously wage this battle and never let folly win. It's an outrageously demanding proposition. But I never said it was easy.

If we were perfectly controlled, there would be no need to test ourselves in sports and no surprises in game playing. For competition is a test of self-control. We are excited by the opportunity to test our ability to control our emotions, resist temptation, behave rationally. He who is best controlled, he who has the most "pride," wins.

17 / Pressure

The price of greatness is responsibility.
—WINSTON CHURCHILL

A CRITICAL MOMENT IN THE 1977 BRITISH OPEN WAS DESCRIBED IN *Sports Illustrated:*

> They went to the 16th tee [tied for the lead] and Jack [Nicklaus] and Tom [Watson] looked at each other. Yesterday and today. Then and now. Domingues and Ordōnez.
> And Tom smiled at Jack. "This is what it's all about, isn't it?"
> And Jack smiled back and said, "You bet it is."

Pressure—you can avoid it, succumb to it, or thrive upon it. You can't deny it. Much as you'd like to disregard the outcome—and know that you can perform better if you do—sometimes the outcome is all that matters. At the Olympic trials, you are selected or you are not. This is what it's all about, say the great competitors: playing against the best when the outcome is significant. When you lose one of these, you never get it back. And every one you win will be with you always. The greater the pressure the greater the pleasure—if you win. This is the true test of whose Child and whose Parent is best controlled, of who is best able to make realistic appraisals (of himself and of the challenge), best able to focus on his own performance, of who is the toughest mentally. To succumb is not only to lose the game but to lose the purpose, the enjoyment, of the game. Courage is required, grace under pressure.

Succumbing is all too common. Fear arises and cannot be controlled. Paralysis, confusion, bumbling ineptitude, panic, or just irritability and preoccupation result. And instead of the best performance of which one is capable, the worst that one can remember follows. Consider the Red Sox down the stretch in 1978. With a sixteen-game lead in early July, a lead that a few said only the Red Sox could blow, they began to look over their shoulders and played the worst baseball in their history. Down to a four-game lead when they met the Yankees in late September, they said, "We've still got a chance," and lost four straight.

As they approached the sixteenth tee in the 1978 British Open, Simon Owen, who had never won anything, was leading Jack Nicklaus by one stroke. "I've been here before," Nicklaus must have said to himself. But Owen hadn't. He bogeyed the sixteenth (while Nicklaus birdied it) and was demolished on the seventeenth.

Of the helmsman ahead in an oscillating wind, Paul Elvstrom says, "The closer you get the more anxious he gets and the more he loses." He is concentrating—on you, on what will happen if you continue to gain, on losing, not on his own performance. It is the recurrent calculation of the significance of the competitor's progress that distracts and interferes: "If he gains now, if he wins this one, then . . ." Tension builds. Bruce Crampton says of tournament golf, "It's a compromise of what your ego wants you to do, what experience tells you to do, and what your nerves let you do." Dave Powlison says, "Every time you heel, you die a little." Fear—of failing, of being overtaken, of losing—is aroused by an inability to keep the boat upright. Fatigue makes "cowards of us all"!

Panic is one possible outcome of pressure. I have seen at close hand various panic reactions among my students at Steve Colgate's Offshore Sailing School. I remember one who, after achieving (with a little help from me, perched on the Soling stern) a near-perfect windward-end start, responded to my recommendation to tack by pulling the tiller up and almost crashing into the boats to leeward! Helmsmen may show their panic by shouting, of which they are subsequently unaware. ("Me? I never shout on the race course!") Crews more often panic by "freezing." Faced with the necessity of getting the spinnaker down *now*, they are unable to find the guy, or the halyard. Animals behave similarly in similar situations. When the headlights of a car find them on a highway, they freeze, or they may rush headlong across the road.

Panic is a Child response to the recognition of helplessness in the face of an overwhelming threat. As fright is originally experienced in response to parental threats, subsequent panic is more likely to occur in the presence of authority. The crew reacting to a poorly understood order (like my student in the Offshore Sailing School) or the helmsman being manipulated by an opponent who is, for example, establishing an overlap at the last moment, is likely to panic. The person who panics has first been made to feel like a Child, and then forced to recognize that he may be unequal to an upcoming demand; he has been made to feel helpless.

During panic, receptor systems fail, incoming information goes unrecognized, motor responses cease, insignificant stimuli provoke inappropriate responses. Control is lost. In primitive circumstances the "freezing" response may be protective; if he is motionless, the rabbit is less likely to be noticed by the fox. In competition, however, "freezing" has the worst possible effect. In sports such as sailing and automobile racing, in which collisions are possible, panic may even be dangerous. And it may occur not just the first time that a particular threat appears, but the fifth or sixth as well. Because panic results in amnesia, the experience of it yields no subsequent benefit.

Although panic runs counter to the conscious desires to assert power and demonstrate competence, it is not totally wasted. In accordance with the economy of utilization of psychic energy, it may be used to express ulterior wishes, and is more likely to occur when there is a need to do so. Through panic one may express an otherwise inexpressible anger toward an opponent, a teammate, or one's parent. After "freezing," the frightened person may lash back against the threat in an irrational manner. Anger is merely a different face of fear, and it is directed against any external control that causes a feeling of helplessness. Panic may also express a desire to "get it over with," to face the worst *now*. If the anticipation of fear is intolerable, the paralysis of panic may provide an escape from that awareness.

Fred Patek, after hitting into the double play that lost the 1977 American League play-offs, mused about fear: "None of us even understands why a player goes into a slump. I think that, all of a sudden, the player is scared of the ball. Maybe you're having a fight with your wife. You lose just enough confidence so that you get scared of the ball. The best thing you can do in a slump is admit you're scared." Fear can be distracting, even paralyzing, but admitting to its presence is the first step toward its conquest.

Many competitors play scared, recognizing fear. When the pressure is on, it is reasonable to acknowledge it. Both courage and effectiveness follow the acknowledgment. Billie Jean King says, "When you're holding the trophy, it's all over. What a relief!" John Albrechtson, while winning the gold medal in the Tempest class in 1976, remarked, "I think I will come back to my fourth Olympics as a freepistol competitor. At Munich our pistol man, Ragnar Skanaker, won on the first day. He had his gold medal and free whisky and was being driven around in a car with chauffeur before we sailors had our opening ceremony. For sailors the Olympics are seven long days in doubt." Such competitors face the demands of their Parent, deny its doubts, feel the tension, but still win.

Denial is often used as a means of avoiding pressure. By denying that winning is important or that one intends to win one can avoid both the fear of potential failure and the depression that otherwise follows. A more appropriate form of defense is to consider realistically in advance the possibility of defeat. Art Ellis says, "If you can't afford to lose, you can't afford to race." Such realism not only reduces tension, but makes winning more likely. Hans Fogh, relaxed after winning Kiel Week, felt that he couldn't possibly win the Europeans as well. Having already satisfied his Parent, he felt no pressure and went on to win again with ease. When Reggie Jackson stepped up to the plate after hitting two home runs in the World Series finale, he thought, "At that point, I couldn't lose. They were going to cheer me even if I struck out. So the last one was strictly dreamland. Hey man, wow, that's three!"

Accepting in advance the possibility of defeat does not mean being willing to be defeated. It merely means recognizing that defeat, if it occurs, can be lived with. It is not the same as Andy Kostanecki's approach to the 1975 Tempest World Championship: "If I don't do well in the first three races, I'm going to take off." Needless to say, his first three races were disastrous, and he took off. Accepting defeat is realistic and beneficial, predicting disaster is unrealistic and detrimental.

No artificial defense against fear is as good as facing it, but any defense is better than succumbing to it. Pregame "psyching" techniques provide one form of defense. The "sports psyching" of Thomas Tutko and Umberto Tosi consists of (1) getting loose, (2) breathing easy (reducing the awareness of tension), (3) staying on the ball (concentrating on the game), and (4) mental and (5) body rehearsal (imagining and practicing effective performance). The major purpose of this sequence is to reduce the distraction and confusion that accompany tension. Jack Nicklaus uses mental imagery, visualizing in advance his swing, the trajectory of the ball, and the landing of the ball in the desired location. The power of such positive thinking is only sufficient to overcome the adverse effects of fear; it creates no capability beyond that which was present to begin with.

The best way to deal with tension is to thrive on it. There are those, like Reggie Jackson, whose performance seems to depend upon pressure. They recognize the significance of the outcome, recognize that all eyes are upon them, and perform at their best. Jackson, the King of October, seems to need an audience before which to prove himself. The motivation of mountain climbers is to demonstrate that they can be as nerveless five hundred feet up as the rest of us are on a curbstone. They don't climb because "it's there" but because they wish to test their ability to stand the pressure. A *Sports Illustrated* article says; " 'Almost' falling doesn't count; almost losing a solid sense of control of yourself when you're 1,000 feet above the ground and gripping a rock with little more than your fingernails counts for everything."

Pressure derives not from what really happens, but from one's beliefs, often irrational, about meaning and impact. All changes are perceived as either beneficial or detrimental, and many are also perceived as indicating the future course of events. Tension is felt whenever a change occurs which is perceived as detrimental *and* likely to continue, relaxation whenever a change occurs which is perceived as beneficial and likely to continue. For instance, on the final weather leg you may recognize the only boat ahead to be slower than your own and to be losing with each tack. Even though your position is astern and losing, you feel no pressure. What is perceived is relaxing, reinforces a positive self-image and a positive view of probable outcome. On another final weather leg you may recognize the boat astern to be faster than your own and to be gaining with each tack. Even though your position is ahead and winning, you feel pressure; a negative image develops, and performance deteriorates.

Garry Hoyt points out that when a helmsman astern is gaining, "he is as much heartened by his gains as you are disheartened—it seems inevitable he will burst through." The potential "psyching" derives from a belief in progression, in inevitability. The tendency is to disregard all previous experience and expect whatever has happened to continue inexorably, without any potential for variance. Those for whom pressure is threatening perceive beneficial change as evanescent, detrimental change as inevitable.

Jack Nicklaus's experiences in the British Opens of 1977 and 1978 are illustrative. In the lead in 1977, he was watching Tom Watson gaining, and recognized the possibility of being overtaken and beaten. Behind in 1978 he was watching himself gaining on Simon Owen, and recognized the probability of overtaking him and winning. When we are gaining, we assume that we will continue to move ahead inexorably to a victorious conclusion. Confident and attentive, in control of both Child and Parent, we proceed to progressively improved performance. When we are losing, we assume that we will continue on the road to disaster just as inexorably. Fearful and confused, controlled by our Child and belittled by our Parent, we proceed to progressively diminished performance. No wonder that momentum carries us forward so well and that the pressure that accompanies its reversal can be so devastating.

18 / The Protestants

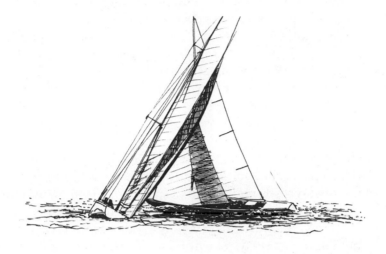

*A winner freely expresses resentment, discharges
his feelings and then forgets it.
A loser smolders with unexpressed resentment
and revenges himself by doing worse.*
—SYDNEY J. HARRIS

THERE WERE FIFTEEN PROTESTS AGAINST THE RACE COMMITTEE FOR ITS
alleged mismanagement of the fifth race of the 1976 Olympic series.
The protestants all claimed that they had been materially prejudiced,
and deserved redress. The British claimed that the race committee
had prejudiced their representatives because it had failed to abide by
the Sailing Instructions, which specified that there would be in each
race a specific distance sailed to windward, on a reach and on a run.
Behind the protests was the implication that the race should have been
abandoned when a major wind shift resulted in a period of calm and
alterations in the sailing angle of the subsequent legs. This was a
unique event—fifteen highly competent competitors all protesting for
essentially the same reason. An analysis of the performance of those
who protested and those who did not should indicate not only the circumstances which induce protesting but the psychological factors
which characterize the behavior of those who protest. Perhaps we can

discover why so few sailors do protest (in this instance there were 15 out of a possible 116).

I observed the racing of the Solings, Flying Dutchmen, and Tempests and recorded their positions at each mark, and subsequently I discussed the race with many of the participants.

One sailing skill which is necessary to the successful management of every race and which should certainly be tested in the Olympics is the ability to predict the occurrence and direction of wind shifts. With complete meteorological data, the help of team meteorologists, and extensive records of previous similar days at Kingston available, each sailor should have been able to predict the typical displacement of an offshore weather-system wind by a lake ("sea") breeze and to deal with it. Before the race Geert Bakker, the Dutch Soling representative and subsequent winner, asked me what I expected would happen. I told him that my own records indicated that the only time in many years a northeaster had *not* been replaced by a southwesterly lake breeze had been in the third race, three days before, and that this freak occurrence would not be repeated. The fifth race was a test of skill—and in some respects, inasmuch as the behavior of the wind was so precisely predictable, a better test of skill than some other races of the series.

The lake breeze was expected to develop during the race; every meteorological source indicated that it was at least likely. The northeast weather-system wind present at the start would die, a zone of calm between the two winds would develop and persist for thirty minutes to an hour, and the lake breeze, at approximately 200°–220°, would appear at the surface out on the lake and proceed toward the course and the shore thereafter. The only question was when this would happen and which way the northeaster would shift as it died. Most winds back as they die, and the northeaster was dying and backing before the race started. By the time the Solings started, the port end of the line was so heavily favored that it was almost impossible to cross on starboard. Clearly the way to manage the first beat was to go left. Those who did (like Dennis Conner, Fazio Albarelli, John Kolius, and Bakker) were far in the lead at the first mark. By the time the third leg became a run (many of the Solings jibed) and the race committee signaled a new weather mark 45° to the left of the original, it should have been obvious that the wind was going to back its way to the southwest. Clearly, the way to handle the second beat was to go left again. The sharp ones—including Bakker, Jorge Sundelin, Boris Budnikov, Claes Christensen, and Valentin Mankin—tacked immediately at the leeward mark and headed offshore. They were well ahead at the second weather mark. By this time the wind had almost disappeared (Poul-Richard Jensen spent nearly an hour within a hundred yards of the weather mark). The lake breeze appeared as a dark line on the southwestern horizon as the Flying Dutchmen reached the second leeward mark. With 10 knots out on the lake and nothing inshore, the mentally tough (Reinaldo Conrad, Hans Fogh, Norman Freeman, Christensen, Mankin, Bakker) headed for the wind at 60°–90° to the course, bore away when they reached it, set their chutes and roared home three and four abreast. The behavior of the wind was predictable, and the proper management of each leg was determinable in advance.

In the twenty-four boat Soling fleet there were seven protests against the race committee. One protest originated with the Italian, Albarelli, who, after the best start in the fleet, led to the jibe mark, then lost ten boats on the second beat, and subsequently retired. Patrick Haegeli, who led the series at the time, and Jensen, who ultimately won the gold medal, were last and next to last at the first weather mark, finished eighteenth and fourteenth, and protested. Of the other Soling sailors who protested, Willi Kuhweide was fourth until the fifth leg and lost eight boats thereafter; David Forbes was fifth from last at the first mark, eleventh at the second weather mark, and eleventh at the finish; Juan Costas was eighth at the first mark, lost nine boats on the second beat, and finished seventeenth; and Juan Torruella was sixteenth at the first mark and twenty-second at the finish.

In the sixteen-boat Tempest fleet the Italian, the Spaniard, the West German, and the American protested. Of these, Giuseppe Milone was seventh at the first mark, lost seven boats on the second beat, and finished twelfth; Felix Gancedo was approximately thirteenth all around the course and finished fourteenth; Uwe Mares, who had been ninth at the jibe mark and twelfth at the second weather mark, retired during the prolonged calm that followed, Conner, who had had a beautiful start and a big lead at the first mark, lost five boats on the second beat and three more thereafter to finish ninth.

In the twenty-boat Flying Dutchman fleet there were four protests, made by the Spaniard, the Frenchman, the Englishman, and the Swede. Of these, Jandro Abascal had been far astern on the first beat, worked up to ninth on the second beat, and dropped to eleventh at the finish; Yves Pajot, who had had two eighths in previous races, was

fifth at the jibe mark and at the second weather mark, but lost ten
boats on the final lap; Rodney Pattison was seventh at the first mark,
twelfth at the second weather mark, and eighteenth at the finish;
Stefan Sjostrom was tenth at the first mark, thirteenth at the second
weather mark, and eighth at the finish.

What did these protestants have in common?

1. They finished poorly—only two finished in the first ten (Sjostrom eighth, Conner ninth).
2. Their performance deteriorated as the race progressed—only
   four finished in a position higher than they stood at a previous
   mark (Haegeli, Jensen, Forbes, and Sjostrom).
3. They tended to lose dramatically (often from a position at the
   head of the fleet)—three boats improved significantly, four
   remained in a mediocre or poor position throughout, while
   eight lost from seven to eleven boats on a single leg. Albarelli,
   who led the Solings to the first mark, retired after dropping to
   twelfth or lower. Conner, who led the Tempests to the first
   mark by a quarter mile, protested after dropping to ninth.
   (The Russian, Vladimir Leontiev, led the Flying Dutchmen
   to the first mark and dropped from second to ninth on the
   final lap, but he did not protest.)
4. They usually made one major error, rather than an abun-
   dance of little errors. Haegeli and Jensen blew the first beat,
   Albarelli, Kuhweide, Costas, Milone, and Conner lost five or
   more boats on the second beat, while Pajot and Pattison had
   their disasters on the final lap.

Haegeli and Jensen were far behind not because of race-committee mismanagement but because they were trapped at the port end of
the line when Forbes hung up on the mark. They had to escape
behind the entire fleet on port, away from the shift. Dieter Below,
who was trapped in the same manner, came back to the left as soon as
he could, and was sixth at the first mark, eighth at the second weather
mark, and fifth at the finish. Conner was first at the first mark because
he made *the* perfect start at the port end of the line and continued left
on the first beat. He dropped to sixth at the second weather mark
because he went right on the second beat—not because of any action
of the race committee. Albarelli was first at the first mark because he
handled the start and first leg as did Conner, and he blew the second
beat by going even farther down the right-sided drain, to eighteenth.

Kuhweide followed him but recognized his error considerably sooner. Forbes was twentieth at the first mark because of his disastrous start, and fought his way back to eleventh at the finish despite the race committee, the calm, and the lake breeze. Mares had gone to the right on the first beat and was a half mile behind Conner at the first mark, long before his decision to retire in the calm. Torruella, Milone, Gancedo, Abascal, and Sjostrom had played the first beat similarly and were similarly out of the race at the first mark. On this leg the wind velocity dropped from 8 to 4 knots and shifted approximately 10°, hardly a variation beyond the capability of Olympic sailors. The subsequent greater variations in wind velocity and direction provided opportunities, ordinarily not available, to recover (as Forbes demonstrated). Pattison (who had been seventh at the first mark) dropped to eighteenth on the last lap because he failed to follow Fogh and Freeman out into the lake after he rounded the leeward mark—not because the race committee failed to provide a beat to the finish.

The people who did well were either, like Bakker (who was never below third), fully cognizant of the strategic implications of the changes in wind velocity and direction or mentally tough enough to put their mistakes out of awareness and concentrate on the leg at hand. Fogh, who had been second at the first mark and dropped to seventh on the second beat, came back to finish third. Conrad, who had had a disastrous first beat and was still fifteenth at the second mark, finished first, and thereby won the bronze medal. Christensen, who had been fifth at the first mark, was second at the second weather mark and finished first. Mankin was third at the first weather mark, third at the second, and second at the finish. The Canadian, Allan Leibel, had been second the first time upwind, dropped to seventh on the second weather leg, but recovered to finish third. Sundelin, who had been eleventh at the first mark, was second at the second weather mark and second at the finish. Budnikov had rounded the first mark fourteenth, but worked his way up to third on the second beat and finished third. Gastao Brun was seventh at the first weather mark and fourth at the second weather mark, and finished fourth.

With few exceptions the leaders at the finish had been close to the lead throughout the race. In particular contrast to the protestants, they experienced no dramatic losses. They were consistent. Five of the Flying Dutchmen, six of the Solings, and seven of the Tempests that finished in the first ten were in the first ten at the first mark.

The Russians and East Germans did well in these conditions, and none of them protested. Among the Russians, Leontiev (Flying Dutchman) dropped from first to ninth, Mankin (Tempest) was never lower than third and finished second, and Budnikov (Soling) came from fourteenth to finish third; among the East Germans, Uwe Steingross (Flying Dutchman) came up from eleventh to finish sixth, and Below (Soling) was fifth, sixth, seventh, or eighth at every mark and finished fifth.

These Eastern Europeans exemplify the character of those who did well in the fifth race. They are mentally tough. They concentrate on what matters, on every leg, at every mark. They are not distracted by the behavior of their neighbors; they do what is strategically correct. They are consistent; they do not make dramatic gains, but they do not have dramatic losses. They persevere; they do not give up when behind or settle for an immediate gain. They are not preoccupied by previous mistakes; they turn at once to the problem of how to get back into the race. They do not become anxious as they see their competitors slipping away. They are not brilliant; they rarely have the lead, but they stay close leg after leg. They are not angered by misfortune; they recognize that it does not discriminate. They do not protest.

The attributes of the "protestants" seem to be the exact opposite. They tend to be brilliant; three of them ultimately won medals (Jensen, Pattison, and Conner), and two of them had previously won gold medals (Forbes and Kuhweide). They tend to do well because of their brilliance, rather than because of consistency. Both Albarelli and Conner had outstanding starts and dramatic leads at the end of the first leg. After splendid success, some "protestants" are prone to disaster. They may be unable to concentrate on what matters at the moment. If their (often brilliant) plans fail, they seem unable to adjust. They appear to become distracted and preoccupied when they get into trouble. They may become anxious when struck by misfortune, and may feel that they have been particularly discriminated against. They seem to become angered when their success, which they undoubtedly regard as deserved, is snatched away by the "undeserved" luck of their opponents. They do not seem to be as mentally tough as many of the opponents who beat them in this race. They tend to protest.

To abandon a race like this one would be to succumb to the increasingly common belief that sailboat racing should be a pure test of boat speed and boat handling. The fifth race was, of course, not a test of boat speed or boat handling; it pitted a sailor's intellect and psyche against the elements and against the fear of defeat. To eliminate the uncertainties and risks, to turn a race into a test of equipment and physical skill alone, would be to remove its most important elements.

The attitude is prevalent that the outcome of participation in the Olympic games is more significant than the participation, that competitors are selected not to play a game, but to win. The external pressures to win—transmitted from the nation to the team to the individual—generate such anxiety, so distract and preoccupy the competitor, that his performance often suffers. When the team authorities focus his attention on the outcome, force him to work only to win, he is more likely to lose. Only the truly tough can withstand these pressures.

And whether the urge to protest originates with the competitor or with his team, his involvement in the protest procedure, the incitement of his resentment against the "system," the arousal of guilt associated with his rebellion against authority, must distract and detract from his subsequent performance. One has to wonder whether the Eastern European team organizations do not deliberately restrain their contestants from protesting, knowing that this action may in itself have an adverse effect upon their subsequent performance.

A more fundamental question is why Eastern European competitors are so mentally tough. (Bob Fisher thinks that Valentin Mankin is the toughest, most imperturbable competitor he has ever met.) It is reasonable to believe that daily training, including experience with defeat, and the constant pressure to excel (their life-style depends upon their performance) weeds out early on those who are not mentally tough. Most probably, too, the Eastern European organizations know what it takes to do well in top competition and select for their training programs in sailing not the brilliant, but the mentally tough.

19 / Anger

Whatever little we have gained we have gained by agitation, while we have uniformly lost by moderation.

—DANIEL O'CONNELL

ANGER USUALLY AFFECTS PERFORMANCE. IF FELT AND DISPLAYED, IT MAY or may not be beneficial; if felt and suppressed, it is usually detrimental. It is often distracting. It may cause a competitor to act in direct opposition to his own interests. Its effect will depend upon whether or not it is displayed, whether it is displayed appropriately, and whether it is perceived as acceptable by the internalized Parent.

The purpose of anger, as evidenced by animal behavior, is to arouse and concentrate the attention of the angered individual on a presumed attacker. It occurs when an individual perceives himself to be threatened—and in most instances the anger-inducing threat is the presence of another individual. In animals anger is clearly associated with fear. The dominant animal does not display anger unless a major threat is perceived; the subordinate animal displays anger with minimal provocation. The more fearful the animal, the more readily it becomes angry. Anger is more likely to be displayed when the animal is surprised. If the threat is subsequently recognized to be minimal or absent, the anger dissipates immediately. The pet dog will turn on his master, growling, if surprised by his sudden appearance, but will immediately thereafter wag his tail happily. The effect of appropriate anger is to warn an attacker that his threat will be forcibly opposed, that if he does not wish to fight, he should depart. It is beneficial in that it provides protection without a fight.

Anger does not appear late in a race, when the outcome is no longer in doubt, or at the start, when the outcome is completely in doubt. It usually erupts in the midst of a race, when a presumably deserved position is usurped. A competitor becomes angry when he approaches the weather mark on port tack and has to bear off behind four sterns, or when he must give room to an opponent who at the last possible moment obtains an inside overlap. Most inclined to anger is the competitor who has successfully developed a large lead and loses it because of a "fluke"—an unpredictable wind shift, the abrupt development of a calm. The angered person regards himself to have been treated unfairly, disrespectfully. The Child within has had what is "his" snatched away by an unjust but all-powerful parent.

I remember becoming angry during a race in a Fall Soling Bowl at Annapolis. We had made a beautiful start in a strong but highly variable northerly, and seemed to be well in the lead halfway up the beat. But the race turned completely around when the fleet astern began to lift and drive by in strong, backed air nearer the shore. As we approached the weather mark on port, Bruce MacLeod, who had been astern and farther offshore, was approaching on starboard. I was furious, having been "unjustly" deprived of my well-deserved (?) lead; now, to make matters worse, Bruce, who "should" have been far astern, was about to pass me (take "my" place) at the mark. I tacked ahead and to leeward of him, but too close—and fouled out.

The expression of anger comes easily to some. I am amazed by the ability of a baseball manager to stand chin to chin with an umpire, shouting over some minor disagreement. He is obviously able to use anger in the manner intended; he attempts, often successfully, to dispel a threat by producing a little show. If the display of anger is brief and appropriate, a facet of showmanship, it may be useful. It may indicate to an opponent that he should not pursue a threatening move, and so dispel a threat. It may have the effect intended by the baseball manager: "Now he owes us one!" Similarly, the racing sailor who displays anger may expect that he will be given a break the next time the boats meet. The baseball manager is probably not carried away by his anger and can subsequently dismiss it with ease. Most people are unable to use it so freely or dismiss it so readily.

Skippers who feel threatened may occasionally proceed from shouting to fighting. One Long Island Sound Soling sailor leaped into a competitor's boat to take a swing at him after a port–starboard incident. (His anger was cooled when he slipped ignominiously and fell into the water.) One American skipper started a fist fight with his crew when in the 1964 Olympics a mistake on the final leg of the seventh race cost him a silver medal. Patrick Pym attracted official attention when, with his paddle, he cracked the hand of a competitor who was pushing his Finn backward at the starting line. Charlie Morgan floored Stan Leibel as he stepped ashore from a race in which he had dismasted Charlie's Star (for the second time!). Incidents like these are rare enough to make good stories. More typical is Paul Elvstrom's attitude. Rolly Tasker accused Elvstrom and Hans Fogh of "hard international sailing" during a Flying Dutchman World Championship. Paul replied, "No—that means jumping into the other man's boat and pulling the mast down! But I would not do that."

The display of anger should be of short duration. Either it "works" or it doesn't. Animals and children do not sustain anger. If the threat is not dispelled, if their anger doesn't "work," they either fight or surrender. But few competitors wish to fight, few are willing to surrender, and even fewer are able to use anger appropriately—precisely and briefly. Hence, the anger of many will smolder, within or without their awareness, hidden from others. Because it cannot be dissipated in surrender or in fighting, it persists. Anger in this form has the most adverse effect upon competitive performance. It may result in irrational behavior, in action or inaction inimical to one's own best interests.

Anger may have contributed to the outcome of the 1976 U.S. Olympic Soling trials. Buddy Melges was leading the series after the third race (as most everyone expected him to be). However, he had failed to report his presence to the race committee prior to the first race, as was required. That error (which might have resulted in a disqualification), and a tenth place in the first race, may have been early indications that he was feeling some pressure. But he must have thought that the first race would be his throw-out, and he had had two firsts in a row thereafter. In the fourth race, John Kolius drove through him on the first beat, and went on to win. Buddy was fourth. As the gun sounded for the fifth race, his mainsheet parted. Although he was reprieved by a general recall, he must have begun to think the fates were against him.

On the re-start, although cautioned by his crew that he was a little early, Buddy pressed across the line and was recalled. He was never able to get back into that race and could only watch as John fought for the lead. Most of the leaders sailed the run on starboard jibe, but a third of the way down, John jibed to port and changed spinnakers. In the final quarter mile the wind backed and picked up to the west. John came roaring through us all to lead by a hundred feet at the mark and win the race with ease. Buddy was eleventh.

Now John had a total of only 23.0 points, while Buddy had 24.0, after discounting a throw-out. It could have been all over on the following day. There was almost no wind at the announced starting time, and little appeared thereafter—a whisper of a lake breeze, a little northerly. The race committee postponed and postponed, but finally, at five in the afternoon, in a northeasterly of 3–5 knots, they sent us off. Buddy was furious; he had headed for home at three thirty, certain that no race committee in its right mind would start a race of the Olympic trials in those conditions at that time. He was over early in the first start, which was recalled, and over early (three starts in a row) again in the one that mattered. He was far astern when Jim Young, Maury Rattray, John, and I led the fleet around the first triangle. If that race had been completed, the trials would have been over, with John winning and Buddy fourth behind Robby Haines and me. Although the race was abandoned before we reached the second weather mark, Buddy's anger undoubtedly continued long afterward. The following day, in moderate air, he made a beautiful and daring start at the port end, was soon in the lead, and—despite a squall and a 180° progressive veer—stayed there. But Robbie Haines went off in the wrong direction on the run and allowed John to move into second. The fates were surely conspiring against Buddy. Now, for victory in the series, he would have to win the final race *and* John would have to finish fourth or below.

The seventh race was started in a light, fluky northerly, and Buddy, probably not pleased by the conditions, was angered by the nonappearance of six members of the fleet, which meant there were six less boats to place between him and John. He forced John into a poor start, moved out into the stronger air to the right, and was close to the lead near the weather mark. But a couple of shifts put him back to fourth before he rounded; he lost another boat on the reaches, and

John came out of nowhere to a hundred-yard lead at the second weather mark.

Now it's difficult to say that anger alone did Buddy in. But he *was* angry—at the race committee, at the boats that did stupid things when they were between him and John, at the boats that failed to appear, at himself for starting the series with a tenth, at the crew who had failed to remind him to check in, at the mainsheet that had broken. All these petty problems—after he had dominated the class for four years. What a shock it must have been, that first awareness that he could lose! It must have seemed that the world was against him, was about to deprive him of what he deserved. He was angry, but he couldn't show it. He couldn't admit to a lack of control. So the anger smoldered within, distracting him, preoccupying him, disturbing his judgment enough for him to make three early starts in a row—one of which surely put the series beyond even his reach. He was still angry months later when he responded (most courteously) to my attempt to analyze his behavior in the trials.

Anger is a problem a quarterback must learn to deal with. When his team is being beaten, when he is being sacked and his running plays are being shut down, he has a tendency to become angry and to "force" the football. Deprived of his power by forces beyond his control, he attempts to re-establish his godlike stature by attempting the impossible. He throws the football when he knows he shouldn't, and is intercepted. Like a child who is told he can't do something but goes right ahead and does it, the quarterback is attempting to prove that the laws of rational behavior do not apply to him.

The helmsman of the boat astern, angered by being beaten, is often unable to sail passively on the course of the boat ahead. Despite clear evidence that the course of the leading boat is the correct one, he elects to try the other tack, the other jibe, a position to leeward, a position to windward. His anger causes him to regress to a childhood level at which no clear distinction between reality and fantasy exists. He hopes to escape from the limitations of reality by escaping from the pattern of rational behavior. Then, he fantasizes, all will be possible: if rational determinants no longer govern, he may succeed.

The angry person is crying, "You can't do this do me! You can't deprive me of what is mine! And if you do, I'll demonstrate my magic, unlimited by reality, unrestricted by reason, and I'll show you! I'm still in charge here!"

The direct effects of anger—distraction, preoccupation, loss of judgment, the inclination to respond irrationally—are bad enough; in addition, often a depressing residue is left behind. Whatever justification there may have been at the time, the anger, the loss of control, become unacceptable in remembrance. The angered individual cannot admit that he was fearful, felt threatened, lost control, acted irrationally, or was subject to intimidation. He subsequently castigates himself for his show of weakness. The anger which could not be directed at its intended object is turned against himself. And so for the next day or days, during the next race or races, in the next similar situation on the water, at the next meeting with the same competitor—whenever the remembrance of the anger surfaces—he is again distracted, preoccupied, impulsive, and irrational. Show me an angry loser and I'll show you a loser.

20 / Depression

When down in the mouth, remember Jonah—
he came out all right.

—THOMAS ALVA EDISON

AFTER THE DEFEAT OF THE KANSAS CITY ROYALS BY THE NEW YORK YAN-
kees in the 1977 play-offs, Fred Patek slumped in the dugout, holding
his head in his hands, alone, beaten. He had hit into the double play
that ended the series. When interviewed a few days later, he said,
"Oh, it's all behind me now. The pain was gone after a few hours, the
deep involvement after a few days. You have to start again. What hurt
was wondering if I had done everything I could possibly do, and
when I finally satisfied myself that I had, I was OK."

Here were all the ingredients that precipitate depression. The
event was significant, and therefore so was the failure. The possibility
of success had been high. There had been a heavy investment of intent
and expectation in a positive outcome. There was a feeling of personal
responsibility. Depression is likely in these circumstances; it may
even seem reasonable. But a strong Adult does not permit it to occur.

Competitors invest a large amount of psychical energy in their
games. They believe in the significance of the outcome; they are

game. Their investment of feeling is partially Parent-derived—a desire to perform well, to demonstrate competence, so as to please and gain the approval of their Parent. This conscientiousness increases their determination, drive, and persistence, causing them to prepare themselves assiduously and return to competition again and again. Without the need to be approved, the likelihood of success would be greatly diminished. Parents are useful, but they must be controlled.

Competitors, hooked on competition, seek the elation, the "high," that comes with success—with excellent performance and with winning. It is not surprising that if they can get so "high" with success, they can get so "low" with failure. Their elation results from the presumption (an intellectualization) that they themselves determined the outcome—that they were victorious because they were better controlled, more attentive, more realistic, than their opponents. Elation is incompatible with the realization that victory came because the opposition performed poorly, made greater mistakes, had poorer equipment or worse luck. Unfortunately, those capable of this misapprehension in victory are usually incapable of avoiding it in defeat. Retaining the presumption that they determined the outcome, they can now only conclude that they have failed. Very few are able to reject this judgment, to really *believe* that winning is self-determined but losing other-determined. The ego defenses used in the attempt to achieve this result—to permit elation in victory and prevent depression in failure—are never fully successful.

Elation arises both from the satisfaction inherent in competent performance and from a sense of having performed in an approved manner—usually by winning. It is consequent to an internal judgment which (as in a diving competition) evaluates both the degree of difficulty of what has been done *and* the degree of success. High marks—elation—are awarded for overcoming strong competitors, in adverse circumstances, by a near-perfect performance. Low marks—minimal satisfaction—are given for winning against a small fleet of neophytes by "lucking" into a big shift on the first leg.

Just as elation is a Parental reward for good behavior, depression is a Parental punishment for bad behavior. To the extent that our Parent gives approval and rewards for drive, enthusiasm, and competence, we must expect disapproval and punishment for failure and incompetence. And, of course, the degree of depression is proportional to the height of expectation. The players who sit slumped in the dugout, or the cockpit, holding their heads in their hands, are those who just missed, who almost won. The tail-enders feel no great depression over one more failure. Their Parents expected no more of them and do not punish them for performing in accordance with their investment. (And that is, of course, why they are tail-enders.)

In those in whom internalized standards are extremely high, and/or in whom the Adult ego is unable to face and overcome the pain of failure, depression occurs and may be protracted and detrimental. These are the competitors, discussed earlier in this volume, with the need to win, the ones who cannot be satisfied by the demonstration of competence, but demand victory and perfection on every occasion. Not only is this need directly detrimental to performance, as has already been pointed out, but the depression with which it is characteristically associated increases its adverse effect.

Self-punishment is sought by some competitors whose Parents, recognizing defectiveness, demand expiation. Others, angered by their opponents (or the gods) and unable to express that anger, turn it against themselves in prolonged self-flagellation. Such behavior is extremely detrimental to further performance. It must be recognized as irrational—that is, serving an ulterior purpose. We must, with Fred Patek, be able to accept failure once we are satisfied that we did everything we could possibly do—*and even when we are not*.

Everyone is defective, everyone makes mistakes ("he who makes the fewest wins"), everyone fails to meet the standards he has set for himself. Everyone must expect to feel pain with failure. But just as it is appropriate for a parent to limit the chastisement of his child to a sharp word or a quick slap, so should the Adult limit the Parent to a quick stab of pain and little more. Mourning for a lost victory, a lost opportunity, should be brief. We seek challenges, risks, and surprises. Prolonged punishment for finding them is hardly appropriate.

Defenses which permit the avoidance of one pain by the substitution of another are sometimes used. For example, a weak ego may cause an individual to surrender early in a contest, failing to recognize that in the long term the pain of guilt may be far more intense and protracted than the pain of tension in sustained competition. Guilt may be engendered by surrender both because it results in failure to perform successfully *and* because of the subsequent recognition that one was unable to "take it," to stand up and fight. Deliberate defeat may be sought not only as a means of surrender but with the unconscious recognition that it will result in guilt and pain. The consequent pain is then used to atone for some previous "sin" or feeling of unworthiness.

Unfortunately, such feelings of unworthiness cannot be expiated, and failure to meet other needs of the personality merely enhances the distress.

Of course, the most effective means of avoiding the pain of failure is to avoid investing one's energies and concerns in the competitive outcome. If one does not care whether one performs well or poorly, whether one demonstrates competence or not, no pain will result. This attitude is clearly inconsistent with that of a true competitor, who believes in the significance of the game and wants to see the effects of the outcome, whether pleasing or painful. But many participants are not game. They avoid the pain of failure by avoiding investment in the development of competence. This avoidance is sometimes overt: "I'm just here for the fun of it!" But far more commonly, it is covert and unconscious: "I would really like to be as good as Hans Fogh (and I could be), but I haven't the time, the money, the crew. . . ."

To be competitive is to invest oneself in the attainment of competence *and* in winning. The more we invest, the greater will be the likelihood of attaining competence and of winning and the greater will be the elation associated with that winning. But we must pay for the advantage; the greater the investment, the greater will be the grief when we fail. We should honor our competitors, and our Parents should honor us, for willingness to make the investment despite the risk of failure. An approving Parent—one properly controlled by a strong Adult—should ask only that we try, believe, dare.

Failure is frequent. Competitors must learn to deal with it. The ability to recover from it is one of the most important of their skills. A high investment in competition means both a greater likelihood of success and a greater degree of grief. Grief is the normal and appropriate response of the abandoned Child. It will subside quickly if expressed and not manipulated by the Parent. The more thinking, evaluation, and analysis is involved, the less effective either grief or performance becomes—and the longer grief persists. Recrimination, self-punishment, or preoccupation, particularly if it continues beyond a reasonable few minutes or hours, should be recognized as Parental in origin. And as soon as the presence of the Parent is recognized, it should be excluded.

The ability to keep the Parent out of grief is essential to competitive success. Competitors cannot allow themselves to become depressed, to castigate themselves for inadequacy, to preoccupy themselves with punishment. In sailboat racing, at least, failure—to recognize a shift in time, to gain the inside overlap, to jibe without losing speed—is almost continuous. One can grieve for a moment, but one cannot allow the Adult to be undermined, to be distracted, to be discouraged. The race is always "from here onward"; the past must be forgotten as soon as possible, and must remain forgotten at least until after the event.

Vic Braden says that a competitor must feel free to make mistakes. He must recognize both the likelihood of failure and the necessity of feeling disappointment and pain as a consequence. But he must not be burdened by the accompanying guilt so that he is unwilling to risk subsequent mistakes. John Veitch, Alydar's trainer, after his horse had been beaten for the third straight time by Affirmed, said, "If you don't know how to lose, you'd better not play this game. You lose many more than you win. Maybe they should charge extra for the thrills. But if you don't get used to accepting defeat, it will drive you crazy. I learned from my father that you should lose the same way you win. And I think you show more class in the way you act when you lose than when you win."

"The thing that stays with you, though, is wondering whether you ever will get another opportunity to play on a world championship team. Some day, when I'm an old guy, will I look back in dissatisfaction and say, 'Well, I almost made it'?" So Fred Patek mused after the play-off loss, and so feel most of those who almost make it. And for the ten who get a second chance (Richard Petty says, "You never get a second chance. The one you lost is lost."), a hundred do not. Pollyanna cannot overcome reality sufficiently to deny this. You had your chance; it's over, and you lost. If you hadn't wanted the contest to be important, hadn't sought the elation that would have accompanied the victory, you could have regarded the event differently— and forgone the joy in the striving, the dedication, the successive satisfactions that accompanied each evidence of progress. If this was the big one, the one you spent months and years preparing and hoping for, its loss warrants a little grieving. You didn't expect or want it to be easy, did you?

21 / Passive Sailing

In the game of life, it's a good idea to have a few early losses, which relieves you of the pressure of trying to maintain an undefeated season.

—BILL VAUGHAN

WHEN THE LEADING BOAT SAILS FARTHER AND FARTHER AHEAD, WHEN the boat on the weather quarter drives inexorably forward to take our wind, when a competitor luffs us just before the gun fires and leaves us wallowing in his wake, our inferiority seems clearly exposed. If we try to gain and lose, our confidence is eroded and our ability to concentrate on our subsequent performance is reduced. Nothing succeeds like success—and nothing fails like failure. Some tactics are bound to fail—at times we must attack without the certitude of success, or be attacked when there is little chance of defense. The ability to appraise situations realistically, to accept the inevitability of failure, to ignore past failures and past mistakes, is essential. But it is also possible to manage a race in a way that minimizes the need for such mental manipulation. Frequently, a passive approach that minimizes failure, and hence the subsequent work of ignoring it, is appropriate.

We race for the Ice Bowl each year, usually on January 1, five miles up the winding Severn River, around St. Helena Island, and back. Critical opportunities to recover or break away are more prominent than in most races; the lead usually changes many times. The race demonstrates more clearly than most the need to stay close, to avoid early mistakes, to forgo ventures that risk taking the boat out of contention.

We detected an oscillating veer just before the downwind start of the 1977 Ice Bowl, jibed to port as we crossed the line, and escaped to the left as the fleet went right. When the wind backed again, we crossed them all on starboard and they jibed into line astern. Tom Davies, in his new boat, was but two boat lengths astern, and Sam Merrick was two boat lengths astern of him. I had exulted in our initial success but now began to worry that Tom would force us higher and higher on the preferred jibe and that after Tom had trapped us in his blanket, Sam would jibe away in the next veer. Sam jibed while the back persisted, and then Tom jibed to stay with Sam. I breathed a sigh of relief (although they were sailing toward the more leeward shore, where the wind was stronger), continued until the wind began to veer, and then jibed. When we all jibed in the subsequent back, I had gained another two boat lengths on Tom and about five on Sam, I was now on the more leeward side of the river, and I was approaching the next bend to the right on the preferred jibe, starboard. Sitting pretty!—and all because the boats astern had elected to try something different, to attempt a gain instead of merely following me.

The determinants of progress while running along a winding river in a warm but oscillating 5-knot wind over cold water are the oscillating shifts, the alignment of the air flow with the course of the river, and the inability of the warm air flow to reach the surface near the windward shore. It is necessary to (1) jibe with the oscillations, maintaining the jibe that will take the boat more directly along the course of the river, at the better (more headed) sailing angle; (2) jibe with the bends in the river, maintaining the port jibe where the course of the river is to the left, and the starboard jibe where the course of the river is to the right (because the channeling never completely aligns the wind with the river); and (3) jibe toward the more leeward shore, since the wind will be strongest there. The best compromise should always be sought, by holding a lifted jibe a little longer if it carries the boat more directly toward the next bend or toward the more leeward shore, and jibing earlier if an oscillation permits such a course on the opposite jibe. If the leading boat is using this strategy, it is highly unlikely that a follower will gain by adopting a different course, by assuming an opposite jibe.

As the race continued, Tom stayed close on our heels but Sam periodically tried something different (apparently concentrating on the leeward-shore advantage), and he fell farther and farther astern. The river hooks to the left and then opens to the right into Round Bay. Tom jibed to port, toward the expected veer, as we held starboard to be inside at the final bend. As he approached the Bay on a dead-downwind course, we had a good angle on port jibe and a ten-boat-length lead. By concentrating on the strategic determinants, we had made the right move again and again and moved farther and farther ahead. By failing to comply with the strategic determinants, by being unwilling to accept the status of passive followers, by taking chances against the odds, my competitors had put themselves out of contention.

Out of contention—unless some dramatic alteration in conditions was yet to come. (That possibility must always be considered— indeed, expected.) Two major obstacles, which almost always cause the fleet to close up and reshuffle, lay ahead: the approach to the island to leeward of a large bluff, and the rounding of the island itself. As we passed to leeward of the bluff, the wind died abruptly. We stopped. The boats astern almost caught us as we scrambled to get the spinnaker down, and they were within a few feet of us when we escaped into the stronger, veered air beyond. However, by the time they escaped we were rounding the island, two hundred yards ahead. Tom (now desperate?) tried to take a short cut when leaving the island, ran aground, and watched the entire fleet sail by. We now had a quarter-mile lead, and it was perhaps even greater when we finished in a 12-knot southwesterly an hour later.

How different the outcome might have been if Tom and Sam (or anyone else) had stayed close on that run, close enough to profit from our stopping beneath the bluff as we approached St. Helena Island. At that point we needed every inch of our hundred-yard lead to reach the new wind before our competitors. Now the Ice Bowl is no ordinary race, but on this occasion its character was typical. The leader, confident of his ability to remain at the head of the fleet, occupied with the determinants of progress, sailed farther and farther ahead. The followers, their confidence eroded by being astern, preoccupied with the possibility of failure, made more and more mistakes, and fell farther and farther astern.

There is, however, always the possibility that the leader will make a mistake, meet an unexpected condition, have a breakdown in boat handling. No one sails a perfect race; few fail to make many mistakes. Each competitor must be expected to commit a certain number of errors in a race. The followers must stay close enough to profit when the leader's error occurs. If you make one error while you are astern, you've used up at least two of your allotment (counting the one that got you astern). The leader can now make an error and still be one up.

John Illingworth points out the frequent need to resort to "passive sailing" when astern in a match race. He recommends that the helmsman of the boat being beaten accept the situation for the moment, perhaps for the leg, and concentrate on staying as close as possible while waiting for a new opportunity. One must, like Paul Elvstrom, believe that the superiority of the opponent is temporary, arrived at by chance, and that when conditions change, when the next mark is turned, one's own superiority will become evident again. Illingworth says that passive sailing accomplishes two things. First, it prevents the boat astern from taking wild chances, sailing a far longer, roundabout course, assuming the obviously wrong tack or jibe. Thus it keeps the boat astern close enough so that when an opportunity to catch up appears, she can capitalize upon it. Second, by avoiding tactics that will probably result in greater loss, it preserves for subsequent races the confidence of the loser. It demonstrates that despite being beaten, he can manage a determined, controlled race, and that the outcome of such a race remains dependent upon his own behavior.

Elvstrom stresses another, practical reason for passive sailing. The aggressive sailor who becomes preoccupied with passing the boat immediately ahead will likely find that his efforts to achieve this result will put him farther behind the leader. Elvstrom particularly eschews efforts to pass a competitor on a reach. To the extent that a follower threatens to pass a boat ahead, he will induce a progressive luff of both boats above the rhumb line and thereby cause both of them to sail a slower, broader course than the leader or leaders. If winning—catching the leader—is the intent, any activity that causes a follower to sail a course less optimal than the leader's is counterproductive.

A realistic appraisal of a leading opponent should indicate that he will make mistakes, will be unprepared for problems yet to appear. A realistic self-appraisal should indicate that you are capable of making fewer mistakes than the leader, of being better prepared for problems yet to appear. (Won't you have the advantage of seeing him sail into them?) A successful competitor must maintain the confidence that his own performance determines the outcome of the race, that, as Robert Ringer says, what the opponent does is irrelevant. Each element of the race must be viewed in terms of the action that should be taken to achieve the greatest advance, regardless of what the opponent does. Perceiving the result of each move as a victory or a defeat, an indication of superiority or inferiority, is dangerous; self-appraisal must be impervious to the implications of success or failure in minor battles, remaining attuned instead to an awareness of previously demonstrated competence.

Each moment of a race is associated with an ebb and flow of confidence. As I broke away from the start of the 1977 Ice Bowl, my confidence was high, for I had been the only one to recognize the significance of the shift and to utilize it appropriately. I was able to calculate the next move dispassionately, to jibe back to cross the fleet at the correct moment. A short while later, with Tom Davies close astern, I felt threatened. I was then in a situation with no possibility of gain, only the possibility of loss. When Sam and Tom jibed away, there was again a potential for gain—and when I did gain, I was reassured, my confidence was enhanced. Each time the boats astern jibed away from me, the potential for gain reappeared—and each time, when I did gain, my confidence and my ability to concentrate on the real determinants of progress were enhanced. How much wiser my followers would have been to maintain the pressure, to continue the same jibe, to keep me in a position in which there was no potential for gain, only a potential for loss. Not only did they take themselves out of contention by the mistakes they made, but they eased the pressure on me, thereby giving me increased confidence and enhancing my performance.

The confidence of my followers must have been impaired when they noticed me take an immediate lead and recognized that they had been on the wrong jibe. It must have been eroded further when, after they jibed away, they fell farther astern. Maneuvers which had a limited chance of success were succeeded by maneuvers which had very little chance of success. Sam attempted a foray closer to the bluff after running into the dead spot in its lee, and Tom tried the short cut across Long Point instead of following me around the shoal. Every time they attempted an attack that was not successful, they became more aware of their failure and of the likelihood of ultimate failure. Their performance deteriorated progressively.

By taking chances and failing and being preoccupied with their failure, they were at once diminishing their own performance and enhancing the performance of the helmsman ahead. And so it is for every meeting between two boats.

22 / Daring and Equanimity

*Show me a thoroughly satisfied man—and I
will show you a failure.*

—THOMAS ALVA EDISON

PERHAPS THE MOST VALUABLE ATTRIBUTE OF THE CONSISTENTLY SUC-
cessful racing sailor is a cool, calm; collected temperament. This permits the retention *throughout the race* of an awareness of the technical
and psychic factors that determine success. It is not difficult to learn
what these factors are and to concentrate attention upon them as the
race begins. But as the race evolves, unexpected problems arise and
unexpected relationships with other boats develop, and these are distracting. It is necessary to maintain a certain amount of disinterest, an
aloofness, from the immediate affair, as if one were riding at the mast-
head, looking down on the situation but not involved in it. Steering is
distracting enough; one must not let competitors increase the distraction.

A number of balances must be struck: between aggressiveness
and passivity, between greed and complacency, between impulsivity
and intellectualization. Most races, and all series, demand these balances, demand equanimity, but there are times and places for marked

variation from the happy medium. If one is behind, greed becomes acceptable; if about to round a mark, aggressiveness to attain the inside overlap is essential; if riding waves, impulsivity is necessary. The effective sailor, whose Adult is in charge, is able to apply the right psychic attitude to the right situation. He is not distracted into complacency merely because he is leading or into greed because the tack opposite to the fleet is enticing. He is daring when daring is required and complacent when complacency is required. If, to do well, he must risk the entire race, he takes the risk; if the position attained is satisfactory, he accepts it and does not take a risk. The effective sailor recognizes when risk taking is justified and when a position is satisfactory. If he "has it made," he doesn't fiddle about; if he needs to move up, he calculates the best method of doing so and takes the chances that are required.

During the 1977 Soling World Championship at Hankø, Norway, we led the fleet for at least a brief period in three races. On each of these occasions, we had had the best, or nearly the best, start—a daring start among fifty-eight of the best Soling sailors in the world. In another of the races we finished forty-second, after a cautious start in the middle of the line. In three races in which we finished twelfth, seventeenth, and twenty-fifth, we had good but not outstanding starts. The start determined the finish, within ten places at least, and only a daring start got us into the first ten.

Clearly, in big fleets of competent competitors, daring at the start is appropriate. At least half the assemblage will have boat speed equal to the best, so one cannot rely upon boat speed to do more than retain the position obtained by the start. It is equally evident that an excess of daring (a weakness of mine) is inappropriate when starting in smaller fleets. Then boat speed becomes significant. If one has it, there is no sense in jeopardizing a good finish by risking disaster at the start.

In the 1977 World Championship I repeatedly threw away the advantages of my daring starts—by continuing to be daring. In the second race, after we had had a huge lead wiped out by the early encroachment of the sea breeze, we fought our way back to tenth and then threw away four places by hunting for wind on the final beat. In the third race we went from third to first on the second beat but held on too far to the left and lost ten boats before we reached the mark. On the run in the fourth race we lost twenty boats when, with the entire fleet on starboard, we jibed away. Instead of dying as they jibed back

against the current, these boats were swept down to the mark by a 20°
back! In the fifth race, after leading the first rounds by a hundred
yards, we maintained our jibe to the right while everyone else went
left, and dropped to fourth by the end of the run. In the seventh race,
on the second reach, we jibed away, down current, and dropped from
fifth to seventh. We undoubtedly made a few gains by daring, but
none when we were at the head of the fleet. The lesson seems obvious
enough: when in a good position in a big fleet, don't mess around—
keep what you've got, take no risks.

In a small fleet daring may be required if a boat-speed deficit is to
be overcome; one will never get past a faster boat by following her.
Awareness of this usually appropriate principle underlay my inappropriate behavior at the 1977 World Championships. I failed to recognize that it does not apply in large fleets, in which there are all sorts of
ways of getting past. Boat speed is infrequently one of them. In a large
fleet the chances of a boat making a mistake are multiplied. The boat
ahead can be relied upon to make at least one mistake (as we so regularly did). While awaiting her mistake, one need only keep in line, following the boat ahead, leading the boat astern.

The validity of this principle was obvious in the final race. On
the second beat, we were about eighth and Erich Hirt and Stig Winnerstrom were just ahead of us and adversely affecting our wind. We
were tempted to tack away from the lifted tack that was carrying us
out into more favorable current. I no sooner told my crew that we'd
hang in there waiting for them to make the mistake than Winnerstrom
tacked away and Hirt tacked to cover. We were now free on the more
desirable tack and beat them both to the next mark. The competition
had been daring, we had been complacent; they lost, we gained.

Whether to risk changing position will be determined by the
boat's position on the course and by the sailing conditions. Attempting to gain one place at the risk of losing two is more justifiable on the
final beat (following which there is no chance of gain) than on the second. On beats and runs, when there is a high likelihood that relative
positions will change in any event, risk taking becomes more justifiable; big gains are possible. On reaches there is little chance for gain;
any change entails a greater risk of loss than of gain, so major variations in management should be avoided. In moderate air, chances of
gain are diminished; risk taking should be minimized. In light air,
major risks are inherent; risk-taking is essential, and courage—
daring—is required.

Some find it difficult to be daring; I find it difficult to be complacent. I can't seem to shut off the desire to try something different, to attempt to gain another position, even while riding down a reach in a chain of boats locked together in their respective stern waves. What I need is equanimity, a tolerance for things as they are when they are good enough, an ability to weigh the risks of loss against the existing advantage. I was sixth or better at the end of the first round in four races of the 1977 World Championship, but I finished better than sixth just once. In only one race did I improve upon my first-round position. At the end of the series I would have been glad to exchange my chances of doing better for the four sixths I gave away.

In big fleets, standings are determined in part by the balance between those who have insufficient daring to get good starts (who start behind and stay there), those who have insufficient daring to get good starts but take appropriate risks thereafter (who start behind but gain progressively as others make mistakes), those who have sufficient daring to get good starts but continue to be daring thereafter (who start ahead and then fall back), and those who dare to start well and are satisfied with their position thereafter (who start ahead and stay there). Desire and drive get you to the head of the fleet, but they must be controlled if you are to stay there.

Equanimity derives from a sense of satisfaction with oneself. Those who have it are able to say, "Look how well I'm doing—how good I am!" Those who do not have it doubt their capacity, feel a constant need to prove themselves, are never satisfied. They feel impelled to seek change. The more stable the situation, the more urgent this need for change becomes. Even when in the lead, perhaps particularly when in the lead, they feel the need for change. But then, of course, making a change can lead only to a position farther back.

The difference between the temptation to seek change for its own sake and a valid need for change must be recognized. As soon as the desire for change arises, the differentiation must be consciously made. Would I be satisfied to finish in this position? Am I aware that a change might be for the worse? Does a better finishing position require a change now? Do the risks of change now justify a maneuver different from that of the neighboring boats? Will there be better opportunities ahead? Should I be satisfied with my present position, expecting that my capability relative to my neighbors will improve later? How much can be gained must be compared *consciously* with how much can be lost. A fifth place with four boats ahead and ten close behind should be accepted as satisfactory. The chance of gaining four will rarely justify the risk of losing ten.

Reality Testing

23 / Realistic Appraisal

*Man blames fate for other accidents, but feels
personally responsible when he makes a hole in
one.*

—HORIZONS MAGAZINE

WE WERE AT THE FIRST RACE OF THE 1977 SOLING MIDWINTERS, BIS-
cayne Bay. At 2:00 P.M., in a maritime tropical Gulf air mass, winds
were south at 8–16 knots. There was 8/10 cloud cover, and little
chance of a sea breeze (100°–140°) developing. The expectation was
that the wind would increase in velocity and veer as a cold front
approached from mid-Florida. We planned to start at the weather end
and tack to the right for the expected veer. We arrived at the line too
early, were nailed by Rick Grajirena, had to wait for a weather boat to
drive over, and finally tacked to port. Those who had tacked to port
with us (except U.S. *674* on our lee bow) were soon left astern. We
belatedly recognized that the skipper of U.S. *674* was Bob Mosbacher, whose return to the class was being hosted by crew Buddy
Melges and Fraser Beer. In a modest veer, Bob was able to tack across
our bow. We carried on, expecting the veer to go farther. It did, and
when we tacked we looked to have the entire fleet. We lost in the
prolonged back that followed, but near the mark we were able to tack

ahead and to leeward of Rick, who had led the starboard-tack bunch out to the lay line. We sailed past the minute orange cone (which turned out to be the weather mark) toward the Whaler carrying the orange flag (which turned out to be the mark boat), thereby giving Rick a lead of four boat lengths.

Rick led the fleet 20° off course on the first reach, and we led them 20° off course on the second reach (trying to find those damnable little marks!), and we had lost about three boats by the time we rounded the leeward mark. The compass showed that the wind was slightly backed as we started the second beat, so we took off to the right once again. This time, as the wind velocity increased from 10 to 14 knots, the veer settled in for good. When we tacked to starboard, only Bob Mosbacher appeared to be close. We met him near the rhumb line halfway to the mark, where he tacked close on our lee bow. For several minutes it was touch and go, but I was determined to hang on in the veer. We finally lifted out of his bad air and gradually worked farther and farther to windward. After we blew a tack, he was just able to tack under us at the mark. He gained a boat length or so on the run and pulled away in the heavier air of the final beat. We finished third, behind Bill Abbott (whom we lost in a poor leeward-mark rounding), with Dave Curtis and others closing in.

I attempted a realistic appraisal of the race, to record the lessons I had learned and prepare myself for the subsequent races of the series. Had I properly judged the strategic variables? Our success to windward on the first two beats was partly due to our getting off to the right in the expected veers. Or had I merely been forced to tack after a bad start? "No, no!" said my crew. "Before the start you told us that you planned to go right." Had I been fast to windward on those first two beats? Or had I just gone the right way? Had I been essentially in the lead as we approached those weather marks? Or had I talked myself into believing that overstanding at that first mark and my crew's inability to get across the boat when we tacked at the second had cost me the lead? Had my technique and determination been superior to Bob's during that prolonged battle on the second beat? Or had he (or Buddy or Fraser) made a wrong sail adjustment? In the heavy air of the final beat, had I failed to make an adjustment that was available to me? Or had I merely missed a shift?

I discussed the race with a number of my competitors. Dave Curtis indignantly told me that he, not I, had been second at the first mark and that he had been unaware of my overstanding. When he described the situation I remembered that there had been a boat inside of us as we rounded, which I had driven over and left astern immediately after setting my chute. I had conveniently forgotten that I had (temporarily) lost a position. Both Dave and Sam Merrick objected to my suggestion that there had been a net veer on the first beat; they felt that a net back had made the left side advantageous. Did that mean that I was very fast and had overcome the twin disadvantages of a poor start and a shift against me to round the weather mark second (or third)? They agreed that there had been a persistent veer on the second beat and that I was lucky to have been off to the right. Was it luck? Or had I followed the oscillations in accordance with the compass and logically discovered the veer? Fraser Beer thought we'd had a good race, that I'd done well to stay with them on the second beat. Either he or Buddy (or both), he thought, had made some inappropriate sail adjustments at the crucial moment, which had allowed me to escape from their lee-bow control. Was my talent and determination of so little significance to the outcome? Sam indicated that he had gained markedly on the run and was close astern at the leeward mark. I hadn't remembered that he'd been around at all! Was my perception that on the final beat I had lost to the boats astern merely a figment of my concern about losing my position? Had I really made the right sail adjustments and been sailing fast?

A realistic appraisal of Patrick Haegeli's win in the first race of the 1976 Olympics is equally difficult. The Solings started on a line that slightly favored the port end, and Patrick had the pin position. The majority of the fleet continued on starboard as Patrick worked out on their lee bow. But as the southwesterly began to back, the boats began to peel off onto port. More and more tacked away. A third of the way to the lay line, only Patrick and a few others were still knifing along on starboard. The mass of boats to the right began to disappear into the haze. Finally the penultimate boat tacked, and there was only Patrick. Disdaining to cover, he continued—on and on. And at last, to the relief of the anxious spectators, he tacked. The wind backed even farther and he led around the weather mark by a hundred yards!

Ashore after the race, I sought out Patrick and his crew to congratulate them on their judgment, their perseverance, and their courage. It was difficult to express my admiration in totally inadequate French. One member of the crew explained: "We had broken the jib traveler. We could not tack to port until it was repaired!" Subsequently I was assured that the long starboard tack *had* been planned, that they had expected the back to continue as it did.

How should this action be appraised? Was it planned or was it pure serendipity? I wonder if even Patrick Haegeli can say for sure. His subsequent behavior in the Olympic series (he won the third race) indicates that he was capable of making and carrying out such a plan. Whether planned or not, was the charge to the left brave or merely foolhardy? Hindsight demonstrates that it was correct but does not tell us whether it was the consequence of luck or of brilliance, whether it was a freak or an example to be emulated.

Appraising reality is an ego function of prime importance to a racing sailor. The decision to tack, to jibe, to modify sail trim, to start at one end or the other of the line, depends upon a realistic appraisal of the external world—on seeing it as it is. Is the boat on your lee bow gaining because of a heading shift (which requires a tack) or because your sails are trimmed incorrectly (which requires a sail adjustment) or because she is faster (which requires no action, only a calm acceptance of the evidence that you need a new jib)? Progress in the attainment of competence and a high level of performance will be forever beyond the reach of a helmsman unable to make such appraisals.

We always distort our appraisal of external reality by including ourselves in it. How we would like things to be, how we feel things ought to be, becomes inextricably confused with how things are. We continue, as we did when we were infants, to place ourselves at the center of the universe, to assume that all events reflect upon us or are consequent to our action or inaction. In making judgments about external reality, we appraise experiences as favorable or unfavorable, as revealing us as we want to be or as we do not want to be, as demonstrating that we behave as we should or that we behave as we should not.

What is needed at any particular point is a simple conclusion based upon a simple perception. The appraisal, however, becomes complex. A boat astern jibes away. Is the helmsman jibing because he wishes to give up the direct confrontation (the attack from astern), because he perceives better wind on the opposite side of the course, or because he wants to lure me into a jibing battle? Shall I jibe to cover his move, or let him go? Do I fail to detect the advantage he sees on the opposite side of the course because I do not want to continue the

confrontation? Am I continuing the present jibe because my preconceived plan remains justified by the evidence at hand, or because I
don't want to respond to a move initiated by my opponent? Appraisal
is never merely realistic. It is almost always colored by meaning, the
significance, of the event to the appraiser.

A strong ego (controlled by a strong Adult) should be able to
  1. Distinguish reality from fantasy (wished or feared).
  2. Judge status, ability, and potential in relationships with others.
  3. Be trusting and respectful of others.
  4. Resist intimidation.

A weak ego will demonstrate its impaired ability to appraise reality by
  1. Failing to distinguish reality from fantasy or denying or misrep-
     resenting reality.
  2. Accepting a fixed position in a contrived pecking order.
  3. Being suspicious of others.
  4. Submitting to intimidation.

We seek to discover our true position in the real world, to determine to what extent we are safe, satisfied, and accepted in it. We avoid
situations in which we feel we don't belong, rewards or punishments
which we feel we don't deserve, people who we feel threaten or do not
accept us. When the real world holds such situations, conditions, and
people, the strong ego detects them and arranges for their avoidance.
The weak ego fails to distinguish those that exist from those that are
fancied: it fears rewards that are justified, seeks punishments that are
unjustified, is intimidated by people who only appear to be threatening or nonaccepting. A weak ego looks for evidence of the individual's
failure to belong, to be accepted, to be deserving. Looking for failure,
it often finds it.

During and after competition, appraisal must be realistic. Confusing what you fear or what you hope for what exists is inconsistent
with successful performance. You must know what *is* happening,
what *has* happened, not what you—or your opponents—wish to happen or to have happened. Consider rationally, one by one, the possible explanations for the events in a race. Disregard those that strongly
support your wishes or those of your opponents. And if your opponents' postrace appraisals are surprisingly favorable to themselves,

recognize their difficulty in making realistic analyses. If you were third, you beat every boat out there but two. Don't talk yourself out of recognition of your accomplishment—and don't let them do it either.

24 / A Particular Opponent

I never saw anybody I couldn't look back at!
—JIM THORPE

MANY SAILORS WHO FUNCTION WELL IN THE IMPERSONAL GAME OF RAC-
ing against the fleet react poorly to the personal threat they perceive
when racing against an individual. When the same opponent is met
again and again in race after race—as occurs when competitors of
equal capability race in a local fleet—or when one-on-one situations
are protracted, each competitor becomes preoccupied with the other,
tending to perceive the race or series of races in terms of beating the
particular opponent, and assuming that the opponent perceives the
situation in the same way. The result is often a feeling of confrontation and hostility which is at the least distracting and may at the worst
force the individual to seek escape, even if it involves surrender. A realistic appraisal, however, indicates that the game is the same, that
one opponent who must be beaten in the last race of the series is no
more threatening than a fleet of opponents all of whom must be beaten
in the first race of a series.

About twenty years ago in a race for International 14's, we trailed Sam Merrick on the final leg by about fifty yards. As we approached the finish line, it was obvious that we would never catch him. "Well, that will make Sam happy," I said. My crew, Tom Guillet, came back immediately with, "We didn't come out here to make Sam happy!" Maybe not, but Sam and I have been making each other alternately happy and unhappy ever since. In local races we are almost always either first or second, and when we race in big regattas away we frequently find ourselves fighting for the same position. We are usually aware of each other's presence; occasionally we become so preoccupied with each other that our performance suffers.

In the 14's I almost always beat Sam, so compassion came easy. When we both took up Solings, his extensive background in E-scows soon made him my equal. I was joyous over his early successes; he was my clubmate, and his success was my success. I lost this enthusiasm, however, when it became obvious that he was likely to beat me as often as I beat him! In 1972 he beat me rather regularly, and I have spent the years since satisfying myself that his advantage was temporary. Each of us now regards the other's capabilities as being approximately equal to his own—which means that each of us wants to beat the other all the time. We accept being beaten by Melges (whose talent is so great); that is honorable defeat. And we accept being beaten (occasionally) by those of lesser competence; that is compassionate defeat. But we don't accept being beaten by each other. To me, and I am sure to Sam, equal means "capable of being beaten." Winning means moving up the pecking order; losing means moving down.

Jack Nicklaus describes how he lost to Johnny Miller in the playoff for the Hall of Fame Trophy. "Miller hit a 3 wood through the trees to eight feet from the cup. I needed to get a chip shot close from an awkward lie. I guess you can say that Johnny's good shot caused me to hit a bad one. So I lost another golf tournament."

Hans Fogh describes the problems of Rolly Tasker in a Flying Dutchman World Championship as follows: "I think it was a big handicap for Tasker that we were always ahead of him at the start. In the last race when he knew we were close to him from five minutes before the start, he became so nervous that he made a very bad start. He really gave up before the start. That is an example of how the tactics can start before the start, where you show people you are better than them. Then they get afraid of you and they don't think that they can beat you. It is a shock that can stop them from doing their best on the course right from the beginning."

Many seem convinced that whatever a champion like Buddy Melges says or does must be right. They are, of course, wrong (as is Buddy occasionally). His tremendous talent easily overcomes and obscures any defects which might result from his being wrong, so few notice. While working for Paul Elvstrom, Hans Fogh admitted that Elvstrom's sails were sometimes suboptimal. The Master could sail anything fast so that he had difficulty distinguishing fast sails from slow ones! The Gunslingers, as my crew Guy McKhann likes to call the top contenders, are good but they're often not right. It is important to recognize that they do stupid things, like the rest of us, that they can be beaten, and that neither their example, their advice, nor their products should be accepted blindly. Their talent is impressive but should not be intimidating.

The realistic appraisal of any competitor recognizes him to be only human. The Australian Finn and Soling sailor John Bertrand says, "Every crew that is competing is capable of defeat," of making mistakes. "Once you're out on the race course everyone is equal." But, he observes, "How many times has the situation arisen where one boat with a good reputation has blown off another which does not claim the same reputation. Many times both yachts are going the same speed but the crew on the second-rater freeze and lose their poise and will always lose out. The crew with the reputation will come out tops each time; since they believe they are the best they lift their game and the also-rans get nervous and slow up." It is not always superior talent that wins; it may be the intimidating perception of that talent that loses.

One type of concern for a particular opponent may be viewed as a variant of the ulterior "game" described by Eric Berne as "If It Weren't for You." The thesis of this "game" is, "I fear to win, to do better than I deserve." It may be played with a specific opponent week after week or with whoever is nearby at a crucial point in a particular race. The player needs the "game" because he is unable to admit that he fears (feels that he does not deserve) to win and resents being forced to lose. To deny what he cannot admit and sustain his belief in his own omnipotence, he undertakes an ulterior "game." He cries (to himself and to his opponent), "If It Weren't for You, I could have won." He takes the view that he was only beaten because the opponent unfairly, inappropriately, developed his skill beyond the "acceptable" level.

One advantage provided by this "game" is the apparent justification for the claim that "I wouldn't do *that* to win"—wouldn't devote *that* amount of time, *that* amount of money, *that* amount of effort in so unimportant a cause. This attitude underlies the resentment of many toward the "full-time" athlete, the prospective (or actual) professional. In many sports, government or commercial support permits a few talented competitors to attain levels of competence far beyond that of the amateurs. The latter, rather than admitting their inability to win against such competitors, seek to justify the defeat their psyches *have already committed them to,* by pointing their fingers: "If It Weren't for You. . . ." And, of course, another advantage is that acceptance and support are obtained from many of the other losers who join in the chorus.

(This is not to say that all those who are concerned by the proliferation of semiprofessional players in amateur sports are attempting to hide their intention to lose. Full government support of racing sailors does reduce the uncertainty, does limit the opportunity for competitors to act out a story whose course and outcome are unknown, and could diminish the fun. If international and Olympic competition become contests solely among the full-time employees of national governments, the fun *will* be reduced. The "best man"—the best trained, the best supported—will likely win, as the nations wish, rather than the man who unpredictably, surprisingly, performs best on the particular occasion, as most competitors would wish. If the Olympic games are to remain games, if they are to be played instead of worked at, amateurs must continue to compete, and some governments must continue to give amateurs a chance to be involved. We must not allow "what is supposed to be high athletic drama to become high finance!")

Preoccupation with a particular opponent, his talent, his aggressiveness, his immediate or his past accomplishments, is always distracting, and is often anxiety-provoking or intimidating. These adverse effects may be either deliberate or unintentional. The latter, which result from some special relationship developed between two competitors in a previous encounter, originate entirely with the perceiver. They are far more frequent than advertent efforts to "psych-out" an opponent. However, such advertent efforts may be effective, and many competitors do act so as to diminish the performance of susceptible opponents. The common denominator, as indicated by Thomas Tutko and Umberto Tosi in *Sports Psyching*, is that "psychouts are 'other directed.' They get you to worrying about what other people think of you, rather than on what you think of yourself." Many of us fall for these tactics; we are provoked, intimidated, distracted, preoccupied, or made to feel guilty in the presence of a particular opponent. To the extent that we react, take notice, become involved with that opponent, we take ourselves out of the game.

In *Winning Through Intimidation* Robert Ringer presents the Organic Chemistry Theory, a principle of behavior he learned from his experience with a self-styled expert in a college chem lab. "Don't allow yourself to be intimidated by know-it-alls who thrive on bestowing their knowledge on insecure people. . . . The only thing that's relevant is what *you* know and what *you* do." Although the lesson was learned from an experience with a psych-out artist, the principle applies equally to experiences with the truly talented.

Provocation and intimidation may effectively neutralize some competitors. Evoking guilt feelings may be more effective with others. Some of your competitors are saying, like the typical five-year-old child, "I'm such a nice kid, you wouldn't beat me, would you?" Many competitors want to make it perfectly clear that they are racing under a handicap. One of the top finishers in the 1976 Soling trials proclaimed repeatedly that his crew members were not only incompetent but unco-operative. "I still don't have the mast put together." "I'm using that old main that blew out last year." "I was testing a new jib that I knew was wrong." "You're not going to use your good sails for this unimportant race, are you?" "I haven't been able to practice for three months." Poor souls! They may be looking for an excuse to reassure themselves, but if they elicit your sympathy, your concern for their problem, they've achieved a psych-out. They have you preoccupied with their game rather than your own.

Marv Hubbard, the great running back of the Oakland Raiders, was asked prior to the play-off game of the 1975 National Football League season, how he expected their opponents, the Cincinnati Bengals, to perform. His reply sums up the only attitude a realistic competitor can take about his opponent: "Listen, Cincinnati is an explosive team; they're going to score points on you. I don't worry about it anymore. If they score in the fourth quarter, well, that's when they score. With the Bengals you expect them to score. You blow out the New Orleans Saints and the New York Giants because after you get ahead they quit. These guys didn't get into the play-offs by being quitters.

"It's like what a pool player told me happens in their big tournaments. When a guy gets on a table and starts running all the balls, the other good pool players just go to sleep and wait for their turn. You can't worry about it."

25 / The Pecking Order

I cannot give you the formula for success, but I can give you the formula for failure—which is: Try to please everybody.

—HERBERT BAYARD SWOPE

THAT EACH RACING SAILOR TENDS TO FINISH IN THE SAME GENERAL POSI-
tion in race after race, that he is committed to a pecking order, is common knowledge. Why and to what extent he manages his performance to assure this result is rarely recognized. A recent article suggests that the pecking order is the result of external forces, chiefly the desire of the existing leaders to maintain the status quo. In fact, it is engineered deliberately (albeit unconsciously) by the joint efforts of all participants. Although every competitor claims to want to win, most seem to find greater satisfaction in standardizing an order of finish. Many make significant progress in their first few years of racing. Some change classes. Finally, each seems to accept his own perception of his ability, assumes a position at a particular level in a particular fleet, and repetitively finishes in that position. Most arrange to beat only those they intend to beat, and to lose to all others.

The ascent of the order-of-finish ladder is associated with a decreasing likelihood of success and decreasing likelihood of satisfaction.

To attempt to win is to be constantly dissatisfied, to constantly struggle—at the expense of great personal commitment—for a slim chance of satisfaction. Most sailors prefer regular satisfaction; they set their goal at a readily attainable level, and finish, satisfied, at that level again and again.

I remember how delightful it was, during my early days in 14's to finish eighth instead of the expected twelfth. How miserable it is now to finish second instead of the expected first! Each competitor rates himself, judges his capabilities, and predesignates an acceptable finishing position. If he fails to attain the finishing position he expected, he is likely to be depressed. If he exceeds the position he expected, he is likely to be elated. Most competitors keep their expectations down at a level at which satisfying results occur more often than depressing results. If a position less than expected is reached, a great effort is made to advance. If a position consistent with expectation is reached, it is accepted. If a chance to beat a competitor who is rated higher appears, it is easily relinquished.

Included in many internalized Parental patterns is an implication that a person should restrain his attempts at gratification, so that he gains only his fair share, receiving no more than what he deserves. Children are taught to be considerate, compassionate, and concerned for the wishes of others, not to be selfish. They are not allowed to deprive another child of something he wants. They are taught not to infringe upon the rights of others. Almost all parents imply (at least) that a child should not obtain what he wishes—should not win— unless he "deserves" to do so. ("You can't have that candy; you've been bad." "Mother will bring you a present because you've been good." Even, "Mother loves you because you've been good.") So the extent to which one can perform well, excel, gain what is wished, win, is restricted by what is felt to be acceptable to others, to be deserved. And depending upon other aspects of parental behavior (the respect given to the child by his parents, for example), the child will feel more or less deserving. By the time he is an adult, each person learns his place, his position, in the hierarchy of deserving. If subsequently he wishes to gain more than he feels he deserves, to reach a level higher than that at which he feels he belongs, he finds that his wish is unacceptable.

A child adopts a pattern of parental behavior because (in part, at least) he fears to continue to oppose his parents. Depending upon his early relationship to his parents, whenever he subsequently fails to conform to that pattern, he may feel guilty, frightened, or depressed. These feelings arise when he finds himself—"undeservedly"—ahead of his usual position. He obtains satisfaction in finishing in that position, beating those he expects to beat, but he experiences fear and distress when he finishes, or attempts to finish, higher up.

It is a sense of "fairness" that ultimately determines the pecking order. Parents engraft the standards, determine the distribution of rewards and punishments, and establish a pattern for the future assessment of fairness. The competitor who has done poorly in a previous race or a previous series may feel that it is fair that he do well in the next. If he does well in the first race or the first part of a race, he may feel bound to do poorly in subsequent races or on subsequent legs.

Examples abound of competitors who win the first three races in a series and then, to atone, finish with a brace of disasters. They are determined to appease their internalized Parents by "knowing their place," "keeping in bounds," "behaving." They may feel compassion for their previously beaten competitors, have an urge to give them a "break". Christopher Lasch in *The Culture of Narcissism* indicates that many competitors view competition as annihilation of the loser. If annihilation is forbidden (and for most it is), winning is forbidden and must be punished when it occurs.

Thus the pecking order is made up of competitors seeking their "deserved" place over a series of events. Sometimes they deserve a reward and permit themselves a higher finishing position than usual. Other times they need punishment and seek a lower finishing position than usual. That the fluctuation is in fact slight is due to the advance recognition that a higher than usual position will result in pain, guilt, and an awareness of a need for punishment. That they rarely feel they deserve a remission of pain and guilt may contribute to their equal resistance to finishing below their usual position!

Since most everyone has the same perception of the proper rank order (based upon repetitive experience), finishing positions do not much vary. Whenever two boats meet on the course and "conquer or be conquered" status is involved, the resolution of the encounter is in conformity with the pecking order. The boat whose helmsman expects to finish ahead will drive over or gain a controlling lee-bow position. The helmsman of the other boat, expecting to finish astern, will surrender, be driven over, or be lee-bowed. Feeling that he doesn't belong, that he doesn't deserve to be ahead, he becomes distracted, preoccupied, and confused, and falls astern. The further above his expected place a helmsman finds himself the more tense and distracted he becomes, the more his mental toughness is eroded, and the more readily he can be beaten. The further below his expected place he finds himself, the more confident and capable of concentrating he becomes. He knows his neighbors in the back of the fleet "should" be beaten. He concentrates on what matters and beats them.

So each member of the fleet works to move the usual leaders forward and the usual followers backward—until every member finds his expected place, the place in which he belongs.

Races are preconceived as easy or tough, and are associated with a particular level of tension. If the competition is vastly superior, the tension anticipated is minimal; one can lose gracefully, since one doesn't have to beat the Gunslingers in order to be satisfied. If the competition is vastly inferior, again the tension anticipated is minimal; one can be certain of winning, and can approach each element of the race confident of superiority. If one should lose, one loss among many wins can be disregarded. The greatest tension arises when the competition is equal. Then the outcome assumes significance: a victory will demonstrate prowess, a loss defectiveness.

Over the years, my performance and that of one of my major local competitors have been approximately equal. Ostensibly, I believe that I should be able to beat him every time—rather than half the time. However, I often behave as if I do not wish to beat him any more than he beats me, do not wish to win more than my fair share of what "should" be an equal distribution of victories. Year after year, near the end of our annual Winter Series, we are approximately tied. He demonstrates the same concern for equity. By determined effort, we have managed to alternate the winning of the Winter Series every year since 1970!

This, of course, represents the ultimate extension of the pecking order. Not only is each competitor committed to preserving his position in the order, but those of equal stature must share their position equitably! Neither of us feels that he belongs in second, but apparently neither of us feels that he belongs in first, either. We work very hard to keep ourselves in position 1½.

One of the most vivid examples of the significance of this feeling of belonging only at a particular level became evident one year when I sailed as tactician in a 5.5-meter regatta. In the first four races we made all the right decisions and our skipper sailed the boat beautifully. With two firsts and two seconds we were sitting pretty, but our skipper was becoming more and more tense. We lost a lower shroud in the fifth race (but finished fourth), and he was barely prevented from switching to an experimental mast. We had a disastrous sixth race, sailing off to the right in a progressive back. But before the final race we retained a dominant lead, needing only to finish close to one particular boat and to place better than eighth. At the start, that boat was buried and we were free at the upwind end of the line. Our opponent tacked to the favored port tack and we covered. He was completely controlled, a hundred feet astern and to leeward—and our skipper tacked to starboard to get clear air! By the time we persuaded him to tack back to cover, the opponent was far ahead on the one-way street to the beach. We eventually caught him and went on to win the event, but not until our skipper had tried several more times to escape from his series-leading position. He seemed determined to get back to a more acceptable position, to avoid winning. He obviously felt that he didn't deserve to win. That he very clearly did was, for him, irrelevant.

This sense of belonging only at a particular level accounts for many disastrous Olympic performances. The pecking order ordinarily determines the finishing order, but it does not determine the entry list. Being selected for the Olympics, however, is a clear designation of position. If the representative feels that his selection was appropriate, that he belongs at the top, he will perform well. If he feels that his selection was inappropriate, he will be preoccupied with the need to atone for the unfairness and will perform poorly. He will feel that he doesn't belong, doesn't deserve to be among Olympians, that it would be particularly inappropriate for him to pass or to beat someone who deserves to be there. (It is evident that the individual who perceives himself as not belonging is rarely able to perceive others as not belonging.)

The pecking order is created, of course, by preoccupation with outcome. If each participant were unaware of the significance of his actions as determinants of outcome, he would make no distinction between the competitor he expected to beat and the competitor he expected to be beaten by. But inasmuch as most of those in the fleet *are* preoccupied with outcome, the pecking order is maintained. Only the sailors who can ignore the significance of their immediate performance can hope to break out of the predicted pattern. An obvious characteristic of the newcomer who is destined to do well is his ability to disregard expected rankings, to disregard outcome, so as to perform repeatedly and continuously at his best regardless of which competitors he happens to be racing against. This behavior is, of course, frightening to those who are mired in the pecking order. They are intimidated by the aggressiveness of anyone who is able to perform well without regard to where he belongs!

Acceptance of a pecking order is a disorder of appraisal. It represents an inability by the participants to appraise external reality. They distort the real world, in which ability to determine strategy and tactics and to handle a boat determines outcome, into a fanciful world in which each participant deserves a certain place in the finishing order. They believe that they are allotted a position in this order and work desperately to maintain it. To escape, they must learn to see the world as it is, to recognize themselves and their competitors as they are. Each competitor is equally entitled to do well. It is right and proper that the helmsman who performs best on a particular day and in particular circumstances should win—not because he deserves to, but because he did so.

Self-Appraisal

26 / Self-Confidence

Men at some time are masters of their fates:
The fault, dear Brutus, is not in our stars,
But in ourselves, that we are underlings.
—WILLIAM SHAKESPEARE

SELF-CONFIDENCE PERMITS A COMPETITOR TO SURVEY THE FLEET ASHORE
before a regatta and predict his finishing position. These boats and
these sailors are incapable of performing at my level. These boats are
capable, but their helmsmen are not. These helmsmen and their boats
are superior and will finish ahead of me. These three or four are at my
level, and I will finish ahead of them. The appraisal is realistic: my
competence is greater, less than, or equal to that of each of the other
competitors and warrants my expecting to perform at the predicted
level. Trust is superimposed: among competitors of equal competence, I will excel. Self-confidence is not a false belief in the certainty
of victory, but a realistic faith that one will perform at the highest
level of which one is capable.

Richard Petty says, "The fact is, I think I have more confidence
than anyone. Most drivers are beat before they begin; they think
they're going to lose, so they're going to lose. Some of them may think

they can win, but they don't expect to win. I know I'm not going to win every race, but I expect to win going into every race." He knows at what level he can perform, and his faith in himself tells him that among equals, he will excel.

Buddy Melges approached the 1976 season with his thoughts focused upon his expected performance in the Olympics. His recent performances in the winter regattas justified his presumption that he would be the U.S. Olympic Soling representative. His faith in himself provided the assurance that among the top competitors, who might at their best be his equals, he would excel. Chris Law, winner of the 1976 Finn Gold Cup in Brisbane, was equally confident of his selection as Britain's Olympic representative. In a *Yachts and Yachting* interview, after the Gold Cup but before the trials, he discussed his expected competition at the Olympics. He had just beaten every good Finn sailor in the world *and* his U.K. rival, David Howlett. Why shouldn't he be confident of his selection? Retrospectively it seems that, since both Melges and Law failed to gain selection, their confidence was unjustified. However, one failure, no matter in how important an event, should not and—if they were truly confident—did not alter their self-appraisal. Their confidence was both justified (by previous experience) and appropriate (to future performance).

Resistance to the effects of recent adverse experience—loss in the last regatta, failure on the last leg—is the mark of the truly confident. The trust remains, the appraisal of basic worth is unchanged. Poul-Richard Jensen, after a disastrous finish in the fifth race, came back to win the following day and take the fifth place in the finale that brought him the Soling gold medal in 1976. His appraisal of his capabilities, his trust in himself, had not been altered by a single adverse experience.

Appraisal of oneself depends in part upon appraisal of the competition. Paul Elvstrom, after winning the gold medal at Melbourne in 1956, was asked by an Australian journalist, "To what do you attribute your victory?" Elvstrom answered, "The others they were too slowly." He raced with Aage Birch for the Dragon Gold Cup at Marstrand in 1958. Sergio Sorrentino of Italy was the fastest and they were the next fastest. The cup would be won by whoever beat the other in the final race. On the last beat they alternately crossed each other until, "by pure luck" says Elvstrom, Sorrentino crossed the line ahead. "When things go like that and it is luck who would win then we know that and we don't have to be disappointed." Elvstrom's confidence, his trust in himself, assures him that he should win, that only luck can enable a competitor to beat him.

The most confident are those who can be most realistic in appraising others and themselves, who have no need to inflate their expectations artificially. Race after race they predict how they will perform; they perform as they have predicted, and their trust in themselves is enhanced. How much more trustworthy they find themselves when, having predicted a third place, they achieve a third place. How much more untrustworthy they would have found themselves when, having predicted a first place, they achieved a third. Repeated failures to live up to expectations undermine confidence, erode faith in oneself. Robert Ringer says, "You either acknowledge reality and use it to your benefit or it will automatically work against you." He developed his Theory of Sustenance of a Positive Attitude Through the Assumption of a Negative Result as a means of maintaining confidence. This theory begins with the observation that no matter how well prepared you are, you will win only a small percentage of the big races, since "there are an endless number of factors that are beyond your control." Hence, the only way to sustain a positive attitude is "to realistically assume a negative result." If this is done, each negative result becomes an educational experience and the result itself can be disregarded. One gains faith in oneself; one *can* predict the outcome; one need not be disappointed in oneself.

Ted Turner described his chances to win the 1977 Congressional Cup in typical fashion: "I really don't have a chance. I am as optimistic as a Polish cavalry officer caught between the Germans and the Russians in 1939." What he meant was, "I don't have to convince either you or me that I'm better than they are. I know I'll do my best, and we'll see what happens." (He won.) Before the 1976 Olympics, I discussed with Jeorg Diesch, the German Flying Dutchman sailor, his chances of winning the gold medal. "I hope to be in the first five today [in heavy air]. I am not the fastest in any condition. Pajot is the fastest in heavy air, Pattison in moderate air, Bilger in light air, but I could be second in any condition." He won the gold medal with ease—by being second in almost every condition. On the same occasion I talked to Hubert Raudaschl, who felt that any of eleven boats could win the Soling gold medal, that any one of them could have a lucky day or a lucky week. I asked him how he would explain the loss, if he were to lose. "The others were better," he said, as he threw up his hands! The confident tell it like it is.

The diffident assume that in a contest among equals they will finish at the bottom. The confident assume that they will finish at the top. In some contests, they may predict a low finishing position, but they expect to perform at the highest level of which they are capable. The diffident expect poor performance, at the lowest level of which they are capable. The falsely confident predict a high level of performance despite a realistic recognition that that level is unattainable or despite a lack of faith in their potential to attain that level. Diffidence interferes with immediate performance. False confidence interferes with subsequent performance because it undermines trust in oneself.

Grandstanding is usually associated with false confidence. I remember one competitor at the 1957 CDA Regatta in Montreal who seemed at the time to be supremely confident. After five general recalls for the seventy-seven-boat fleet, he announced that he would sit out the next start! As the rest of us struggled tensely into position, he dangled his feet over his transom and jeered at us from a position a few boat lengths to windward of the starting line. He rejoined us for the seventh general recall! After a Buzzards Bay Bowl race in a howling southwester, Ron Ormiston was asked why he didn't take down his main after he rounded the final mark and recognized that the entire fleet was capsized astern. "We expected to dump and thought it would be easier to take it down then!"

Self-confidence is not assuredness of winning; it is assuredness of doing one's best—every time. Its major benefit is that it permits one to leapfrog ahead in expectation and accomplishment. The remembrance of having beaten each of three boats on each of three previous occasions indicates to the confident competitor that all three can be beaten in the next race in which they participate. When on a subsequent occasion another boat is beaten for the first time, the confident competitor predicts that because she can be beaten, henceforth she will be beaten. When his prediction is fulfilled, he looks ahead to the next boat to be conquered, feeling no need to consolidate the gain. Each subsequent performance will be as good or better than the best previous one. The confident competitor sails through the pecking order, while the diffident falls back after each advance or makes no progress at all. The confident competitor views each accidental advance as an indication of enhanced competence, while regarding a setback as the consequence of a readily correctable mistake.

The confident competitor assumes that he is personally responsible for the outcome. If he does well, his competence is revealed. If he does poorly, he recognizes his failure to have been the consequence of his own mistakes or of something beyond anyone's control. My crew Guy McKhann says that his son, who is a wrestler, has never been beaten. His foot slips occasionally, or the referee makes a poor call—but he has never been beaten.

27 / Believe in Yourself

*Don't be afraid to take a big step. You can't
cross a chasm in two small jumps.*
—DAVID LLOYD GEORGE

THE 1976 OLYMPIC SOLING TRIALS WERE CONDUCTED AT ASSOCIATION
Island in light air. On most mornings, before the start, Robbie Haines
(with Lowell North crewing) would come alongside and suggest a tuning session. When the air was light, we were distinctly faster. Lowell
would get down to leeward, scratch his head, and twitch a little jib
sheet here, a little backstay there. But no matter what he changed, he
could not get their boat up to our speed. One morning after we had
slipped away in a particularly impressive manner, I turned back and
called over that I hadn't guaranteed not to demoralize them. "That's
OK," replied Lowell, "we appreciate your help." Several times we did
the same thing to them on the course—but in the trials they almost
always finished ahead, and they barely missed selection (while we
dropped to seventh at the end of the series). We certainly hadn't demoralized them. Indeed, despite speed that was frequently inferior,
they sailed a better series than (almost) anyone else in the fleet. What

self-assurance they must have had to ignore their handicap and get on with the job!

To believe that you will perform at a level higher than that attainable by your competitors frees you of anxiety concerning the minutiae of the race, the one-to-one conflicts with other boats, the technical aspects of sail trim and boat handling. The apprehension which accompanies the loss of self-assurance must always be detrimental. The competitor who is overtly apprehensive may be inattentive to significant changes in strategic and tactical conditions or may experience episodes of total unawareness. John Bertrand says, "You must believe you are capable of winning and in fact believe that you and you alone are the very best sailor out there. If you don't believe this, then at some critical stage of the race, the wrong decision will be made."

Pete Reiser says, "You need to have inner conceit." Roger Staubach exudes this feeling; he *knows* he's the best. Bob Whitehurst, after he came ashore from winning the fourth 470 race of the 1976 Olympics, announced, "We rounded the weather mark in the lead and just left 'em." "Where were you when I was losing?" he prodded the reporters around him. He left little doubt that he expected to win the races remaining. Dennis Conner, when I interviewed him during the same Olympics, said that he perceived himself as a winner. He felt that each competitor recognized his proper finishing position, and that it was important for a winner to establish his position early in a series. Terry Crowley, the Oriole pinch hitter, tells himself each time he goes to the plate, "I'm the best man for this job." Success reinforces innate self-assurance; the success of these obviously self-assured competitors indicates that the inverse is also true—self-assurance breeds success. One can doubt that they are able to maintain this inner conceit continuously, but it is clearly beneficial when they feel it.

Peter Barrett and Dick Tillman once arrived in Bermuda barely in time to rig their borrowed Finns, yet managed to finish 1–2 in the first race. Upon returning ashore for lunch they noted the terrible condition of the bottoms of their boats and proceeded to polish them energetically. In the afternoon race, apprehensive because of their now-recognized handicap, they finished among the second ten. John Albrechtson seemed to become more and more tense as the 1976 Olympics proceeded, although he led all the way. It took the full-time efforts of Borje Larsen (and other members of the Swedish team) to keep John assured and at ease—but they succeeded, and he won the Tempest gold medal. Self-assurance is obviously a subjective perception; it need not be based upon any real superiority, and it can be lost in the presence of actual superiority.

The Washington Redskins played the St. Louis Cardinals on October 26, 1976, in a game which ultimately determined their entry into the play-offs. They won 20–10, chiefly because the Cardinals fumbled eight times. The Redskins' total offense was 133 yards, their quarterback was sacked eight times. They made one touchdown after recovering a fumble on the six-yard line, one touchdown on a punt return, and two field goals after recovering fumbles. Coach George Allen said afterward that his Redskins had played the best game of their careers! He may have believed this; whether he did or not, he thought it was important that his players believe it.

John Bertrand says, "It is extremely difficult to win a yacht race with a slower boat. However, if you *believe* your boat speed is excellent, it becomes very difficult for competitors to pass you." I asked Paul Henderson how he was doing in his Flying Dutchman at CORK 1973. "I have a very slow boat, but I am sailing brilliantly," he replied. Australian Ralph Doubell talks to himself as he runs. While leading the finals of the 800-meter dash at the 1968 Olympics, he was telling himself, "You're going to win! You can feel it in your muscles." During the 1975 Soling World Championship at Chicago I remarked to Bruce Goldsmith that Richie Stearns was sailing very well. Bruce replied, "Oh yes, I've been working with him. Really got him tuned up!" Richie finished tenth, Bruce forty-fourth! Self-assurance derives from an inner strength, a state of mental toughness, that is impervious to the recognition of an inferior performance, the presence of a superior competitor, or the threat of failure.

A display of self-assurance is intimidating to others, particularly those who are not self-assured. When competitors are intimidated—that is, lose *their* self-assurance—their performance suffers, to the benefit, of course, of their self-assured opponents. Thus, as in many aspects of competition, a gain is doubled; to the extent that self-assurance benefits its possessor, it is detrimental to his opponent. This is the George Allen thesis: act as if you are above the usual limitations on performance, *and* thereby intimidate the opposition. The unhappy truth is that the less competent and diffident will easily be intimidated, and their performance will suffer as much in the presence of bluster as in the presence of genius.

To believe in oneself is to have one's Adult in control. One senses neither the helplessness that one's Child feels nor the belittling that one's Parent expresses. But there is an ebb and flow in every competitive activity, which alternately strengthens and threatens the Adult's control. The confident, mentally tough competitor handles most threats without allowing either his Child or his Parent to assume command. However, his belief in himself, his ability to maintain control over his fears, and his resistance to the tendency to belittle himself, are tested periodically, and at no time so much as when he is far behind or way ahead.

When a competitor falls behind, his Child feels abandoned and his Parent focuses attention upon his defectiveness. When he moves ahead, his Child feels secure, his Parent approving, his Adult supported and confident. He delights in risk, relishes challenge—at first. But these feelings do not persist. The Child of a leading competitor begins to feel possessive, becomes anxious to keep rather than risk what he has attained. His Parent reminds this individual that he doesn't deserve to be in the lead. Fearful and guilt-ridden, he becomes distracted and ineffectual. Meanwhile, the competitor who has fallen behind discovers that defeat is not nearly so bad as he had expected. Perhaps with the aid of denial and intellectualization, his Adult works through the initial grief. His Child becomes reassured that it has not been abandoned. His Parent is satisfied; he has suffered enough. His Adult has faced the pain and the fear, has found itself sufficient, and is once again poised for performance, risk, and challenge.

This ebb and flow of confidence and effectiveness is particularly evident in events which take place as a series. Then there is time between games or races for the significance of the previous performance to be recognized and for an accommodation to be reached. The winner of the early games may later be oppressed by both Child and Parent, and tense, fearful of losing, may be easily defeated. On the other hand, the early loser may have accommodated his grief, atoned sufficiently. Freed of Parental pressure, at ease with his Child, relaxed, confident, and daring, he may subsequently perform at his best. Comebacks are not surprising; among competitors of equal competence, they are the rule. The farther behind one falls, the easier it is to perform competently. Many a World Series has been characterized by this behavior. The failure of the Baltimore Orioles to win after attaining a lead of three games to one in the 1979 World Series is a dramatic case in point.

The result of these psychological oscillations is usually performance that displaces the standings of the competitors toward the median. Those ahead fall behind; those behind catch up. However, some individuals progress in one direction or the other. Those with strong, belittling Parents can believe in their worthiness only when they are handicapped. But when "doing it the hard way," from a position far astern, they may progress inexorably to victory. Other competitors, whose Children are in the ascendance, lose faith in themselves when behind. Shorn of the success they believe should be theirs, fearful of being abandoned, they surrender.

Recognition that being in the lead is threatening benefits the knowledgeable competitor. He is better able to pass a competitor ahead both because the latter feels threatened and because he, making the gains, feels advantaged. And by "going at the opponent's strength," he makes the resulting defeat all the more devastating. This technique is exploited in many sports, notably long-distance running, automobile racing, and cycling. Not only does the competitor astern often obtain a physical advantage, but he maintains a threatening relationship, ready to pounce upon the "helpless" Child ahead.

Early in a contest the Adult gives the Child full rein, enabling the participant to believe in himself and in the joy of seeking an external prize. Later, when he is in the lead and threatened by his Parent or behind and threatened by the external world, his Adult may weaken, lose faith in itself, and permit the Child's fears to surface. Then the competitor fears to lose what (Child-like) he feels he owns, avoids risk, and ceases to play. The person with a stronger Adult, recognizing that fluctuations in success are to be expected, accepts his present status, makes but minimal adjustments in self-appraisal, and performs confidently "from here onward" whether he is ahead or behind.

28 / The Power of Positive Thinking

And if things don't look so cheerful
Just show a little fight
For every bit of darkness
There's a little bit of light.
—"THE BLUEBIRD OF HAPPINESS"

WHEN I ARRIVED IN BERMUDA IN 1960 FOR THE PRINCESS ELIZABETH CUP, Brownlow Gray asked, "What makes you think you're going to win?" I was confident that I would, and I was genuinely surprised that Brownlow should be doubtful. Since the previous September, I had won four major regattas in a row, beating the best in the East and Canada. There seemed little reason to doubt that I would beat the Bermudians as well. However, while I remembered my recent victories, Brownlow remembered *Salute*'s disastrous debut in Bermuda the spring before. My confidence was built upon a demonstrated superiority. With my new boat I had been faster than those who had previously dominated the class. My performance had created my confidence. Despite Shorty Trimingham's reminder that "nothing makes a helmsman look better than a fast boat," the series demonstrated that my confidence was not only warranted but highly effective. We won—with four firsts and one second!

The range of accuracy in self-appraisal is likely to be large, and it

152

seems advisable always to adopt the appraisal which is at the upper limit. Utterances made in public should always be favorable to oneself—and will usually be accepted. The trick then is to accept one's own public appraisal. This is not just whistling in the dark.

Most competitors believe in the power of positive thinking. Consciously or unconsciously, they use it, with varying degrees of appropriateness. John McKay told his Tampa Bay Buccaneers, "I guarantee you the Packers are no better than you are. You can beat this team. But you've got to block somebody!" His positive thinking was certainly inappropriate, but it was undoubtedly useful. John Wohlhuter, contemplating Olympic competition against John Walker and Filbert Bayi in 1976, said, "The best man doesn't always win. Knowing that, it gives you hope." Think of the positive elements, even if they are few. Steve Riddick apparently came to positive thinking only after he won an Olympic gold medal. Contemplating a future sprint he said, "I could run if I had to, but I don't have to. I ain't got to prove nothin' no more."

Confidence is enhanced by a favorable perception of one's ability, especially when it is shared by others—crew members, competitors, advisers. But ultimately it depends upon performance. Those who usually perform well, expect to perform well; they become confident. Crews of winning helmsmen adapt well to helmsmanship. They have the confidence that characterizes those who are accustomed to winning. During practice before the 1976 Olympics, John Kolius had clearly been the fastest. I asked him who would win. He replied, "We will." I remember the confidence with which I approached the 1964 Prince of Wales Cup at Lowestoft. We had done progressively better in each of the preceding races of P.O.W. Week. I knew that in our conditions we could beat anyone there—and we did.

Confidence must have a valid basis, however. It disappears rapidly when it is unjustified. Fran Tarkenton and the Minnesota Vikings talked big before losing the 1977 Super Bowl. They were "up" for this one. "We're going to win," said Fran. But when it was all over, he explained things differently. They *had* been confident, but "you have to have a couple of good plays early to keep up that emotion. After the kick recovery and fumble, our emotion left us."

The concept of being "psyched up" represents a belief in the power of positive thinking: "If I keep telling myself I'll do well, I'll do well." This attitude may provide some benefits before a contest, but without the reassurance of early success it cannot be sustained. As

Fran Tarkenton recognized, the first setback destroys the belief and its supportive power. Those who "protest too much" their superiority seem to fall the farthest when a reversal occurs. Although the appearance of confidence may derive from a belief in one's capabilities, it may represent only a belief in the value of believing in one's capabilities, or in demonstrating a belief in them.

An appraisal of one's own stature and potential should always be as favorable as possible, but it should never be unrealistic. One of my Soling crews has a distressing habit of predicting that "we'll win every race." When we fail to do so (as we almost always do) he becomes discouraged, loses his enthusiasm, and performs less effectively. Expectations should be valid. Failure to fulfill an excessive expectation (a likely occurrence) will have a more adverse affect than an initial belief in a lower level of performance. Satisfaction is the goal of participation and the sustainer of confidence. And satisfaction will be less likely if the level of performance necessary to achieve it is unrealistically high. Progress, doing better than expected, is satisfying. Failure is not. Progress leads to confidence; failure leads to belittling of oneself. Thus, an unrealistic assumption of confidence leads to its diminution.

I remember a race at Annapolis in which Dave Curtis led around the final weather mark. We were third, two hundred feet astern, and followed him down the run on starboard jibe. The boats astern followed suit until, a third of the way to the finish, stronger air (the sea breeze) appeared to the left and they began to jibe to port, toward it. We jibed to protect our position, but as the wind filled in from astern, we had to sail considerably higher to match their speed and gave up considerable distance down the course. When we finally broke free to the left, the wind began to fill in from the right (where we had been), and the boats to starboard that had forgone the jibe moved up rapidly. Dave, who had appeared to be in a hole when we jibed, had continued on his original course. While we had been sailing nearly perpendicular to the rhumb line, he had gained another two hundred feet. His confidence had been immune to the threat that I had felt and responded to. He knew that he was already doing the right thing, that his present course would provide a favorable leeward position from which to meet the sea breeze, that the wind was as likely to reach him where he was as anywhere else. I expect that even if he had been passed by the mob astern, he would have behaved in the same way in the same conditions on a subsequent occasion. His confidence was valid, and he recognized its validity; it would not have been undermined by one reversal in one race.

Thomas Tutko suggests that if confidence is insufficient, it can be stimulated by reassurance, that a coach may help a competitor in this respect by recognizing and rewarding him when he shows confidence. A good crew can provide such reassurance and support to the helmsman, and this *can* be of temporary benefit. Tutko also suggests that the competitor who lacks confidence should avoid placing himself in a situation where there is a high probability of failure. As that situation seems to exist whenever a starting line is crossed, the suggestion hardly seems practical. However, it is reasonable to avoid increasing the probability. Doing the obviously wrong thing just to try something different, tacking or jibing away from the fleet, not following when astern in situations where there is but one way to go, will increase the probability of failure and diminish the confidence felt during subsequent legs and races.

The power of positive thinking is only as great as it is realistic. A strong Adult cannot be misled. The truth will out—and soon—on a race course. Confidence is gained when it is earned. Since it is of great value, we need not wonder that everyone pretends to have it. But only the experience of a high level of performance provides it. And the only means of attaining a high level of performance is to set one's standards realistically, to experience the satisfaction that attends each measure of improvement, to make progress one step at a time.

A basketball coach at LaSalle College tried to put positive thinking to work for his players. He schooled them in psychocybernetics, the use of visual images of a desired result. His players dutifully practiced the art prior to games and while resting on the sidelines. Against archrival Villanova the technique was put to the test. With three seconds remaining and his team behind 70–69, LaSalle's Darryl Gladden was fouled. Villanova called time out before the free throw to put pressure on the freshman. The coach told Darryl to relax, close his eyes, and do his psychocybernetics. Darryl looked at him wide eyed and said, "Coach, this is no time to screw around!" Everybody on the bench broke up. The resultant break in the tension, not the power of positive thinking, permitted Darryl to sink both ends of the one-and-one and win for LaSalle 71–70.

29 / Embarrassment

No one can make you feel inferior without your consent.

—STEPHEN LEACOCK

AS PAUL ELVSTROM SUGGESTS, ONE MUST ASSUME RESPONSIBILITY FOR successful outcomes and deny responsibility for defective ones. All the good must be remembered and incorporated into a positive self-appraisal. All the bad must be forgotten. Future performance depends upon the capability previously perceived. The player must manipulate his past or his past will manipulate him. He must resist embarrassment.

Hans Fogh, after winning CORK 1978, said that he hadn't expected to win, that to win, he thought, one must expect to do so. He had won the two big regattas in Europe that preceded CORK, and he must have known that he *could* win CORK. He was at ease, with nothing to prove, no possibility of embarrassment. Peter Hall won the last race to move from fourth to second in the series. Though he had had some (for him) embarrassingly poor races earlier in the series, he too was at ease. He had faced his embarrassment, found it acceptable, and no longer fearful of embarrassment, went on to win. Billy Abbott, having been in the top four of every one of the previous eight races, in position to win it all, fearful of embarrassment, *was* embarrassed. The final race was his worst of the series. Embarrassing events, whether remembered or expected, must be ignored.

The successful player accepts his mistakes, appraising them and himself realistically. He feels that he belongs, that he deserves to be in the competition. Those who have doubts that they belong—in the competition, in the lead—are subject to embarrassment. They feel that their competitors are particularly aware of them and are jeering at their defectiveness. Those who are self-assured, as illustrated in the following anecdotes, are resistant to such concerns; they continue to recognize that they belong even if they perform poorly.

Slim Dawson was en route to Marion, Massachusetts, for the Buzzards Bay Bowl when he heard the sound of fire engines. He soon discovered that the fire engines were following him—and that he was towing the fire, in his 14! He had flicked a cigarette into the mattress upon which the boat rested and had never noticed the smoke blowing astern until the bottom of the 14 was gone. Unembarrassed, he appeared to enjoy the watching and partying of that year even more than the victory of the year before. I don't know whether the owner of the Dragon that escaped from its tow on a Canadian superhighway responded similarly. As his wife slowed for a curve she witnessed with horror the boat passing her, crossing the median strip, cruising against the traffic in the far lane, and finally coming to rest unscathed alongside a pump in a gas station!

Sometimes, although embarrassment does not develop before a regatta, it is arranged in advance of the event. After having won the first three races of a spring 14 regatta, I announced that the only way I could lose this one was to capsize in the first race on Sunday and disqualify in the second. I capsized in the first one as predicted but having led the fleet by a large margin to the final weather mark in the second was convinced that I had escaped the disqualification. When the following helmsmen hailed that I had rounded the mark on the wrong side, I assumed that they were attempting a last-ditch ruse to catch up. But when I reached the committee boat, I learned the sad truth and recognized that I had fulfilled my prophecy.

It is difficult not to be intimidated by an adverse experience in a race, difficult not to allow it to diminish one's self-appraisal and one's performance thereafter. I remember racing a Penguin, which I had built in my bachelor officers' quarters, against a fleet of antique lapstrake dinghies at Matsushima, Japan. I had asked to be included in their race and expected to beat them with ease. They knew the waters, however, and soon left me mired in the seaweed as they sailed away gleefully. The representative of the conquering U.S. Army sailed home with his tail between his legs. Paul Henderson described a disastrous race in a CDA Regatta: "I was so far back, I met people I didn't even know were in the class!" Don Allen was sailing with Don Barnes in a similar situation. When asked by his skipper what he thought they should do, he replied, "I don't know. I've never been this far back before!"

I visited John Kolius on the morning of the fourth race of the 1976 Olympics. He didn't want to talk to me or anyone else, didn't want to hear any cheering comments. There was a great stir when he realized he had forgotten their battens. "He is embarrassed," said his wife. He felt that his poor (by his standards) showing to date, had let down the side, had failed those who expected so much of him. He didn't completely shake off that feeling of embarrassment until the final race when it was almost too late. David Forbes, 1972 Star gold medalist, who had dominated the Solings in 1975 had a showing far poorer than Kolius's. Halfway through the series he too was embarrassed. "Stu, did you ever have a series where you just couldn't seem to do anything right? We'll have to do better before we can show ourselves in the bar!" He did do better, much better, but he had to shake off that embarrassment first.

Among my most embarrassing times in a 14 was the day at Oakville, on Lake Ontario, when I capsized five times in the residue of Hurricane Audrey. In the first race of the Emerson (in which U.S. and Canadian teams compete), I capsized while in last place and managed to wrap my mainsheet around the leeward mark in the process. I did little better the rest of the day. Walt Lawson tells the story as follows: "How come you came to upset in the lake so often, Mister?" "I didn't come to upset in the lake, I came to . . . !" An equally embarrassing incident which adversely affected the remainder of the series was in the 1957 Princes Elizabeth Series. In the first race I had a beautiful port-end start but couldn't quite lay the anchor line of the committee boat. I tacked with the intention of going astern of the one boat on my quarter that I couldn't clear. Unable to free the mainsheet sufficiently, I attempted to tack back at the last moment, hit the windward boat amidships, and capsized her. She turned out to be the boat of Andy Shoettle, who had just won a medal in the 5.5's at Melbourne, and whose crew was the aide-de-camp of the governor-general of Bermuda! I wished that I could sail back to the club under water.

Bill Abbott must have felt similarly when he was introduced to King Constantine on the grand stairway of the Royal Thames, in downtown London. Bill had tucked a club ashtray under his arm, and when he stuck out his hand to shake Constantine's, it went crashing to the floor! John Cuneo was certainly not adversely affected by his embarrassment at the Kiel Olympics. The Australians' meteorologist had provided a chart overlay to indicate likely wind variations. After winning the Dragon gold medal, Cuneo was asked why he so often took a course opposite to that of the remainder of the fleet. Only then did he discover that he'd been putting the overlay on upside down!

You must expect to make mistakes; you should be at ease with failure. You must expect to be involved in embarrassing situations. A sense of humor is needed, an ability to laugh at yourself. If you feel that the rest of the world is watching, looking for a chance to jeer, embarrassment will not only occur but persist. If you feel that your reputation is affected by every action then every minor error will provoke anxiety and diminish performance. A realistic appraisal of the world will indicate that it is not sitting around with its eye on your every move. A realistic appraisal of yourself will indicate that no one action will alter anyone's opinion of you, nor should it influence your opinion of yourself.

Embarrassing situations will arise. You cannot avoid the occasionally jeering responses of your competitors. Your Adult must not permit your Parent to echo their judgment. You can and must avoid a reduced appraisal of yourself. You must not allow an error or a deficiency to be either intimidating or distracting. Such occurrences must not be allowed to undermine performance during the remainder of the race or series, or in subsequent series. The situation may be embarrassing, but it must not cause embarrassment.

30 / Honesty Is the Best Policy

I am different from Washington; I have a higher, grander standard of principle. Washington could not lie. I can lie, but I won't.

—MARK TWAIN

SAILING IS ONE OF THE FEW SPORTS IN WHICH THE PLAYERS GOVERN themselves. There are no umpires, field judges, linesmen, or referees. Each player determines for himself whether he has complied with the rules and penalizes himself (withdraws) if he recognizes that he has failed to comply. The race committee establishes the boundaries (the course), tells the players when to begin, and sends them on their way. Thereafter, except for recording the finish, the only time that officials take action is when a player protests. In other words, only at the request of a player do officials enter the game in a manner that alters its outcome. This is the sport as we believe it to be, as we wish it to be. To the extent that the game is indeed played in this manner, we see ourselves as trustworthy and honest.

Unfortunately, under the guise of protecting us from ourselves, the rule makers have progressively insinuated officialdom into our game. They urge race committees to detect fouls, to protest suspected infringements, to satisfy themselves that players have observed the rules. They have created a rule to encourage players to spy on one another and protest the infractions they happen to observe. They have created rules that permit national authorities to disqualify players for any period they deem fit and permit race committees to disqualify players from entire regattas for conduct considered undesirable. These rules tells us that we are untrustworthy; they imply that without supervision we would be dishonest.

Most of us took up sailing, in part at least, because we understood that the game was ours, that our fellow players were trustworthy, and that rules, not officials, governed our behavior. Attempts to legislate morality alienate the honest majority, diminish the significance of their example, and either fail to reach or encourage the dishonest minority. In fact, to the extent that the rules recognize the presence of the latter, they are granted a semblance of acceptability.

The celebrated case of Patrick Pym (International Yacht Racing Union vs. Pym) typifies the manner in which officialdom has misappropriated the game. Pym is alleged to have taken a paddle to the hand of a competitor who at the starting line attempted to push his own Finn forward while thrusting Pym's backward. One can easily imagine Pym's shock that a fellow player would so blatantly ignore the rules, and one can as easily understand his momentary fury at this violation of the code. What is difficult to understand is the IYRU's response: to disqualify Pym (for an extended period) and apparently to ignore the cause of the incident! Obviously, the officials were more concerned that a player would attempt to regain one of their misappropriated powers (the power to penalize) than they were to assure that the game was played according to the rules. The precedent set is also typical: it demeans the competitor who insists upon upholding the rules, while ignoring or at least failing to influence the one who violates them.

My own sense of honesty was defined by an experience in 14's in Canada. I had done poorly in the early races of this, my first, CDA Regatta but found myself up with the series leaders in the final race. As we approached the second weather mark, one of them crossed me on port. The crossing was obviously closer than either of us had expected, and he called back to me, "Did you have to bear away?" Surprised by the question, I answered, without thinking, "Yes, a little." I had borne away, but I was uncertain whether I had had to do so. "Sorry about that," he called, bore away, and headed for the beach. I immediately wished I'd had the presence of mind to say "no," for I felt that it was most inappropriate for him to lose the series (Canada's most prestigious) because of this questionable mischance.

What a revelation this episode was, and how impressed I was! One of the outstanding sailors of the class had asked and accepted the word of a newcomer regarding a crucial determinant of the series outcome. "Did you have to bear away?" If you did, I must retire. No ifs, ands, or buts, no arguments, no complaints, no railing against the fates. Take it ("like a man") and go home. The outcome, the chance of winning (which cannot come until next year and may never come again) is less important than compliance with the rules of the game. "This is the way we play in this class (is there another way?)."

Could any lesson be taught better? Could the young newcomer be influenced to behave honorably by a better technique? How proud I was to be a 14 sailor. A few years later I retired from the Toms River Cup when, a quarter mile in the lead, I touched a mark. I remembered my experience at that CDA, and how much more important it was to play the game than it was to win it.

Recognizing that truth is not easy. People are not born honest, willing to forgo advantage for principle. The young child is selfish, possessive, acquisitive, unwilling to give up anything he wants. At first everything he comes into contact with is assumed to be his own plaything. By his second year he begins to understand who owns what but he continues to assume that when he possesses something it becomes "his." Even a four-year-old must be expected to "take" whatever he wants. Six-year-olds are likely to steal candy in the supermarket and to lie when confronted with evidence of their misdeeds. An eight-year-old may take money from his mother's purse to impress his peers with his purchasing power. By age ten the child should have ceased to steal and lie, but he may still stretch the truth a little. He may in secret do things that have been forbidden, keep things that he has "found," modify the rules to assure that he will win.

His progress in this evolution toward honesty depends upon his parents—on the example they set (which determines the character of his internalized Parent) and the attitudes they display toward him (which determine the nature of his internalized Child). If they are dishonest themselves, behaving one way and telling him to behave in another, he will be unable to gain control of his natural impulsiveness and possessiveness. If he finds that those around him invade one another's privacy, "borrow" without permission, lie in dealing with outsiders, he will continue to do the same. A parent's request for him to be "unselfish," to share, may be confusing when he has been told that he cannot "share" someone else's possessions. To the extent that he learns that to be loved he must be approved and that to be approved he must be successful, he may assume that success is more important than honesty. If his parents cheat, if they condone his cheating, he will learn that cheating is an acceptable means of gaining approval. His internalized Parent will require him to gain approval first and worry about the accompanying guilt second.

Parents must set limits to counter the persistence of impulsivity and possessiveness, they must set an honest example to assure the internalization of an appropriate Parent, and they must be respectful of the child to assure against acting out, rebelliousness, and retaliation. They should avoid excessive criticism, even of dishonesty, since this leads merely to self-belittling. They should see that the child has chores, to increase his feeling of responsibility and his respect for himself. Honesty is an acquired trait, but it is a social necessity. Parents who fail to raise their child so that he is honest are not only risking that he will be socially unacceptable, but depriving him of a major source of satisfaction.

People who fail to develop a persisting sense of honesty may excuse themselves by citing the old saw, If I don't cheat and my opponent does, I am only cheating myself. In reality they are only demonstrating immaturity, displaying the arrogance of an infant. "These rules are meant for others; I do not have to comply with them. I establish my own rules." They may be retaliating, revengefully getting even for their parents' disrespect. They do not play games. Instead, they may attempt ruthlessly, vindictively, to "destroy" their opponents. Their involvement (which is not play) is at the expense of others.

The rules of yacht racing are so framed that outright cheating is difficult. One cannot cut across from beat to reach, ignoring the weather mark, without being noticed! John Oakeley's implication, in his book, that taking undue advantage of competitors is acceptable caused Jack Knights to wonder "whether Oakeley would have to be dragged from the wicket towards the pavillion even if all three stumps lay spread-eagled behind him." Some competitors seem to believe that if one can avoid detection one is justified, outside or in advance of the game, in adversely affecting an opponent; "split pins removed, screws undone, wet varnish applied to the underbody" are mentioned by Knights. My only comparable experience was when, leading in the

Swiss Championship, I arrived at the dock to find my bailers opened and the boat full of water. Subsequently, in the same regatta my closest competitor, while reaching but without luffing rights, luffed intermittently so as to force me above my normal course and eventually caused contact between my spinnaker and his pole. This resulted, as seemed to be his intent, in my disqualification.

Fortunately, such behavior is rare. Ordinarily, cheating will be in the form of taking undue advantage of a less competent, less experienced, or less aggressive competitor or of continuing in a race after illegally and adversely affecting another boat. But it is as unreasonable to allow a competitor to force an undeserved advantage as it is to disqualify him for gaining an inadvertent one. Few, if any, will persist in taking advantage once a statement or an action indicates that this conduct will not be tolerated. But some are willing to grab whatever they are given—an opportunity to drive over at the port end of the line, room at a mark after the belated establishment of an overlap, freedom to tack too close. There is no doubt that such moves are common, but I have never met a top-level competitor who didn't forgo them when the victim objected. This is the type of behavior that warrants a protest if direct action is insufficient.

The variations in people's honesty are due to differences in childhood experience, differences in the parental image that has been internalized. They are not subject to modification by the external demands of the rule makers. We resent the intended interference and the disrespect these demands imply, yet the rule makers continue to invade the game. This conflict smacks of the parent–child relationship. The disrespectful, perfectionistic, distrustful parent (the IYRU) belittles us by pointing to isolated examples of our inadequacies and demands that we comply with artificial parental requirements. The threatened child (the yachtsman), unable to be perfect, resentful of the disrespect shown him, rebels against the demands. And the immature yachtsman, who most needs the support of the IYRU, retaliates against the belittling by acting out the forbidden behavior; he cheats. How much better is the response when the immature are left to their peers, who, by example, can lead them to a better self-image and a recognition of the value of mutual respect.

Paul Elvstrom describes an attitude which most of us approve. He was racing in 5-0-5's at La Baule in 1956. "That was a very, very exciting race where three crews played tactics together—altogether the best race I ever sailed. I remember when Jacques capsized, he had the wind on the port side and we came on starboard and had to bear away from him, so there was a discussion afterwards. If Jacques was disqualified from that race, we would win the World Championship. There was no protest, only a discussion, and I remember that inside I didn't like it but, because I would have liked to win, of course, I was feeling it could be fun if he became disqualified. But I must say that I was very happy nothing happened because it would have been a dirty way of winning."

During the 1976 Olympics, Dave McFaull told me how much he liked the "good guys" in the Tornado class. He and his crew had been wearing sweaters on the outside of their life jackets during the early races of the series (in which they won the silver medal) and there was some talk that this violated the class restriction on movable ballast. Dave told me that Jorg Spengler, the German representative, who ultimately won the bronze medal, came to him and said that someone might protest if they continued to wear the sweaters—but that no one would do so if they stopped. Good guys!

Game playing is the real test of honesty; indeed, it is limited to those who are honest. The dishonest person is unable to play, unable to limit his behavior so as to comply with the established rules, unable to obtain satisfaction from testing the performance permitted by the rules. The rules establish the boundaries that separate the world of play from the world of work. To disregard them is to make the game meaningless, to be left out of it. The real world is a confused mixture of shades of gray, ranging between right and wrong. Only in games can we escape into absolutes. Most players recognize this pearl of great price. There may be acceptable deviations from complete honesty in the real world. There can be no deviation in a game.

31 / A Feeling of Distinction

I turned around and looked at the boat and it dawned on me that I was ready.

—BUDDY MELGES

AMONG A GROUP OF COMPETITORS, ALL OF WHOM FEEL CONFIDENT AND assured, all of whom enjoy the advantage this state of mind bestows, one will possess in addition a feeling of distinction, a feeling that he will certainly win, that he cannot lose.

This feeling is an extension of the "inner conceit" described by Pete Reiser. It concerns the particular occasion, not merely capability and not merely self-worth. It concerns winning or finishing in a high position—victory over competitors—rather than performance. It arises in head-to-head conflicts, final rounds, crucial races: "Right now, I will conquer." Not "I *can* outperform him, not "I am better than he," but "I *will* beat him, now, here, on *this* occasion."

This feeling of distinction is not limited by rationality; it does not depend upon the results of previous meetings. It is a feeling of being special, different from all other competitors, unrestricted by the laws of probability, unique. Its hallmark is disregard for previous evidence of failure: "Although last time he beat me, although just now he passed me, just now I made an error—*now* I will win. *This* time it's my turn."

In most games, certainly in sailboat racing, one must expect to make mistakes, to get behind. Sail trim is always wrong; it must be constantly adjusted to deal with changing conditions. One usually does not get the best start and must instead work through from astern. Every boat save one loses the first race, and yet must set about winning the next ones. The situation in which one must disregard evidence of defectiveness and recover from failure is usual, not exceptional. The test is less of the ability to excel than of the ability to recover. This is why winning is 90 percent psychological. The basis for performing well may be up to 90 percent physical, but performing well is not nearly so important as recovering from having performed poorly.

Rationality alone should be sufficient to prevent the erosion of confidence and assurance that tends to accompany a failure. One obviously should not judge one's competence or oneself on the basis of any one performance. But it is difficult to resist the implication that because one is performing poorly, one is defective, and because one's competitor is performing better, he *is* better.

Children learn to seek acclaim rather than self-satisfaction—and in the absence of acclaim they feel defective. They develop a need to win, and belittle themselves when they lose. The morality of modern culture causes belittling if one is not "good," and the prejudice of modern culture causes belittling if one is not "right." One is competent, effective, good, right, if one is approved, and incompetent, defective, bad, wrong, unless one is approved. Without external recognition, only an unusually strong ego can retain self-respect, can develop the feeling of distinction.

This feeling is more than self-assurance. It is self-assurance related to a specific occasion—a feeling of euphoria, of control, of possession, of dominance of a particular event. It cannot be forced, organized, or developed. Some days it is there; some days it is not. It is usually associated with winning because (1) it thrives on adversity, pressure, and failure; (2) it prevents the distraction that accompanies the fear of losing; (3) it renders logic and the laws of probability inoperative, and dismisses mortality; and (4) it eliminates fear, enabling one to attack the opponent where he is strongest, to dare to undertake any risk.

Jack Nicklaus says, when his next putt is worth $50,000, "That's why I'm here, to have the opportunity to make a putt that means that much." When he pushed ahead on the eighteenth to win the 1978 British Open, someone asked, "Who would you rather have play this final hole?" He'd been there before, losing with the final stroke or winning with the final stroke, and was at ease with the pressure. The same pleasure characterizes Paul Elvstrom's response to pressure. He describes a race in which he was behind on the final beat: "We went to port and were waiting for a good wind shift. We went on and on and on—and suddenly it came. . . . I knew that the wind was going to come back sometime; it was a matter of waiting for it. . . . But that was fun because that made the whole race exciting." He was pleased to have had the opportunity to demonstrate his ability to recover.

Henry Bossett says, "One guy is liable to win the first two races and you feel you've had it. But you have to be able to spring back, to get through the whole series, to win." Jimmy Connors, when he gets behind, remembers his great comebacks of the past and recognizes that he can do what others cannot.

Knowing that trouble will appear anyway, the truly self-assured appear to seek adversity. Buddy Melges starts off regatta after regatta with a handicap. He won CORK 1974 without showing up for the first race. He took a tenth in the first race of the 1976 Soling trials and a disqualification in the first race of the 1978 U.S. Championship, and won the 1972 trials after a DNF in the second race. The Lindsey brothers, Allen and Peter, who had won every race they entered during the preceding year, won the 1978 U.S. Youth Championship after a disqualification in the first race.

Once behind, one may find it easy to believe that one belongs there. When Bruce MacLeod beat me at the Midwinters in Florida, I wondered (momentarily) whether he would do it again at the Spring Soling Bowl in Annapolis. Brownlow Gray won the practice race for the 1960 Princess Elizabeth Cup, and I wondered whether he would do the same in the actual contest. I won both the subsequent regattas because I experienced a feeling of distinction, a feeling that my success would not be limited by logic. Unfortunately, I felt no such immunity to failure when I raced at Kiel in June 1978. I assumed that Hans Fogh, whom I hadn't beaten since 1974 (when he was second to me in the Atlantic Coast Championship) would beat me, as he had done every time we'd met in the past year. At Kiel he was far ahead in every race, and I found myself accepting this relationship as reasonable. In the absence of a feeling of distinction, it is easy to succumb to logic.

When things get tight, says Hale Irwin, "feeling is the key. Thinking can be an enemy." Those who think that they are only human, that they may fail, are more likely to do so. Tom Watson finally overcame a reputation for "choking" when he beat Jack Nicklaus, head to head, on the final holes of the 1977 Masters Golf Tournament. He had blown big leads on the last few holes of Sawgrass and Heritage, presumably because he recognized his humanity, his lack of distinction. After the Masters, Nicklaus was asked whether something Ben Crenshaw had said about him ("we're not as scared of him as we used to be") had affected his play. Watson, who was standing nearby, stepped forward: "Let me say something about that. I'm always afraid of this man." "No, he's not," said Nicklaus, smiling. "He's not afraid of anybody. That's why he won." The feeling of distinction eliminates fear, dismisses mortality.

Vince Lombardi, Jimmy Connors, Bill Tilden, Muhammad Ali, all have said that the way to victory is to go at the opponent's strength, to take his best shots—and show that they have no effect. Once a player begins to feel that his best is not good enough, the contest is over. Most players tolerate the expected amount of adversity—a slight loss, a temporary setback—and remain confident that they will recover. When they are shown that their best can be beaten, however, they fold. I remember pressing a Canadian 14 sailor closely for the first five legs of a long-distance race in 14's and then planing over him on a close reach. Once I got past, it was all over; he was a quarter mile back at the finish. Perhaps Buddy Melges is trying to put us all in this position. "I'm giving you your best chance, giving you a whole race," he appears to be saying, "and I'm still going to beat you." Remembering how often this has happened, we are impressed, if not intimidated.

Hale Irwin also says, "When I'm playing well, I'll try a risky shot that makes the difference between winning and second." Perhaps this says it all. If you have that feeling of distinction, you do not feel limited by your actual competence or that of your competitors. You do whatever needs doing; you dare, and your daring is not distracted— not by fear and not by intimidation. And behaving so, you win. The feeling goes with success. More valuable—and more elusive—is the ability to experience it after failure.

Frank Gifford wonders, "Fourth and one—should you go for it? Suppose you miss. That can take a lot out of a ball club." Should one take a chance that risks an obvious, incontrovertible, defeat? In golf, as Hale Irwin observes, you have time to think about a bad shot before the next one; "momentum" may be lost. That mystical attribute so discussed by sports commentators seems to depend upon continuous gain, the absence of the slightest setback. In team sports, where the collective psyche may be more fragile, less susceptible to a feeling of supernatural confidence, momentum is ephemeral. In individual competition a feeling of distinction carries one of two players through a setback. The failure is disregarded, the risk is taken as if success had been continuous. The player who avoids taking a risk because he fears to fail, who feels depressed by adversity, who recognizes that his past failure indicates the probability of future failure, will lose. The player who ignores the loss and seeks the risk, who delights in the opportunity to overcome adversity, who feels immune to probability, will win.

Memory, Attention, Conception

32 / The Previous Race

*I have made mistakes but I have never made the
mistake of claiming that I never made one.*
—JAMES GORDON BENNETT

DURING A RACE THERE IS ONLY SUFFICIENT TIME FOR WHAT IS AHEAD;
the race is from wherever you are onward. Preoccupation with anything other than the immediate determinants of success is detrimental.
The mistake of the past leg must be accepted and ignored. The mistake of the past race must be accepted, and after it has been analyzed,
evaluated, and stored in memory, ignored. Subsequent success will be
markedly influenced by how realistically that acceptance, analysis,
evaluation, and storage has been accomplished.

The fifth race of the 1976 Olympics is a dramatic case in point.
As we know, fifteen competitors in the Flying Dutchman, Tempest,
and Soling classes thought that the whole race was such a mistake that
they protested its handling by the race committee. How four subsequent medalists dealt with their own perception of it is illustrative.
One of them won that fifth race and proceeded to markedly improve
his performance thereafter. One had a disastrous race from start to
finish and yet went on to win the gold medal. Two others had been in

contention for the gold medal but after their disastrous finishes in the fifth race experienced, at least temporarily, a dramatic deterioration in performance.

The events of the fifth race were sufficient to affect anyone's psyche. A northeasterly wind is unlikely to survive against the lake breeze at the eastern end of Lake Ontario, and this occasion was no exception. The race was started in about 10 knots of air, with the wind backing progressively from 10° to 340°. By the end of the first beat it was down to 4 knots and had backed to 320°. The zephyrs that remained backed farther and persisted longest to the left—the south. The boats that were able to slip off in that direction were soon in the lead. The three fleets fused and then congealed in a calm that persisted for over an hour. The tail-enders were convincing themselves that the 4½-hour time limit would expire when the lake breeze (at 210°) appeared in a slowly advancing line to the south. Everyone turned toward it, but a half hour elapsed before it had filled in sufficiently to send the jumbled fleets, under spinnaker, rushing home together.

Rodney Pattison, after finishing 1–2–4–3 in the first four races, led Jeorg Diesch by 0.3 points (and the rest of the fleet by a country mile) going into the fifth race. He took the lifted port tack in the backing wind to round the weather mark seventh (Diesch was third). As the wind died and backed farther, Pattison dropped to twelfth. At the beginning of the run he sailed almost perpendicular to the course toward the expected lake breeze. An hour and a half later they reached the leeward mark together. He finished eighteenth and protested. The following day, still only 2.0 points out of first but aware of his vulnerability, apparently preoccupied with his failure of the day before, he struggled in the strongest (and truest) breeze of the series to a twelfth. Now thoroughly shaken, he surrendered to Diesch, finished eleventh in the finale, and barely salvaged the silver medal.

Among the Tempests, Dennis Conner had a similar experience and a similar response but recovered much more rapidly. He started beautifully at the port end of the line in a transient veer, held on until the back returned, crossed the fleet, and led by a quarter mile at the weather mark. He must have thought, as he disappeared down the reaches, that this would establish him in the lead, would demonstrate his superiority. And then he sailed off to the right, the wind died, he crept around the second weather mark sixth, the lake breeze appeared, and he finished ninth. He must have been furious. His first opportunity to vent that fury was in a protest against the race committee. In addition, he protested because the Russian Soling skipper, Boris Budnikov, had been towed home by an unauthorized powerboat. Neither protest came to fruition, which may have angered him further. The following morning he rushed out of the harbor early (to ease his tension?), made his worst start of the week, was forced to tack, tacked poorly to the wrong tack, tried to set his chute on the first reach when no one else did, broached, and staggered around the jibe mark eighth—by far his worst position on the first round of any race in the series. About this time he must have ceased to rail against the fates as he marched progressively back to fourth. By the following day he had apparently accepted the world as it was, sailed a brilliant race, and almost forced his way back into the silver.

The winner of the fifth Flying Dutchman race was Reinaldo Conrad, of Brazil, who had been fifteenth at the first weather mark and fifteenth at the second weather mark. He made the correct choice at the final leeward mark, however, turned left immediately, and picked up the lake breeze first (before some of the early leaders had even started to move). He had been 8–9–18–6 in the first four races, completely out of the contention, but this victory, this evidence of his ability to make the right move, restored his confidence. Instead of thinking himself lucky, he apparently perceived this accomplishment as an indication that he belonged at the head of the fleet. He finished 3–3 in the final races and took the bronze medal!

By the time the Solings started the fifth race the wind had backed so much that it was difficult to lay the port end. When David Forbes hung up on the mark, he took half the fleet, including Poul-Richard Jensen, out of the race. Jensen, who had been third, a mere 7.3 points out of the lead, rounded the weather mark next to last (just ahead of series leader, Patrick Haegeli). He was fourteenth as he approached the second weather mark, but lost two places as he drifted within a hundred yards of it for an hour and a half. In the end, he finished thirteenth. He must have been as distressed as Pattison and Conner by this unjustified result, but he apparently made no unrealistic reappraisal of his stature. He went out and won the heavy-air race the following day, leading at every mark. And in the finale, demonstrating his relentless determination, his certainty that he deserved to win, he marched from tenth at the first weather mark to fifth and the gold medal.

Now of course much of this is surmised (although the actual events were all observed), but the subsequent dramatic changes in performance must have been influenced by what had happened in the fifth race. Those who appraised their experience as revealing an underlying deficiency fell apart thereafter. Conrad, who appraised it as revealing a previously hidden but actual competence, was then able to demonstrate that competence. Jensen apparently appraised it as no more than it was—one race among hundreds in his career, some of which had been won, some of which had been lost—and went right on racing as he always did, competently. To the extent that a competitor was angered by the experience, and particularly to the extent that he allowed that anger to preoccupy him thereafter, his subsequent performance suffered. To the extent that a competitor allowed the experience to confirm a positive conception of his ability, his subsequent performance improved. To the extent that a competitor realistically appraised the event as but one race among many, only partially subject to his control, he continued to perform to the best of his inherent ability.

33 / Concentration

*It is not necessary to hope in order to undertake,
nor to succeed in order to persevere.*

—CHARLES THE BOLD

"YOU CAN'T THINK AND HIT AT THE SAME TIME," SAYS YOGI BERRA.
His wisdom is being belatedly recognized by many analysts of athletic
behavior. We have been grossly misled over the years by leaders in almost every sport who have told us that what we must do is concentrate. In a recent article in the *Olympian*, Helen Hull Jacobs gave example after example of great athletes of the past who owed their
success to concentration, to thinking about what they were doing. But
it now seems clear that thinking about what one is doing is the best
way to ruin one's performance. Concentration is needed prior to performance, not during it.

What has been called "concentration," and recognized as extremely beneficial to athletic performance in the past, is a state of
unawareness of anything but that which matters. It is a state of non-
distractibility, of nonpreoccupation with extraneous particulars, but
also of not thinking about what is being done. It is quite evident that
the best players in any sport perform without thinking about what

they are doing (to the confusion and dismay of all those who think that thinking ought to be beneficial). Buddy Melges is not one of the world's finest sailors *despite* his lack of awareness of what he is doing (as has been suggested), but *because* of his lack of awareness. He doesn't stop to think about what he is doing; he does it automatically, without interference. He has been quoted as saying, "I love to involve completely my mind, my body, and all my senses with the boat and her path in the water. I very seldom watch the sails; rather a blank stare at the horizon forward gives me the angle of attack." He once told me, when I asked for the secret of his success in sailing to windward in waves, that he tries "to keep the horizon level"!

This Yogi Berra-ism was totally unintelligible to me at the time, but I now reckon it to be one of the most important lessons a sailor can learn. Don't think about it; "a blank stare at the horizon" will let it happen! Tim Gallwey's *Inner Game of Tennis* is dedicated to this proposition. The body responds to plans developed prior to the action; it does not require reminders from conscious thought. During play, judgment should be suspended in favor of trust in the body to accomplish the desired result. Conscious direction of attention to the action itself interferes with the previously learned automatic interplay between perception and response.

We've all walked carelessly and at full speed along a line on a sidewalk, never varying from our chosen path. But when we attempt to do the same thing on the top of a wall or along the edge of a dock, we take each step with care and stumble repeatedly. Our Parent is interfering, reminding us of our limited capabilities, analyzing the risks, preoccupying us with the consequences of our action. Any self-focused attention—criticism or praise of what has or is being done, considerations of success or failure, attempts to "concentrate" upon the movement of our body—distracts us from what we are doing and diminishes our performance. Athletes have tended to believe that they must tell their bodies what to do and then criticize or praise the results. The batter's slump, the sailors' race when "nothing went right," the quarterback's multiple interceptions in a single game, all result from this same inappropriate assumption. Praise and criticism are Parent-related concepts, the residues of a Parent–Child relationship that has no place in Adult game playing. During performance one benefits from being totally in the present, disregarding the past (what *should have been* done) and the future (what *should be* done).

It is no good to tell an athlete to concentrate. It might even be better to tell him not to concentrate. Distraction and preoccupation are what need to be avoided; in other words, one must avoid concentrating on something else. Nick Martin claims that he achieves maximum speed in his 470 by keeping his mind on the *idea* of boat speed and that if he is forced to think of anything else, he loses speed—his automatic neuromuscular responsiveness is distracted and made less effective. When someone is said to "lose his concentration," the meaning is that he has *begun* to concentrate on something else—that he is now preoccupied with a particular awareness, whereas previously he gave himself up to an unself-conscious, unaware immersion in what he was doing.

"Loss of concentration" may be transient, the result of a momentary distraction, or it may be persistent, the result of preoccupation with trivia or competitors or the weather or a thousand other things. I have learned only with difficulty that one of a helmsman's major responsibilities is to avoid distractions. Watching the crew to see whether they are doing something wrong, or involving myself in the solution of a breakdown problem, always interferes with my steering. Confusion under tension is a common problem. This arises out of preoccupation with fear, usually the fear of failure or of revealing some inadequacy; then concentration develops, upon the threat rather than upon the task at hand, and bumbling confusion results.

Sometimes preoccupation is so great that it amounts to mesmerization. I remember on the final windward leg of the penultimate race of the 1973 Swiss Championship watching my major opponent steadily gaining. At the leeward mark he had been several hundred yards astern, in about seventh place. I had assumed that the series was in the bag, but now he was coming on strong in the dying air, passing boat after boat. As I looked astern and to leeward, I became mesmerized by his progress. He was pointing higher and footing considerably faster than I, "making land" rapidly. As I calculated the effect of the loss of each boat that he passed, it seemed that I could not take my eyes off him. How could he go so fast when, in the previous races, I had always been faster? What was I doing wrong? How had I trimmed the sails differently? I was, of course, contributing greatly to his progress; not only was he sailing faster in better air, but I, mesmerized by his progress, was slowing my own boat considerably. I awoke barely in time to save my lead, but not before he had gained about five places.

Frequently, "concentration" is attempted as a way of assuring optimum performance—and the opposite is achieved. A boat tacks on your lee bow and is about to establish a safe leeward position. You focus your attention upon what you are doing. You begin to ask questions. Am I meeting the waves correctly? Is the jib trimmed correctly? Are we heeling too much? Should I point higher—or lower? This "concentration" upon questions, problems, solutions, is distracting. Steering is hampered. Your boat begins to fall back. An awareness of the imminence of failure appears. Tension is added to distraction. Fear arises and disaster follows. "Concentration" must be avoided.

Sometimes a "loss of concentration" is associated with a state of unawareness, from which one awakens belatedly to find that the game has been lost. The individual in this state makes no analysis of the conditions, gives no thought to what is at stake, develops no plans for the game, before the start. He goes through the motions without an awareness of the present or the future. The fact that he is not thinking about the present does not mean that the focus is appropriate. His unawareness may be complete, extending to automatic behavior as well as to thinking. This state is probably protective; it enables him to avoid the anxiety associated with the fear of losing or the fear of winning. It makes the feared winning much less likely and provides a perfect excuse for the feared losing.

Actions requiring pure skill are best performed without thought. Jumping, hitting, throwing, are affected adversely by the attention paid to them. Sailing, and many other games, require both skill and thought. The elements of performance requiring skill must be let alone, allowed to happen without thought. Thinking must be applied to the question of what is to be done next. Thus one should be steering automatically while considering the possibility of tacking in the developing header. When a means of attacking and blanketing the boat ahead has been determined, one rounds the mark and hoists the spinnaker without thinking about rounding or hoisting. What is being done is ignored; concentration is upon a plan for the next move. Once the plan is completed, the decision made, attention is diverted to the following tactical and strategic problem. The muscles are left to their own devices.

According to Jack Nicklaus, "the difference between the professional and the weekend golfer is that the professional has the ability to concentrate after he hits a bad shot. He has enough savvy to go down and play the next shot and not worry about the one that's behind him." A better way to describe this behavior is to say that the professional does not concentrate upon the last shot (or the impact of the present one upon the eventual outcome). He clears his mind from thinking and allows his body to behave appropriately, without distraction, while hitting. He doesn't "concentrate" upon the ball, the swing, or the green. A recent parody of tennis psychology in *Sports Illustrated* suggests that if concentration is 94.6 percent of tennis, the dedicated student should spend "12 hours a day standing at the baseline concentrating on a tennis ball that has been placed eight feet in front of him!" This nonsense is revealing; concentration is accomplished in advance of the action, in the preparation of a plan, not during the action.

Paul Elvstrom tells a story about crewing for Albert Desbarges in a Star regatta. "You sail, I will tell you where to go," he told Desbarges. After the race, which they won, Desbarges said, "I have never been so tired in a race and I have not seen *anything*." But he was steering, according to Elvstrom, "better than I could have done," which showed that "you cannot concentrate on sailing the boat and also see where everything is. . . . If the helmsman is so clever that he can feel the boat and it never stops for him, then he has time for tactics also. [Then] his crew must understand how to adjust the jib and the mainsail together." Distraction is the problem. The helmsman and the crew members must know their responsibilities and not allow themselves to be distracted by concern with the responsibilities of the other.

Golf, football, tennis—many sports—are performed intermittently: there is a stroke, a down, a serve, and then a period of rest. During the rest period, concentration *upon the next action* is appropriate. No thought is given to the previous action and no thought to the ultimate significance of the action to come. When the plan has been determined, the decision made, the mind is wiped clean and the body allowed to act without conscious supervision.

Only a few sports (perhaps the equestrian) are as continuous as sailboat racing, requiring that a significant action (in this instance, steering) be performed while the next step is considered. The effective helmsman must reach the point where his steering becomes automatic, where concentration is not only unnecessary but recognized as undesirable. Instead, he must pay attention to tactics, strategy, sail trim, heeling angle, and so on. He must use conscious thought to develop plans to deal with these problems, and then, during the execution of the plans, he must ignore them, instead turning his mind to the next problems. Attention shifts intermittently, as in tennis, but there is never a moment of rest. The previous move, the significance of the present state, the ultimate result, all are ignored—as is the action being taken.

34 / Grace under Pressure

There is no point to anything you do—or anyone else does—unless you give it meaning yourself.
—JEFF LOWE

BYRNE'S STANDARD BOOK OF POOL AND BILLIARDS DESCRIBES THE PROPER ATTITUDE for a player who has failed or lost: "When you miss a shot during a game, step away from the table with good grace. Redouble your resolve and await your next opportunity without morbid brooding about the shot you missed. If you lose, so what? It's only a game. Don't explain to the winner how lousily you played; congratulate him instead on a fine performance—after all, he beat a terrific player."

When you congratulate the fellow who defeated you and he points out that he didn't notice the huge shift on the final beat, implying that his excess of talent won the day, you needn't take refuge in the conclusion that the entire event was unimportant. Instead, you *realistically* recognize that even someone with little understanding of the game can win on a particular occasion, and you *supportively* recognize that he has just revealed that you are the better player. Grace under pressure.

To permit appropriate analysis of problems, the conception of what has occurred must be realistic. To permit the maintenance of ego function, it must be supportive. Full awareness and total realism are not always beneficial. Failure to recognize the imminence of being passed from astern may permit greater attention to performance. On the other hand, this failure may prevent the assumption of a defensive posture that would prevent the opponent from passing. Compromises between realism and supportiveness must constantly be sought.

The courageous individual conceives of himself as significant, of his behavior as important. He feels that what he does and how he does it matter. He wishes to create something which in his absence would not exist. He wishes to place his stamp upon the situation. He wishes to remember his own behavior as contributing to, even determining the outcome of, an event. The less courageous individual wishes to be uninvolved, to have no effect upon a situation. The courageous person conceives of a situation as significant—whether it is passing a single boat or losing a local fleet race—and of his involvement as essential to its outcome. The less courageous conceives of a situation as unimportant—he is only a single competitor, the fleet race is only local—and of his involvement as incidental. One cares, the other does not. Neither of their conceptions is realistic, but the difference between them is important. One of the two will perform well and may win; the other will perform poorly and will almost certainly lose. Grace under pressure is a matter of conception; a conception appropriate to long-term interests and to excellence leads to graceful performance.

Many have described how it felt to be in the huddle with John Unitas ("like being in the huddle with God"). There was never any doubt about the significance of the game and the significance of each individual's play. They mattered. And when a receiver returned to the huddle after dropping a ball, he knew that the enormity of his failure would be fully recognized.

Conceiving the event to be important and one's contribution to be important is essential to athletic success, but the conception can be carried too far. Witness George Allen, coach of the Washington Redskins, "the Snake Oil King," as described in the *Washington Post* by William Gildea and Kenneth Turan,

> telling one and all about the winning they're going to do, how putting up with his rah-rah ways will lead them to greater glory. . . . [But] you can only go to the well so many times. The first time he says this is the most important game of your lives, you believe it. Maybe you'll believe it the second and third time,

too. But the twentieth time you start to wonder. If you ask for the superior effort week after week, after a while you don't get it. . . . He is so megalomania-
cal about winning, so insistent that victories are, if possible, more important
than life itself, so willing to twist everything twistable, to blame everyone
blameable, that he shreds the last vestiges of illusion owners have about being
involved in sport. . . . Owners inevitably take the path of least resistance; they
kill the bearer of bad news and let their illusions live another day.

Allen's conception was both so unrealistic and so outcome-
oriented that it was ultimately detrimental to the performance of his
team. The truth will out. When you are a leg astern, there's no use
belaboring yourself with the significance of the event or the significance of your behavior to its outcome.

On the other hand, you get no more than you conceive of. My
conception in 1972 was that without hiking aids, crews could be expected to hike only intermittently during a windward leg—and I
asked no more of them. Buddy Melges's conception was that what
crews had to do, upwind and down, was to sit on the topsides with
their hands beneath their thighs—and he expected them to do so. A
year later I had my crews hiking continuously when we were sailing
to windward, but not until 1976 did I finally recognize that they
should be expected to hike continuously while close reaching as well. I
never got any more than I conceived was appropriate.

Similarly, one's conception of the capability of one's opponents
will be reflected in the outcome. During the final race of the 1978
Atlantic Coast Championship, I conceived that I had a good chance to
beat Dave Curtis for the series if I got ahead and covered him carefully. I reckoned that Peter Hall and Peter Galloway had finished so
high up in each of the previous races in similar conditions that they
could not be beaten. So while leading on the final beat I covered Dave
Curtis carefully and ignored the threat of Sam Merrick, who, in fifth
place, appeared to be sailing into a good angle to the right. I finished
second (behind Merrick), 3.0 Olympic points short of first, and was
fourth in the series, ahead of Dave Curtis, but 2.0 points behind Hall
and 2.3 points behind Galloway! On a grander scale, the British fleet,
after near victory in the naval battle of the Gallipoli Narrows early in
1915, fearing that the Turks were well prepared, failed for over a
month to follow up the advantage gained. The Turks, completely demoralized and convinced that they would be overwhelmed if the fleet
attempted to break through the following day, regained their courage,
and ultimately defeated the subsequent combined land and sea in-
vasion. You get no more than you conceive of.

Because of differences in motivation, competitors have different conceptions of their sport. Many conceive of sport as a means to an end, to secondary gain rather than to concurrent satisfaction. Their expression of this view may operate as a form of gamesmanship, with some competitors, who believe in the game, becoming intimidated by the implication that the activity is not a game and that they don't belong in it.

A recent letter to the editor of *Yachts and Yachting* was entitled "It's Not the Racing, It's the Winning that Counts." Many modern competitors behave as if the act of racing were insignificant: they fail to participate in the last race when they have already won or lost; they lodge a protest when a wind shift or some other vagary of the sailing conditions causes them to have a poor finishing position. Rick Barry says that money is breeding a new generation of "gunners" in basketball: "Kids have the wrong idea. Scoring is overemphasized. You'll never see a youngster get in a defensive position or practice passing. Pro basketball is not played as well today as it was 10 years ago. We're playing the playground game—run, jump, shoot." Thomas Tutko, codirector of the Institute for Athletic Motivation, viewed the Yankee victory in the 1977 World Series as a "triumph of greed." And Michael Novak, author of *The Joy of Sports*, felt that the fans' dislike of that victory was consequent to its "profaning of something good."

Val Howells, describing the evolution of single-handed ocean racing, correlates it with Dr. Johnson's statement that "no man but a blockhead ever wrote except for money." Howells says of single-handed sailors, "There were those who soon realized that the competition was getting hotter and that, as there could be only one winner in a fleet of perhaps 50 starters, there might be other, better ways of pursuing fame and fortune. And so began the Nautical Flagpole Sitting Era. Several attempts were made to *row* the Atlantic. One was successful, others not. Some hardy souls sailed to Iceland in an open boat. Another sailed the Atlantic in a 12 foot dinghy. Chichester declared that he was going to race the clipper ships to Australia . . . and upon arrival in Sydney, the skipper of the winning boat in a one-boat race was awarded a knighthood!"

Clearly, many conceive of sports as a means to a reputation as a winner, and to money, fame, glory, "success." This is not an impaired conception; it may well be appropriate—realistic and serving the individual's long-term interests. That it is not the conception shared by most of us—that game playing is not intended by us as a means to success—doesn't make it invalid. Nor does this conception make invalid our utilization of games for the joy of participation. That some destroy their game by ensuring that the outcome is certain should not prevent us from enjoying the uncertainty, the challenge, the surprise inherent in our own performance. To the extent that we conceive of a game as a game, it *is* a game—even if we are likely to be defeated by those who have ceased to play.

Object Relations

35 / Live and Let Live

Really great men see something divine in every other man and are endlessly, foolishly, and incredibly merciful.

—JOHN RUSKIN

SAILBOAT RACING IS NOT THE ONLY SPORT IN WHICH PARTICIPANTS EXhibit a code of honesty and consideration going beyond the rules of the game, but it is an excellent example of this common circumstance. Only a small minority of sailors fail to adhere to this code (and to the racing rules). Unfortunately, however, the rule makers and the protest and appeals committees have frequently acted as if the minority typified the sport. In the classes I've sailed in, and among the sailors with whom I sail, there is no need for concern. The other guy has always either learned how to play the game or moved on.

The code, which few verbalize and almost no one has ever recorded, goes like this *and goes no further:* We are playing a game, the object of which is to finish first. We do not interfere with our competitors except for the purpose of assuring that we finish first. In order to finish first we attempt to do the following:

1. Sail faster
2. Sail a shorter course

3. Sail a faster course
4. Obtain an advantageous position at critical times—at the start, at mark roundings, at the lay lines, and so on
5. Control a particular opponent (deliberately affect him adversely) at critical times—at the finish, in the final race of a series, and so on

The code permits the use of the rules for the purposes listed—to facilitate finishing first—but no further. Live and let live. Give the other guy the same break that you'd like him to give you. Don't use the rules to take an advantage that does not contribute directly to finishing first. At the start, push the opponent up, but not so sharply or so high that he is touched. On the windward leg, tack so as to grant the competitor clear air. Wave a close-crossing port-tacker across. On a reach, arrange with the opposing skipper to avoid a luffing match. *Never attempt to disqualify an opponent.* The gentleman's agreement, which is generally adhered to, implies that to do otherwise would be unacceptable—regardless of what the rules permit.

The rules, as distinguished from the code, were originally designed to prevent collisions; they designate the boat that has right of way and define which is the burdened boat when two boats meet. To achieve this result without excessive complexity, the rules are, of necessity, artificial. They were not designed to coincide with the code, and in fact they permit activity in direct violation of the code. But they provide a game of tactics superimposed upon the game of speed and strategy—a highly desirable addition. They can and should be used to prevent an opponent from taking a shorter or faster course, to obtain an advantageous position, or to control an opponent at critical times.

The rules authorize one competitor to take another out of the competition temporarily or permanently—to get him off the course, slowed, or disqualified. Any competitor, regardless of his competence or potential to finish first, is authorized to behave in this manner. Paul Elvstrom has said that in any race any competitor who wishes to disqualify any other could do so. Only the existence of the code prevents this from happening.

In a variety of common circumstances, one boat is helpless, at the mercy of the other. No boat is immune to these dangers; every boat at some time will be to windward on the starting line, astern or on port on a windward leg, overlapped to windward on a reach. If the boat in control is merciless in these circumstances, the boat at risk can be driven out of the race.

Similarly, a helmsman who commits an error is at the mercy of his competitor. A port-tack boat may come into the close proximity of a starboard-tack boat unawares. A last-second tack is made to avoid a collision; the starboard-tacker has to luff slightly. The port-tack boat has made no gain that a proper tack into a controlling lee-bow position would not have provided, yet she is at risk of disqualification if the starboard-tack boat protests. A boat ahead and to leeward on a reach broaches; the boat astern is unable to avoid brushing the leeward boat's shrouds with her spinnaker. If there is a protest, she can be disqualified. Two boats are nose to nose, side by side, battling to see who can steer better, whose rig is better trimmed. The windward boat's mainsheet breaks; her boom touches the boat to leeward. If there is a protest, she can be disqualified. A leeward boat luffs to round the windward mark in the teeth of the starboard-tack parade. The boat immediately to windward luffs head to wind, but the leeward boat's quarter touches her as the latter bears away around the mark. Although the leeward boat made the error of not allowing for the leeward-going current, the windward boat can be disqualified for not granting her sufficient room; the rules prescribe—nay, according to their most recent modifications, demand—that when such errors are committed the non-right-of-way boat be removed from the competition, whether or not she committed the error.

The code, in complete contrast, requires that when a boat is helpless she be treated mercifully. Elvstrom says that a protest should be lodged only if the error of the opponent is deliberate, that to protest for other reasons, with the expectation that he will withdraw or be disqualified, inappropriately deprives the fleet of a competitor. No one works harder than Elvstrom to intimidate, to dominate, his competitors, but he draws the line short of disqualification.

It should be clear that in many circumstances—port–starboard, windward–leeward encounters—protesting is tantamount to disqualifying the opponent. Under the rules the accused must prove innocence—which is often impossible.

The exercise of compassion is altruistic, and altruism is certainly a characteristic pattern of human behavior. We all wish to reach out, to make contact with one another. Showing compassion is one of the most certain and reassuring signals that we are open and receptive to contact. But altruism is not the only basis for the code. Many who subscribe to it show little compassion. The code is also founded, at least in part, on the concept of *quid pro quo*. If I treat you with compassion, with respect, you will be more likely to treat me similarly the next time we meet—as we surely will—with you in the controlling position. I do not wish to find myself at your mercy without a little advantage—this present evidence of my compassion. Even more practical considerations arise. If I touch you while luffing at the start, I may myself be slowed or trapped by the collision. I don't want you to tack on my lee bow, so I'll be happy to bear off and wave you across. The code not only provides a pleasant milieu that contributes to the fun of racing, it is of real practical advantage.

The belligerent may reject this description of the code as applying only to losers, and may be pleased that others will take no unfair advantage of them while they go about the business of winning at any cost. The timid may cheer this description as defining the way they've always hoped the game would be played, and may use it to justify their timidity. Both would be wrong. Winners do sail by the code; they do not race to win at any cost. And the code is designed not to protect or support the timid, but to maintain the quality of the game. The competent can readily distinguish between a tack made dead to windward that provides an optimal position for the tacking boat relative to the fleet and one that is made for the purpose of hurting a particular opponent. Every helmsman should feel free to act in his own best interest; no helmsman should feel constrained, as the timid may be, to delay or avoid a maneuver that will have an adverse effect upon another boat—merely because it may have that effect. The helmsman who sails the tactically correct course will be not resented but admired.

There are competitors seeking to protest, protests intended to disqualify, and protest committees ready to accomplish the disqualification. The result is diminished competition and an unpleasant atmosphere. What is needed is greater compassion, greater support of the code, greater willingness to live and let live, with fewer protests when the protested boat is helpless, greater restraint by protest and appeals committees in dealing with such protests, and some major revisions in the present rules.

36 / Trusting

*It is more shameful to distrust our friends than
to be deceived by them.*
—DUC DE LA ROCHEFOUCAULD

"ONE OF THE NICEST SIGHTS OF THE 1976 WINTER OLYMPICS," *SPORTS
ILLUSTRATED* reported, "was that of a French girl and a West German girl
hoisting a Canadian girl to their shoulders and all three of them grin-
ning delightedly. The moment spoke of sport that is fun and competition that is its own reward. Rosi Mittermaier had just been beaten by
0.12 second out of a third gold medal, which would have made her
the first woman ever to sweep the Olympic Alpine events, and there
she was, saluting her conqueror, with happiness all over her dimpled
face."

The black-and-white nature of competition, its establishment of a
separate world, is attractive in part because it permits trusting, a
pleasantness that is absent from much of the real world. Most competitors trust one another, enjoy one another, enjoy playing together.
Trusting is characteristic of winners. Bruce Jenner says, "I love my
competitor because he brings out the best in me." Rosi Mittermaier
exults for her conqueror. It may be that distrust is characteristic of

losers. I note at least that those who are the most unwilling to accept help, most inclined to suspect their opponent of some secret advantage, are from the back of the fleet.

Highly competent competitors tend to be at ease with their opponents. They are willing to share their understanding of the game, and do not fear to benefit their rivals. My survey of the attributes of racing sailors demonstrates that trusting characterizes world-class competitors. The range of scores (on a scale of 10–30) was 19–28 (average 23.6) for twenty-five world-class competitors, while the range for local sailors was 16–23 (average 19.6). Competence must be enhanced by trusting, else world-class competitors would not demonstrate it.

Competition is play with others. It is asserting oneself, displaying one's competence, so as to effect a response in others. And the response desired by most competitors is approval. The successful competitor restrains his desire for this response, subordinates it to his desire to demonstrate competence. But he still wants approval. He selects competition as a realm in which he can regularly receive a precise assessment of his competence, and looks to his competitors, who believe in the game as he does, as the best judges of that competence. He returns to competition repeatedly, and seeks to perform well, partly in order to please them. He knows that all the world loves a winner, and believes that his competitors will love him when he wins. (And like Rosi Mittermaier most competitors do exult at a display of competence, even when it's not their own.) For those who are deeply involved in competition, the approval of their competitors is more significant than that of anyone else. Because they expose their competence to their competitors and grant their competitors the power to accept or reject them, they must trust them.

Trusting frees the individual from distracting concern about the motivation of others. It is essential to teamwork within a crew. Most importantly, it permits an understanding of what is to be expected from one's competitors. One assumes that they will act rationally, do what is necessary to move most rapidly and by the shortest route to the finish. One knows what to expect from them. One trusts them.

In the final analysis, trusting is what matters, not being trustworthy. Trusting frees the mind to concentrate on the race, avoiding preoccupation with irrelevant matters. The mentally tough competitor assumes that what he himself does determines the outcome of the race. He is unintimidated by the aggressiveness of his competitors, free of jealousy for their sometimes superior performance. He recognizes that they are acting in their own best interest, without specific regard to him. He is not being selected as a target for their attack.

Trusting permits learning. When ulterior motives are suspected, the suggestions of others are questioned, their assistance is rejected. Most competitors are pleased to share their knowledge. Few attempt to keep secrets. (Those that do usually have little to offer.) One of the most pleasant aspects of competition is "spinnaker-booming" in the bar, and much "how-to" communication takes place in this manner. What sails the other fellow was using, where he had his jib leads set, in what conditions his rig performed well or poorly—all this information and more is available to the trusting. Without the acceptance of this means of communication, the knowledge would never be transmitted.

Trusting depends upon knowledge of what a competitor can be expected to do. When he does something unexpected, he seems untrustworthy. Actually, in such an episode he is merely clarifying his role; thereafter, with his behavior understood and anticipated, he can be trusted. I recently started a club race by assuming my customary position ahead and to leeward of the small fleet coming down the line toward the favored port end. Suddenly I discovered that a newcomer to the fleet was tacking beneath me and I was being pushed over the line! The roles were reversed at the 1978 Soling Midwinters when Buddy Melges, finding me on his lee bow, attempted to drive over me and caused a collision. These are examples of episodes that provide clarification and should not be seen as demonstrations of untrustworthiness. In the future each of us will be able to behave so as to prevent similar mischances; each will be more trusting, more certain of what to expect from the other.

Some competitors in some situations cannot be trusted. Peter Barrett tells the story of a competitor in the 1968 Olympic regatta who while reaching was repeatedly luffed by an opponent. He was able finally to convince his opponent that if the latter stopped the luffing, which was to their mutual disadvantage, he would cease to attack. No sooner had the opponent ahead settled down to a normal course than his follower roared over his stern wave and passed him to windward! In some sports behavior like this would be only a minor deviation from the code. Dave DeBusschere, former all-star forward of the New York Knicks, says, "In all my years in basketball, I saw a lot of fights on the floor but not once did I ever see a sucker punch thrown. What's happening [now]? Is it that athletes are losing respect for each other and a sense of fair play?"

Because competitors are so committed to trusting one another, because they rely so much upon one another for approval and evaluation, they become particularly incensed by any breach of that trust. Having been so exposed, so vulnerable, so dependent, they are extremely hurt when their trust is repudiated. The mutual regard and mutual need for support resembles that in a marriage—as does the violence of the response to rejection. It is not surprising that fighting breaks out among professional athletes and that disagreements among amateurs lead to smoldering resentments that persist for years.

Among competitors who should not be trusted are those who are playing ulterior "games," usually unknown to themselves. A common game that interferes with trust is "You Can't Do This to Me." Here, a Child is saying, "I can, if I want to. I am not confined by rules and rationality." He is seeking to escape the Parental admonition "You don't—you mustn't—play the game that way." The thesis of the game is, "They can't push *me* around." The competitor who barges in between a close-hauled boat and the committee boat, who tacks too close ahead of a starboard-tack boat on the approach to the weather mark, who forces his way inside at the jibe mark without obtaining an overlap in time, may be playing this "game." He may be claiming, "I have a perfect right to be here, look how hard I've tried," or ". . . how deserving I am, how unfair it is for me to be deprived unjustly." And, of course, if the innocent victim protests (verbally and/or officially), the "game" player may retaliate with a belligerent exchange that he finds altogether justified.

Another "game" played occasionally by both top competitors and enthusiastic neophytes is "I'm Only Trying to Help You." The expert who offers his advice or gives a talk to the fleet may be playing "I'll Help You If You Don't Improve." He delights in admiration and attention but doesn't want his admirers to become threatening. The neophyte, mindful of his proper place in the pecking order, is happy to co-operate by playing "I'll Listen and Act Impressed, If You Don't Require That I Actually Improve." This "game" is so popular that many people can be "trusted" to play it.

On one occasion, a competitor of mine, angered because I had beaten him in four straight races, protested my having tacked too close and complained bitterly to the race-committee chairman when he failed to hold a fifth race. The following day he lost to me five times, by even greater margins. Although an angry opponent becomes less trustworthy, in the normal sense, he need not be *dis*trusted. As his anger develops, his performance deteriorates; he becomes less, not more, threatening. He can be "trusted" to do poorly.

Richard Petty and David Pearson have been major rivals in superspeedway racing for many years. At Daytona in 1974 Petty was "drafting" Pearson (riding close astern in the vacuum made by the car ahead), with the intention of "slingshotting" around him to win. Petty tells the story:

> I was where David wanted to be, so he reversed things. We came down the front stretch at 190 or 200 mph and when we went into the first turn of the last lap David suddenly let off the accelerator and slowed. I had to swerve as hard as I could to avoid running over him but couldn't help going right by him. Then he accelerated and got right on *my* tail and drafted me around until he made the slingshot pass I'd wanted to make on the fourth turn, and he won. . . .
>
> It was smart, I suppose, but it wasn't right. We have unwritten rules we live by, and he broke one of them and could have killed us both. The thing that hurt is I trusted David more than any other driver. When I'm drafting him, he could make a right turn or run through a fence and I'd follow him. I trust that if something—cars spinning or something like that—happens in front of him he'll make the right move, so I'll move with him. . . .
>
> Things are all right between me and David now. We aren't buddy-buddy, but we can talk to each other, we respect each other, we enjoy racing each other. And we don't do dumb things week after week in an effort to beat each other. It was something that happened and it hasn't happened again and it's history. You can't carry a grudge around with you and race the right way.

What is evident here is that even professional racing drivers trust one another, recognize the need to trust one another, and are shocked when that trust is violated. Petty says, "He's lucky I didn't hit him or do the same thing back to him when he got behind me, or swerve over and knock him into the infield when he went past me. I was so mad I might have done anything—I was too mad to drive right or I might have had a chance to hold him off." *You can't compete effectively unless you trust your opponent.*

37 / "See What You Made Me Do!"

*I do not feel obliged to believe that that same
God who has endowed us with sense, reason, and
intellect has intended us to forgo their use.*
— GALILEO GALILEI

WANTED: Trusting, nondistracting crew whose Child wishes to be reassured. Will provide Parent, discipline, recognition, and appreciation.

IDEALLY, THE SKIPPER AND HIS CREW REGARD EACH OTHER AS BROTHERS,
companions, peers. Each perceives himself as an adult, perceives that
his Adult is in control, believes that he can relate to those around him
as an adult. Each recognizes his influence upon the other, recognizes
the other's need for respect. Both recognize the supremacy of the
skipper—the necessity of catering to the skipper's psyche. Where this
situation exists, crew and captain function well together. But the relationship of skipper and crew is often more like that of parent and
child, and those who are ill at ease in this relationship have difficulty
in their role while sailing. When choosing a crew, the skipper, particularly if his own ability to play parent is impaired, must consider the
possibility that the crew's behavioral determinants will not comple-

197

ment his own. He cannot advertise in the manner suggested above, but he can screen the candidates to assure compatibility.

The mentally tough crew member recognizes the significance of his contribution and needs no reassurance. Most crews, however, aware of their mistakes, concerned that they are not appreciated, require some evidence of respect—and often complain bitterly when they don't receive it. Brian Burland crewed for Hartley Watlington, four-time winner of the Princess Elizabeth Cup, the year I won that prize. When they capsized astern of me in the final race, the usually taciturn Hartley was swearing—disrespectfully—and Brian told him that he would "not swim back to the boat" until Hartley spoke civilly!

Rod Johnstone in a U.S. Yacht Racing Union newsletter cautions skippers about their behavior toward crews. He implies that few skippers are realists, willing to accept a performance consistent with their own abilities and experience. Many, he says, behave like Captain Bligh. They are unconsciously (or consciously) angry, resentful that their image may be tarnished by the ineptness of their crew. They shout and scream because they feel threatened, because they are frightened, because they have stuck out their necks in assuming the role of skipper and fear to lose their heads if they don't succeed. Many other skippers assume an idealist/fatalist role. They demand a perfect performance from themselves and their crews during the race, and afterward intellectualize their way around any recognition of their failure. This behavior clearly indicates a disorder of appraisal, for regardless of one's level of competence it is unrealistic to expect to sail a perfect race.

A revealing cliché is, The skipper wins the race, the crew loses it. (There is also the variant, I wouldn't want to be a single-handed sailor; there'd be no one on whom to blame the defeats.) Crews are used for a variety of ulterior purposes. I know a skipper who seems to arrange for a green crew in regattas he expects to lose. He is playing a variant of the "game" Eric Berne calls "See What You Made Me Do," which appears to be a means of providing, in advance, an excuse for failure. The skipper can justify his expected (intended) loss to himself and to others by blaming the crew: "I have this poor crew member who needs constant supervision, is distracting, fails me at critical moments; I couldn't be expected to win." Underlying this "game" may be resentment regarding a particular individual, the crew of a competitor, a particular regatta, or sailboat racing in general.

Sometimes a skipper actually wants to avoid the race but feels unable to do so. The competition may be too strong, the weather conditions may be adverse, the competitive juices may not be flowing, the usual crew may be unavailable, and so on. To justify lashing out against a world (a parent) that forces one to compete in such situations, a fall guy is needed. Hoping to vindicate or justify his position, he blames the crew for the outcome. I remember one day when I awaited, to the last possible minute, the arrival of a crew member and then angrily picked up a kid off the dock. We actually did very well in the early part of each race, but there always came a time when a semidisaster "caused by the kid" occurred and we went down the drain. It took me a few days to recognize that I had blown the races deliberately, using "the kid" as the excuse. I really hadn't wanted to race in those circumstances, but couldn't admit that I was inadequate to the task.

Some skippers set up their crews more directly: "Which way do you think we should go?" "Are you sure the jib-sheet tension is right?" Or when being overtaken by a boat planing over their stern wave: "Don't let that spinnaker break! Now you've done it. We've lost him." "See What You Made Me Do!" Even if the "game" is not played overtly in the bar ("we were doing fine until Joe blew the spinnaker") with eyebrows raised in knowing conviviality with other skippers, it can be used to assuage inner concerns regarding loss of power.

In some cases the version played is "Now I've Got You, You Son of a Bitch," with the skipper taking the role of the punitive parent. He arranges for the crew member to do something beyond his competence or in an impossible circumstance and then complains bitterly of his incompetence. This is likely to be played when the skipper is, in fact, jealous of the particular crew member's superiority or presumed superiority (perhaps following a situation in which the latter could say, or imply, "I told you so"). It provides justification for the skipper's otherwise unjustified anger, avoids confrontation of his own deficiencies, proves that "people can't be trusted," and permits a belligerent outburst.

Crews who continue to sail with skippers who behave in this manner have some need to play the abused child, to be punished. Some are playing "Why Does This Always Happen to Me?"; they are trying to establish their pre-eminence in misfortune. They often complain about their skipper ("he gets so excited, he doesn't know what he is doing"), but continue to sail with him. "You Got Me into This," involving a desire to displace responsibility for fancied incompetence, may warrant continuance of the relationship for some crews. They may be content to play "See What You Made Me Do" because they know that it's the skipper's "game" and that the skipper is really responsible.

Of course, crews as well as skippers can play "Now I've Got You, You Son of a Bitch." I feel uneasy as crew, and therefore rarely accept this role, because I am concerned that the skipper (parent) will "catch" me doing something wrong. (Because I am so anxious to avoid mistakes, I am actually very good as crew!) But this awareness leads me to understand why crews may wish to play "Now I've Got You, You Son of a Bitch." If they have the feeling—usually mistaken—that their skipper (parent) is trying to discover their errors and show them up, they may use the "game" to turn the tables on him and thus overcome their sense of being found at fault. One of my crew members played it with me recently. We had rounded the jibe mark in about 18 knots, barely ahead of the fleet. As the spinnaker filled on the new course, I was very concerned (being fearful of being overtaken) that we might broach in the gust that abruptly appeared. I shouted, "Guy, guy, guy!" meaning, of course, "Vang, vang, vang!" The middle man put his hand on the guy but did nothing until the gust had subsided and I realized that I'd been giving the wrong order. He knew that releasing the vang was the primary trim requirement in this circumstance, but as I had ordered something else, he was excused from doing what was correct—"Now I've Got You, You Son of a Bitch." He presumably felt vindicated for all the times I had failed (or appeared to fail) to recognize his contribution.

Keith Shackleton shows the crew's attitude in a famous vignette from one of his K. Humphrey Shakewell articles:

> "Ready about! Ease luff! Up plate! Shorten horse! Tighten foot!"
> "Would you please pass the tranquilizers? The tourniquet is not quite tight enough—I am still losing rather a lot of blood. You will find the telephone number of my psychiatrist penciled on the back of the sailing instructions."

The poor mistreated crew, unappreciated and unrespected! When I told one of my crew that after a tack he wasn't getting over the side quickly enough, he replied that he was doing his best. I told him that his best at that point wasn't good enough! Crews must align themselves with skippers whose aspirations are at their own chosen level. When the competition is at the highest level, it is rare that anyone's best, skipper's or crew's, is good enough.

Mike Peacock echoed this attitude at the time he saw four new members inducted into the Crews' Union (of the British International 14 class): "There go four more guys who won't hoist a spinnaker or go out without a reef if the wind is blowing more than 10 knots!"

If the skipper or the crew members fail to recognize that they are playing "games" with one another, if they resent the position of parent or child in which they have placed themselves and require vindication, the result will be tension within the narrow confines of a small boat—and a serious compromise of performance. The external stresses and recurrent crises of sailboat racing are sufficient occasionally to break down the best of ego defenses and overcome the most mentally tough. When the "games" played or roles assumed by skipper and crew are incompatible, disaster must follow. Even a defective relationship between two crew members may be hazardous. After the fourth race of the 1973 Soling World Championship at Quiberon, France, my French middle man told me that my French foredeck man would not eat dinner with him, let alone sail with him again! The middle man had been told by the foredeck man that he was "bad"; he had exceeded his authority (taken a parental role) in translating my orders into French!

It's easy enough to describe how skippers should behave to their crews, how crews should behave to their skippers, but it's impossible to change them into something they are not. Skippers are skippers in part because they have strong internalized Parents that drive them to assume responsibility, take charge, demand perfection. Crews, in many cases at least, have a dominating Child that disdains responsibility, resents control, acts rebellious. Each *should* be respectful of the other, should take pains to become trustworthy and to demonstrate trust. However, it is nearly impossible to remake an ego. What is needed is realistic recognition, by all those involved, of the roles they wish to play. And crews must recognize that inasmuch as the skipper goes with the boat they'd better either find the right one or learn to get along with the one they've got. Even "Now I've Got You, You Son of a Bitch" skippers can find crews willing to play "Why Does This Always Happen to Me?" The crew not interested in that "game" had better look elsewhere.

Skippers should assume the responsibility of analyzing their crews sufficiently to assure that they are willing to play the skipper's "game," to match the role the skipper assumes. The crew's efforts to support the ego of the skipper contribute mightily to the successful performance of the team. The skipper's efforts to support the egos of his crew detract from the performance of the team because they distract him from sailing the boat. When he worries about bruised egos among his crew, he is impairing his own performance. A crew member who expects his extraneous needs to be attended to is compromising the boat's performance. He should be replaced.

38 / Teamwork

Do not use a hatchet to remove a fly from your friend's forehead.

—CHINESE PROVERB

They were now committed together, all of them were encompassed by the same risks, the same hardships, and the same hope. Any weakness in one man weakened them all and each little triumph was a shared accomplishment. One man was best with a rifle, another at cooking, a third with his physical strength, and all these matters were established without pride or jealousy and were fitted into a pattern. Everything depended, of course, upon their liking and respecting one another, and this they evidently did. Burke was the unquestioned leader and even when they doubted his judgment they thought his leadership was more important than any error he might commit. Wills was their navigator and technician. None of them would ever have dreamed of contesting his calculations . . . he was so thorough and painstaking.

In these words Alan Moorehead describes the party of four from the Burke-Wills expedition which made the final dash across central Australia to the Gulf of Carpentaria.

A group of sailors embarking upon a day of racing is not so dissimilar from these explorers setting off into the Outback. What lies ahead is unknown. The only certitude is that challenges will be met that will require the complete trust of each member of the party for every other. Nowhere is the trust that the crew must feel for their captain and for each other better described than in this account of the attitudes of Burke's company. The significance of each member, the need of the group for his unique contribution, must be recognized. That he has idiosyncracies, that he makes mistakes, that he is sometimes wrong, must be accepted and must not diminish the loyalty and trust that is felt and demonstrated. The crew must think the captain's leadership "more important than any error he might commit." The skipper must never dream "of contesting . . . calculations" by an expert member of his crew.

I described the ideal racing crew member in *Advanced Racing Tactics:*

> He must forgo the pleasure of watching the race, of appreciating the beauty of the sky and the water, of analyzing the determinants of strategy. He must concentrate on the jib telltales, the spinnaker luff, the compass, knowing that to look away is to let down the team. He must tolerate—he must willingly accept—the skipper, the skipper's anxieties, the skipper's complaints, occasionally the skipper's profanity. . . . He does not think in terms of sacrifice; he delights in adversity for the opportunity it provides to make an even greater contribution. By being indefatigable in his own efforts, he establishes a standard that demands the utmost of the other members of the crew. His only question is, Are we doing our best? He believes wholeheartedly, unquestioningly, in victory. He not only accepts the leadership of the skipper, he insists that his authority be maintained. He supports the skipper, encouraging him even—particularly—when things are going badly. . . . [He] senses the skipper's mood, his response to the situation, and complements, restores, or re-creates the attitude appropriate to victory.

The mental toughness of each crew member, his ability to play without excessive Parental interference, largely determines how well he will perform. However, his performance will also be affected, adversely or beneficially, by the behavior of his associates. For optimal performance, an affection—in ideal circumstances, a feeling akin to devotion—must develop among crew members. The ability of crew members to establish such a relationship determines whether or not a group of individuals can function as a team. Teamwork depends upon their having an easy, pleased, unpressured feeling about one another and about the competition. No extraneous needs, no personal concerns, may intrude.

Each individual in a relationship needs a realistic understanding of his role and his responsibilities. Each needs to feel accepted, respected, appreciated. Each needs to feel that his contribution is recognized and appropriately rewarded. Each needs to know what the other expects of him and what limits the other wishes to set upon his behavior. In no relationship is this more true than in that between skipper and crew.

The unique element of this relationship is the far greater significance of the skipper. In the absence of the crew member, a substitute must be found. In the absence of the skipper, the boat will not sail. A tense, distracted, unhappy crew may blow the jibe and lose a boat. A tense, distracted, unhappy skipper will blow the entire race. The whole team will suffer if the skipper's psyche is disturbed.

The skipper should make his crew member feel significant, having him participate in the preparation and organization of the boat, rewarding him when he does well. The willingness of the crew member to sacrifice will depend upon his own perception of the significance of his contribution. The skipper must be explicit in defining what he expects and must provide training (that is, plenty of practice) in doing what he expects. He must communicate in a manner that will be both completely understandable and reassuring. (I found after the third race in the 1973 Swiss Championship that I was completely confusing my French middle man, who was named Paul—pronounced *pole* in French—when I ordered, "Pull the pole, Paul"!) The crew member must know that he is appreciated and respected. Respect is demonstrated by setting a high standard and then assuming that it will be met.

The good crew deserves a good skipper—but it is the attitude of the crew that really matters. To the extent that the crew member learns his job and can perform it without supervision, to the extent that he creates no distractions, to the extent that he makes his reports without disturbance, he frees the skipper to do *his* job. This is the most important contribution that he makes: he can be ignored. The great crew member accepts being ignored as a compliment (which it is); he never grumbles about a lack of recognition. To be ignored he must practice, must perfect his performance, so that even in the most critical and most desperate circumstances he can function without supervision. It is his stability under pressure, his ability to maintain order amid chaos, instead of contributing to the chaos, that gains him the respect he seeks. In addition, he must be ready to respond to orders. Only the skipper knows the over-all plan, can see the big picture, recognizes what must be done to gain a critical position. His orders, designed to modify the routine, must be instantly and fully obeyed.

However, the crew member can do far more than merely be nondistracting. His words and his attitude can be supportive in a way that maintains and, if necessary, restores the skipper's confidence and determination. To the extent that he knows his skipper, he can join with him in developing and strengthening the latter's ego defenses. If the skipper needs to deny the evidence that his boat is slower, the crew can avoid presenting such evidence during the race, saving it for the postrace critique. When I told Marion Mecklenburg, who crewed for me, that a particular competitor was always faster under spinnaker than I was, he responded, "Don't tell me that, I don't want to hear it." His answer jolted me out of my complacent resignation and, with a few appropriate trim adjustments, we forged into the lead. Red Mc-Vittie, noting that her husband, after sailing with a visiting expert, had positioned the centerboard differently, brought them out of their "slows" by asking, "Who do you think you are, George O'Day?"

A positive attitude supports the skipper; enthusiasm is infectious. But a false optimism, a lack of realistic appraisal, interferes with learning and leads to more intense depression when the inevitable failure follows. The crew member should leave to the skipper the ultimate expression of optimism. He must report accurately, as did the cavalry scout, "There are hundreds of Indians on all sides of us," and leave to his leader the reply, "They'll never get away from us this time!" The wise crew modifies the report so as to make the news as nonthreatening, as impersonal, as reasonable as possible.

Dennis Toews, everybody's choice for crew of the decade, noting that the luff tension is a bit loose, says to his skipper, Hans Fogh, "How do you like the Cunningham?" There is no implication that a big problem exists, that the skipper should have noticed the defect before, that the luff tension is wrong. There is no intention to show off that he has discovered something Hans forgot, to interrupt his train of thought with complaints. Bill Robinson, owner/crew of a crack International 14 in the 1950's, says in his classic treatise on crewing that the crew must know when to encourage the skipper and when to restrain him. Tact and discretion are essential; in no circumstance must antagonism arise. "This," says Robinson, "is the responsibility of the crew." In other words, the crew member has the game in his hands; he can manage the skipper to achieve any result he wishes! Crews should recognize the significance of their behavior and manage it accordingly.

The problem, for both skipper and crew, is that they feel unable to request the kind of behavior they would like. Every skipper recognizes that he needs a loyal, trusting crew that will believe in him, support him, encourage him, that what he doesn't need is a crew that second guesses, doubts, and deprecates him. But he cannot ask for such loyalty. He can only hope that his behavior will warrant it. To the extent that he feels that he has to seek this loyalty, he will be preoccupied with the concern and function less effectively as a consequence. By the same token the crew member is unable to request that he be treated with respect, be made to feel significant. Each must recognize the other's needs and provide for them without their having been mentioned.

Each crew member must be trusting. He must, without either request or suggestion, believe that his teammates trust him, respect him, are loyal to him. To be suspicious is to destroy the team. Trust, and suspicion, are attributes derived from early experience and not susceptible to conscious modification. To be trusting one must have been trusted as a child. The members of successful teams trust one another not because they believe they should, but because that is the kind of people they are.

Part Five

Defensive Functioning

39 / Denial

Ah, Love! could thou and I with Fate conspire
To grasp this sorry Scheme of Things entire,
   Would not we shatter it to bits—and then
Remold it nearer to the Heart's Desire!
—THE RUBÁIYÁT OF OMAR KHAYYÁM

COMPETITORS, EXPOSED AND UNDER PRESSURE, ARE OFTEN UNWILLING
or unable to accept the real world. They use a variety of means, defenses, to manipulate reality so as to make it "nearer to the Heart's
Desire." The real world and the competitor's aspirations often collide
in a manner that is threatening, frightening, depressing, or painful.
The mentally tough competitor may be able (and should be able) to
accept these feelings, recognize their cause, and proceed with his performance despite them. Ideally, then, defenses would be unnecessary.
However, few are so mentally tough that they would not be more
handicapped by apprehension than by some manipulation of reality.
Most achieve a compromise by subverting reality in denial, repression, rationalization, intellectualization, "game" playing, or some
other defensive technique. These defenses protect the ego from
threats and fear. But they *are* compromises, attempts at short-term
solutions to acute problems, and may not be in the long-term, best interest of the psyche.

Defenses reassure the psyche in regard to its "life fear" and "death fear." Some individuals (in whom the Parent is in the ascendancy and who have "life fear") are particularly concerned to be pleasing, to be approved. They fear the guilt which accompanies behavior (or the threat of behavior) inconsistent with their Parental standards. They may utilize some form of defense to avoid recognition of a loss of approval or to avoid behaving in a manner that might result in a loss of approval. Other individuals (in whom the Child is in the ascendancy and who have "death fear") are particularly concerned to maintain their independence, their power. They fear the anxiety which accompanies behavior (or the threat of behavior) inconsistent with the maintenance of self-determination. They may utilize some form of defense to avoid recognition of loss of power or to avoid behaving in a manner that might result in a loss of power. Some defenses are more likely to be suitable and to be used for protection against fear of loss of approval; others are more suitable and more likely to be used for protection against fear of loss of power.

One common form of defense is the continuous modification, during the course of an event, of the individual's feeling about its importance. This modification of affect permits an appropriate modification of effort. If a given phase of an event or an element of performance is associated with great desire and great significance, the effort expended will be great. If it is associated with little desire and little significance, the effort will be minimal. The sports psychologist Thomas Tutko believes that "it is the very nature of a player not to participate when all is lost, not to put out totally."

This adjustment of effort is a defense that prepares the ego to experience elation with success *and* to avoid depression with failure. Prior to the game or race, when desire is acceptable because success is possible, the event is conceived of as significant. The ego is prepared to enjoy the elation which will accompany the desired outcome. An effort appropriate to this outcome seems justifiable. Late in the event, when failure is imminent, the conception of it is altered: the event is now assumed to be insignificant and the desire to perform well, to win, is denied. The ego is prepared to tolerate, to accept with reduced pain, the anticipated failure. Only a minimal effort, appropriate to the insignificance of the event, now seems justifiable. The body is required to "act out" the belief that it doesn't matter. To continue to perform well would be to deny the denial, to imply that the event mattered, to cause the ego to feel the pain that would accompany a significant failure. Performance is deliberately caused to deteriorate for the sake of short-term ego protection.

A more common and usually less harmful defense is "joking around." Bermuda's Charlie Berry was the great exponent of this technique. He always had a quip ready to indicate to the rest of us, and to himself, that an event was of little consequence. Then there was the Viking funeral given to the Tempest *Gift 'Orse* by owner Alan Warren after his dismal showing in the Kingston Olympics. After crossing the finish line in the last race, he doused the boat with paint thinner and ignited her. Team coach John Maynard commented, "It shows what a tremendous sense of humor these guys have after doing so badly. With people taking the Olympics so seriously, this kind of puts everything back in perspective." To grandly deny the signifi-cance of their failure may have been appropriate for *Gift 'Orse*'s crew, but it was a marked discourtesy to all those others who, a few hundred yards away, were playing the last and most exciting seconds of the most significant of all sailing games.

According to Leo Durocher, in 1972 one of his players, the most talented in baseball, wouldn't listen. "[He] was getting called out on pitches that were outside by this much. He'd come back to the bench, still screaming, and heave his helmet and bat. I'd try to tell him he was hurting himself. 'You're getting a raw deal. . . . They're waiting to see if you've learned your lesson.' He never did. That was his way. How dare anybody criticize anybody for doing it their way?" He was afraid to submit to direction, fearful of giving up his independence, his power. Like a two-year-old, he was incapable of accepting author-ity. And his defense was denial: they have nothing to teach me; I have nothing to gain by admitting their power. This is one of the most crippling forms of defense; the transient protection it provides from the threat of others' superiority is gained at the expense of a total in-ability to learn from those others.

During competition, an individual continually reassesses his per-formance to determine what should be continued and what modified. Although a realistic assessment might indicate that performance is defective and that at the moment nothing can be done about it, such an assessment is often denied. When out on a limb, far to one side of the fleet, one can easily forget the many times the lift continued and the race went down the drain. But once denial has taken over, once the initial irrational step has been taken, there often is no turning back. Upon the denial that the lift will persist is superimposed a denial

that one looks pretty stupid going the wrong way, along with a denial
that the wind is unlikely to oscillate back in the time remaining and finally a denial that the race matters anyway. Not infrequently the feeling seems to be even more irrational, as the crew (or the psyche) is
told, "I wanted to go this way." (I can, if I want to!) "And these are
the [irrational] reasons I am doing so!"

Hale Irwin says that you can always blame the caddy (he specified the wrong distance) or the crowd (a baby cried). Sparky Anderson
and his players furiously blamed the umpire for a bad call when they
lost to the Dodgers by eight runs! Phil Esposito points out that when
you are losing you notice that you have the same referee with whom
you lost before, but when you're winning, "who cares who the referee
is?"

The most adverse effects of denial or repression of painful awareness are experienced during competition, but postevent denial, because it prevents learning, may also be damaging. How regularly we
hear denial after the race is over: "If the wind had only come back at
the end of that beat, we would have won by a mile!" "My crew is
useless; they never give me the information I need." "If I had used my
other jib, we would have been dynamite." "We sat in this hole for an
hour while the whole fleet sailed by." What is being denied is personal
responsibility, and what goes unrecognized is how one should have
behaved in order to avoid the failure. Some competitors effectively
block the acquisition of any bona fide experience by denying almost
everything that happens to them. One of my backgammon-playing
friends tells me that no backgammon player will ever admit having
been beaten by a better player!

A dull complacency—staleness—may deny the significance of
recent failure (or recent success) and at the same time interfere with a
realistic appraisal of performance. On the other hand, the institu-
tion of a dramatic change may also represent a denial of what really
happened, a denial that one was beaten (or victorious). The excitement that accompanies the planning of a new approach may be satisfying merely because it preoccupies the psyche and thereby protects it
from some painful recognition. It is tempting to be "daring" and to
think that because the conditions will be different in the race to come,
or because the boat felt wrong at the end of the last beat, a sweeping
modification of sail trim is indicated: "I know that this jib [or "this
degree of mast bend," "this amount of mainsheet tension"] never

worked before, but *this* time, despite the evidence of experience, it will." And it is equally tempting to be complacent: "I will concentrate on testing the current [or "obtaining information on the weather," "repainting the bottom"] and will ignore the evidence that I need more speed to windward." It is easy to believe that daring is reasonable, even courageous, or that complacency is rational, even a sign of strength. Either response may be used to deny that one fears the present (or previous) state—whether of success or failure—and either response may result in failure in the race to come.

Postevent denial may also be used to deny the significance of the behavior of others, for self-punishment as well as self-protection. Roger Staubach, after the Cowboys lost early in the 1978 season, said, "I was in a rut in the Washington game, a poor one for me. I blame myself for that loss."

To the extent that competition is counterphobic, it is rooted in denial. The competitor who is made anxious by the threat of conflict constantly seeks to reassure himself that he can handle it. He is forced to return to the fray again and again, never quite overcoming the fear and never quite assuring himself that he *is* handling it satisfactorily. He denies to himself that conflict makes him uneasy, that exposure of his competence is frightening, and that his anxiety is the cause of his problems. "I blew that mark rounding because the spinnaker sheet wrapped around the boom (not because I panicked when the helmsman astern demanded room)." "I tacked away because the wind seemed stronger to the left (not because the continuance of that side-by-side contest with my major opponent was intolerable)." "After I tacked on his lee bow, he tacked away, and I didn't cover him because I was on a lift (not because I didn't want him to feel that I was close-covering him)."

Denial is useful if it diminishes an anxiety that would otherwise have been handicapping, if performance is better than it otherwise would have been. It may provide hope for the future and diminish depression from the past. It is useful in manipulating one's conception of significance. It may help one to maintain equanimity in the face of fear. But it is irrational, and therefore it results in unrealistic appraisal and inappropriate remembrance. It interferes with learning and blocks the acquisition of competence. Successful competitors use it only as a last resort and rarely or never use it during performance. Bert Jones walks off the field *after* an interception acting as if it had never occurred. Ted Marchibroda says of the *upcoming* game between his injury-riddled Baltimore Colts and the world-champion Dallas Cowboys, "What a plus if we win. There will be a new feeling of confidence on this club!"

40 / Intellectualization

If, of all words of tongue and pen,
The saddest are, "It might have been,"
More sad are these we daily see:
"It is, but hadn't ought to be."

—BRET HARTE

JEFF LOWE, AFTER CLIMBING FROZEN BRIDALVEIL FALL, WAS ASKED THE classic mountaineering question: "Why?"

"One of the biggest problems about climbing is to feel that what you are doing is OK and that it *is* worth doing. In fact, there *is* no point to anything you do—or anyone else does—unless you give it meaning yourself." Competition is what we intend it to be and is as significant as we imagine it to be. Our involvement begins as an intellectualization. It is not surprising that we continue to intellectualize throughout our competitive lives.

Intellectualization is used to assist in the accomplishment of many goals, but it is chiefly a defense against the threat of helplessness; it permits the belief that one is determining one's fate. It obviates at least temporarily the feelings, which accompany losing, of being powerless, helpless, and insignificant. Its paradigm is, You can't beat me; I'll beat myself.

The intellectualizer fears that when something goes wrong, his

Parent will point an accusing finger, that he will feel like the helpless, frightened Child he unconsciously remembers, that he will be "caught" being "bad" once again. He arranges in advance to be uninterested in the problem, to be busy playing another, more significant "game," or to be pointing his own finger toward the real villain.

To intellectualize is to displace concern from an emotional issue to an intellectual one. An intellectual preoccupation is substituted for the emotional awareness of being threatened. The technique is highly protective during intense competition. Many competitors say that their anxiety is intense until the game actually begins, until they are able to occupy their minds with plans, appraisals, and responses—to intellectualize.

The best example of the method and effectiveness of intellectualization is in the training of the combat infantryman in days gone by. The soldiers of the famous "thin, red line" of the eighteenth-century British army were trained to fight "by the numbers." With the enemy charging at them, they formed a double line. While those in one row were firing (on command), those in the other row were cleaning, reloading, tamping, priming their muskets—until finally it was their turn to elevate, aim, and fire them. During the prolonged period of preparing their weapons, they never looked up, never paid any attention to the enemy—who might be but a few feet away. It was evident (to their officers, at least) that the best way to reduce the fear aroused by the onrushing foe was to preoccupy the soldiers with an intellectual exercise. If they learned that what really mattered was how well they adhered to commands, how efficiently they performed each of the intricate actions necessary to reloading, they would be better able to ignore the imminence of death—*and* be more effective. It is logical to suppose that, if they had spent their time between shots alternately watching the enemy, who was shooting at them, and attempting to reload, the result would have been mostly misfires.

Intellectualization is more than denial (which merely avoids the issue). Intellectualization creates a whole new issue with which the psyche can become preoccupied. It doesn't so much deny or ignore the game as to put it into "perspective." Prior to the game the intellectualizer can discuss at length the merits of his opponents, their equipment, their ability in the existing conditions, and his own potential. After the event he can discourse at length on the reasons for his poor performance. He is so pleased by his demonstration of competence in

analytic technique that he can ignore (for a while at least) his demonstration of incompetence. A variation on the theme is the loser who
congratulates himself on being a great loser: "I'm proud of my ability
to lose. Losing is an important skill. Without us losers, where would
all those winners be?" Intellectualization is not just excuse making,
not a means of explaining failure as due to bad luck, poor crew work,
poor coaching, or poor equipment. Intellectualization is a godlike
reorganization of the real world, a smug, satisfied, lip-smacking demonstration of power, which, for a time at least, is believed.

Rationalization is a form of intellectualization. The reaction of
the 1970 Princeton hockey team to its 1–22 record was described by
E. M. Swift in an article for *Sports Illustrated*. This team was initially
surprised by losing and came belatedly to rationalization: Their "0–6
record did not seem so bad after eating roast goose at Christmas dinner. The team's troubles seemed trivial when compared to, say, those
suffered by Joseph and the Virgin. Or the goose." Later, "where some
teams try to sit on a one or two goal lead, Princeton began protecting a
one or two goal deficit. 'Nice loss,' they would announce to one another." On one occasion, "the Cornell puck carrier, who was opposite
[Princeton defenseman] D'Ewart, threaded a perfect pass between his
legs to his wingman. . . . The rest of the team and the fans in the first
few rows clearly heard D'Ewart call out, 'Nice pass!' to the Cornell
player. When D'Ewart returned to the bench, Quackenbush
[the coach] asked him dryly if he was enjoying the game. D'Ewart
nodded."

The most effective form of intellectualization involves the creation of another game, another contest, the rules for which guarantee
a victorious outcome. Many competitors pride themselves on their
toughness. My ex-Marine crew Tom Guillet, while hiking on a long
beat, would cry out, "Pain, pain! I love it!" Dick Tillman says that the
ability to stand pain is the measure of desire and the determinant of
victory in Finn racing. Though it must contribute in a positive fashion, preoccupation with tolerance of pain can become a game in itself:
"you may have won the race, but I am tougher, more tolerant of pain,
than you. So I win (*my* game)."

Jack Nicklaus wonders how Arnold Palmer can continue to turn
up for tournament after tournament, knowing that he may not even
make the cut. Palmer appears to have adapted to the loss of his skill by
concentrating on the camaraderie associated with tournament golf. He

is playing a game played by amateurs the world over—"being one of the boys." Nicklaus cannot understand how anyone can so deny the significance of golf and of the display of golfing skill.

Many of the most competent sailors seem to have a surprisingly limited understanding of racing strategy. They develop fast boats, get good starts, and keep ahead of the fleet. They ignore the causes of wind flow, disparage the ability to predict the time and direction of shifts, spurn the postrace analysis of what happened. And indeed, those who do occupy themselves with these considerations may be intellectualizing. They do not win, for they are not, in fact, concentrating on the factors that determine victory. They are working to win another game, one of their own creation. In my youth, I often continued far to the side of the course, disregarding my opponents, because I "knew" which way the wind would shift. And I still catch myself saying, "Well, we may have blown that one, but I did predict what was going to happen!" The intent is to retain control: "I'm not certain how this game of chance will come out. If I lose, I'm going to feel vulnerable, powerless. So I'll substitute this other game (predicting wind shifts) that I know I can win. And if I do lose, I'll know that it was because I followed my 'scientific' plan, *not* because I was beaten."

A more subtle type of intellectualization is the preoccupation with minutiae. One can suppress tension by concentrating upon compass readings. One can block anxiety by watching the crew packing the spinnaker. One can eliminate apprehension by examining lines that have been improperly cleated or are dragging over the side. Awareness of the need to win, the fear of failure, can be avoided by perfectionism. One can be as distracted by a perfect jibe (when one needs to conduct jibes perfectly) as by a disastrous one. Perfectionism is a game: "I'll show you (my parent) how perfectly I can perform, so that I won't have to show you that I can win and so that you won't notice if I lose." And, if a concern for present perfection is insufficiently preoccupying, one can always recall a previous imperfection.

But intellectualization, any manipulation of reality for protective purposes, is detrimental. Winning an invented "game" gets in the way of performance, interferes with the display of competence. Modifications of memory and perception that are developed for the purpose of avoiding pain are unlikely to contribute to appropriate decision making. When approaching the lay line in a lift, one remembers the few occasions when there *was* a header ahead, and a stronger wind—and one conveniently forgets the many times that the lift continued. Obviously, this manipulation of perception and memory serves not to win the race but to lose it and provides but transient protection from the ugly recognition that defeat is imminent.

A famous saying which refers to defensive players in football states, You can't get too smart, or you're going to get burned. In other words, if you get too involved in intellectualization (analysis, classification, organization), you lose your feel. In football, you figure out what's going to happen, commit yourself to an appropriate response, and when something else occurs, find yourself unable to adjust. In sailing, instead of tacking to cover, you cross ahead and continue in a lift—only to find that the lift persists and the opponent is now ahead and to windward. The Parent determines what ought to be, how the ideal game should be played, and disparages the Child if he merely relaxes and enjoys it. But when the game is turned into an intellectual exercise and tension is eliminated, the responsiveness of the Child is lost in the organizational maze. After a failure on the water, I am often chided about how I will "write this one up," how explain it. If I were less able to salvage my sense of power through the opportunity to analyze my failures in print, I might be more able to respond freely and appropriately on the water. Baseball player Larry Hisle says, "I have had the tendency to put too much emphasis upon intelligence when I'm playing, to put too much thought into it rather than letting my instincts and reflexes play for me." Intellectualization merely adds to the distracting efforts of the Parent to get us to do it "right."

Jack Nicklaus extends these concepts in an article describing how he thinks children should be introduced to golf. He says that most weekend golfers, including parents, suffer (and their game suffers) from paralysis by analysis. "If [a child] enjoys what he's doing—and most children I know like spontaneous physical activity—he'll get better at it simply by watching and copying how other people do it." In teaching a child to play golf, Nicklaus says, "avoid too many specifics, especially making a child position-conscious. Rather, emphasize freedom and fluidity of movement. . . . Hit it hard and long and worry about direction later. . . . Whichever way you choose to guide a child, be sure to impart a sense of fun." Intellectualization is the adult's Parent attempting to reorganize his aspirations, conceptions, and sensations. "If this Child is not managed continuously, he'll get hurt," says the Parent—and proceeds to manage him, deceiving everyone into believing that the manipulation will enhance competence. "Not so!" says Nicklaus, in effect. "And not only will it have an adverse effect upon competence, but the game will be no damn fun!"

Peter Hamill, in describing the headmaster of a boys' school, told me, "When he just acted he did fine, but when he stopped to think he got into trouble every time." The general principle for competitive activity is let the Child do it. Once you start thinking about it, particularly during competition, you may very easily confuse extraneous needs with competitive desires. And if in addition, in order to satisfy an ulterior purpose, you superimpose an intellectualization, the acquisition of competence will be further impeded. Playing the game well requires acceptance of the risk of losing. If the risk is removed through intellectualization, both the game and the competence of the player are diminished.

41 / Magical Thinking

*People are usually more convinced by reasons
they discovered themselves than by those found
by others.*

—BLAISE PASCAL

ROBERT RINGER, IN *WINNING THROUGH INTIMIDATION*, SAYS, "DON'T TELL
me how fast you get out of the starting blocks, I'm only interested in
where you are when the race is over." Fair enough, but many of us
resort to magical manipulation in the hope of modifying this truth.
Often we suppress the feeling or the awareness that the present situation is frightening or demeaning. Sometimes we magically project our
own feelings upon others. Sometimes we attempt to undo what obviously exists by a ritual or an incantation. We often displace our anxiety concerning a major problem onto one of lesser significance. And
we regularly rationalize, make excuses, to avoid recognition of failure.
To the extent that we are unaware that they are irrational, these
magical techniques protect us from pain and depression. But because
they are irrational, they interfere with performance and with learning.

A common technique that facilitates self-assurance is the resort to
a "secret weapon": "If I install this new mainsheet cleat, I'll win tomorrow." "If I replace the topping lift that failed and lost last week-

end's race, I am bound to win next week." In the privacy of one's own garage, the evening before the big event, it is easy to believe that all is possible. That one has not won the event in nine previous tries is easily dismissed before the belief that the new jib will solve the speed-to-windward problem. A variant of this technique is the appeal to the "law of averages," the view that "now it's my turn": "I lost the last three; therefore, I'm bound to win this one." When I sailed 14's, I used to have a new "secret weapon" almost every weekend—a cutaway centerboard head to facilitate the board's cocking to weather, jib-sheet leads outside the gunwale, a new Highfield lever on the shrouds. I never returned from a regatta without a new idea that would guarantee victory the next time out. I apparently feared to enter a regatta without a secret advantage. I was unwilling just to play the game, without something up my sleeve. I finally caught on to what I was doing when I began to hear how pleased my opponents were that I had another "secret weapon." "Don't worry about Walker; as soon as he gets going well, he'll try something else." I may have eliminated prerace anxiety but I was actually diminishing my performance.

Those who require secrets, who are unwilling to share what they learn, are revealing, rather than hiding, their need for protection. Mystery is inherent in the game; the mentally tough competitor has no need to add to it. And those who refuse to share, who are preoccupied with the significance of their own secrets, miss the greatest opportunity of all—the opportunity to learn from their opponents.

Continuous practice, participation in event after event, can result in boredom, a loss of the belief that winning is meaningful. The competitor feels tired and irritable, complains about trifling problems, and expresses increasing anxiety about his chances. The realization that competitive success is not worth the sacrifice of all else may come as a frightening surprise to some who have dedicated themselves to preparing for a particular event. Here magic may be useful. Although actual skill cannot possibly be benefited by ceasing to practice, getting completely away from the activity is the only solution. Paul Henderson and Dennis Toews, who had been preparing assiduously for the 1976 Canadian Olympic trials, were losing to their major rivals in late 1975. They decided to lay off completely until the following spring. At the time we wondered about their reasoning, but their subsequent performance demonstrated how right they had been. They regained their former enthusiasm, recovered their belief that being selected was worth their sacrifices.

There are those who act surprised whenever they fail to win. They remember the race at CORK in 1969 when in light air and a big chop they straightened the mast, eased the outhaul, and motored through the fleet to win on the final beat. And the time at Annapolis in 1972 when in 30-knot gusts they played each shift right and won by half a leg. And the way they drove over Bill Johnson on a close spinnaker reach in 1974! They have been capable of winning every leg of some course in every possible condition, so why not today? Why shouldn't they grimace, curse, and roll their eyes when, for some unexplainable reason, they find themselves back in the pack? They constantly feel they are sailing below their capabilities and cannot understand why they are being beaten by inferior rivals!

The delusion that success on one occasion implies success on every occasion is what keeps many people in competition. They had their moment of glory. It did happen! So why shouldn't it happen again? This is useful magic, and it is far more likely to be associated with success than is the realistic appraisal of the same situation: "I have only won once in the last thirty-two regattas; therefore, it is unlikely I will win today." Buddy Melges's appraisal of Peter Galloway's performance at the 1976 U.S. Soling trials may have been unrealistic, but it was undoubtedly reassuring to Peter. "Galloway thinks he's Jesus Christ! He's pointing not five degrees, not ten degrees, but fifteen degrees higher than anyone else!"

True panic is a loss of all defenses, but a "panic party" may be a deliberate defense against panic. It is often a means of displacing the horrifying awareness that the race is about to be lost with the less distressing awareness that, say, the crew has pulled the spinnaker up through the topping lift. For the next three minutes a rational involvement with winning the race is replaced by a heads-in-the-bilge preoccupation of all those on the boat with the question of why and how the spinnaker halyard became attached improperly. By the time they return to consciousness of the tactical situation, the realization that they've blown another one has lost its sting. Each can distract himself with silent vituperation of the others, until all hope is gone and a scapegoat has been selected. Mike Lennox referring to Paul Henderson's orders, is said to have asked, "Which string in this boat is 'the bloody thing!?" Ron Palm during one panic party aboard his Soling shouted the ultimate order: "Pull anything!"

I remember a Spring Soling Bowl in which the current was stronger and therefore more adverse to the left, the wind was stronger to the right, and the possibility of a veer existed. I decided to start at the weather end and to tack to port as soon as possible after the start. However, I was unable to gain a position right at the committee boat and was therefore unable to tack immediately. When I did tack, to go astern of the boat to my right, she tacked simultaneously—and I was in her dirty air. I tacked back and for some time could find no good opening into which to tack again. I soon found that I was one of only a few boats continuing to the left, out into the adverse current, away from the wind and the shift—with most of the fleet to my right heading for the advantageous side ahead of me. I was later asked by several of my puzzled competitors why I had continued to the left (and "down the drain"). At the time I had been unaware of any clear reason for doing so, and I belatedly recognized how irrationally I had behaved. Even though I had failed to gain the ideal position, to be the first boat on port tack, I need not have continued on a progressively more disadvantageous course.

In retrospect, my motivation is clear. I did not wish to reveal that I had been defeated, that I had not executed my plan properly, that I had been controlled by competitors who would have forced me to eat their dirty air all the way to the lay line. I chose instead to defeat myself, to control the situation by avoiding it, to deny that I was being manipulated. I had been able, through magical thinking, to make myself believe that despite all the evidence to the contrary, something good (a back, a stronger wind) would miraculously appear out in the bay—and that instead of being last (as I was, when I reached the mark), I would somehow be catapulted into first!

My wife tells me she has never met a racing sailor without an excuse. To hear most of them tell it, they are never beaten—they always beat themselves. I have one competitor with whom I often tune. No matter which of us gains, he always claims he was the faster. Any failure on his part to come out ahead he attributes to some change in his trim or in his manner of sailing on that particular occasion. Whether he is able to believe what he says, I can't be sure, but I do know that he apparently never recognizes that I continually make adjustments which affect my speed one way or the other, so that the results are determined by my behavior as well as his. Recently, after I marched away to a hundred-yard lead in a short race, he pointed out that *his* rig "bounced about in the chop at that wind strength." It's rational to recognize that one's own behavior contributes significantly to outcome, but a rationalization to believe that *only* one's own behavior determines outcome.

The temptation is always to have an excuse, always to protect oneself. We would have won—except for the breakdown, the crew work, the bad shift. We had excellent speed—except for the run, the second beat, when the wind died. We had excellent starts—except for the third race when we were pushed over early and the fifth race when the boat on our lee bow worked up under us. I remember one of our local boats coming back to the dock without finishing the second race because the bolt that held the mainsheet block to the end of the boom had given way. And I remember only a few weeks later noticing Billy Abbott finishing a race at CORK (in third place) with exactly the same problem!

It's reasonable to recognize, that next time (without the problem, after learning from the present experience) you can do better. But you should not believe that the misadventure is really an excuse. Similar problems are occurring in all the other boats, and some of the others are winning. Ultimately, you have to cut out the magic, the excuses, and the blame and sail the race.

42 / Doing It the Hard Way

Ah, but a man's reach should exceed his grasp,
Or what's a heaven for?

—ROBERT BROWNING

THE COLTS AND THE REDSKINS, MANY OF WHOM REMEMBERED THEIR days of glory, met on November 6, 1978, for what turned out to be one of the best of the Monday-night football games. The first quarter was a standoff, with both offenses looking weak, and the only score a Redskin field goal. Neither quarterback completed a pass until Billy Kilmer lofted one of his "dying swans" and the Redskins were up by 10. Bert Jones's passes were still being dropped, but he engineered a march on the ground that took the Colts to the Redskin goal line. There a short pass to Reese McCall gave the Colts a score and a greatly improved self-appraisal. When they came out for the third quarter, they were fired up. Jones threw a bomb to Roger Carr and the Colts led 14–10! But at the start of the fourth quarter, Jones was sacked and was helped from the field, his throwing arm hanging limp from his bad shoulder. Disaster! The only hope was that somehow the Colts' defense could keep the Redskins out of the end zone for fifteen more minutes.

But no. On a series of penalties, short runs, and wobbling passes, the Redskins drove to the Colts' goal line, and John Riggins went over for the touchdown. The game was as good as over. The Colts' fans had lost all hope when Jones came back, clutching his throwing arm but passing beautifully! Completion after completion followed as the Colt line provided perfect protection and the Colt receivers outplayed the defenders. Finally, Roger Carr, going at full tilt, caught a perfect pass in the corner of the end zone to give the Colts the game, 21–17. Jones, still clutching his right arm, grimacing in pain, waved to the crowd with his left hand as he left the field.

A great game! Virtue triumphs! The good guys come from behind, overcome disaster, achieve the impossible, snatch victory from the jaws of defeat! How often this script is repeated—as if disaster were an advantage. Within reason, it is. Any fear that victory might be undeserved is instantly eliminated. (One's Parent is off one's back!) Any fear that defeat might be unacceptable is allayed. One cannot be expected to win after disaster. There is no longer any need to appease the gods for the temerity of seeking victory. How relaxed the Colts must have been, how free of fear, how free of guilt. All they had to do was play; all they had to feel was the potential for joy.

For the Colts, disaster was a welcome accident (some said Bert Jones played his injury to the hilt, their implication being that he knew what a beneficial effect it would have upon his team and how guilty the Redskins would be made to feel). Many competitors seek disaster—as a means of avoiding guilt, of allaying anxiety, of inducing relaxation. Some are so burdened by oppressive, belittling Parents that they can achieve effective performance only under the handicap of injury, a previous defeat, or a hopeless position in the standings. Disaster may be deliberately generated as a means to appease the need to be deserving or to atone, ahead of time or afterward, for an undeserved success.

According to an article in *Sports Illustrated*, rock climbers describe themselves as continually doubting whether they have made their goals challenging enough. If they succeed, the accomplishment cannot be significant. They must deserve success by achieving the impossible. "At the top of a cliff, the climber will often ask himself, 'Did I really earn the right to feel this good?' " His response, I think, is likely to be, "I have not demonstrated sufficient competence to justify this challenge of the gods."

Disaster may be an attempt to avoid guilt in advance: "I think I may win; I fear to do so. I will, through disaster, either fail or justify the win." Alan Warren claims that he always sails better in heavy weather. "The more it's blowing the more we enjoy it and the more relaxed we get. If a bad situation comes up, I know how to get out of it. I even like it when things go wrong." You pay your way in advance, doing it the hard way, and then you can relax and enjoy it! Paul Elvstrom says winning easily is "not really fun, not for the winner and not for the others. In the Finn (in reasonably strong winds) I only had to start and sail around the course. I mean it was only hard work for me—it was not fun." He felt guilty. He had so many advantages, was so godlike compared to his mere mortal competitors, that his victories were undeserved. Nothing is proved, nothing acceptable, unless it is done against superior competitors, in the most difficult conditions, and in the presence of major handicaps. Only then will the Parent cease its belittling and allow the full display of competence. Thomas "Hollywood" Henderson, the Dallas linebacker, flaunts his omnipotence in advance, derogates his competitors, announces to the world how thoroughly he and the Cowboys will beat them. That few competitors are so able to free themselves from their Parents, to risk offending the Gods, is revealed by opponent Mean Joe Greene's comment before the 1979 Super Bowl: "I wish I had the guts to say what he says."

After victory has been achieved, or after initial success, the need to atone for the undeserved advantage may require disaster. Many competitors must follow a victory with a defeat, and become a threat only after a defeat. Young Tom Watson, after winning the British Open by defeating Jack Nicklaus, blew two major tournaments in succession although he led each at the beginning of the final round. He must have felt unconsciously that he was too young, that he had come too far too fast, that he didn't deserve such easy victories at this stage in his career. The tension built, and he couldn't concentrate on what mattered. At Heritage in March 1977, he lost a four-stroke lead on the first four holes of the final round and then pumped one into the water, made a double-bogey five, and trailed by two strokes. He covered his eyes and ducked his head, knowing that he had again done it to himself, against his conscious will. But now that he was behind, relieved of his guilt, he was able to play well, and he finished second, only one stroke behind. I must have felt similarly on the day when, in my new *Salute*, I had finally found the right sail trim and the right crew (a big one) and in an 18-knot lake breeze at the LSSA Regatta in

Toronto, walked away from a fifty-boat fleet. It was too easy. An hour later, with the help of the zone of calm between the dying lake breeze and the encroaching offshore wind, within a hundred yards of the finish, I managed to dissipate a quarter-mile lead and finish second.

Bob Gardner, hotshot of Lake Ontario, says that sailing is "hours and hours of boredom, punctuated by brief moments of terror." And Ben Cullenbrander of the Royal Canadian Yacht Club says, "Everything I've learned in yachting has been through the eyes of disaster." There are secondary gains: disaster is innately exciting, once experienced it is subsequently more readily recognized and managed, and its immensity provides a clear advantage during discussions in the bar. Perhaps its finest contribution is the opportunity it affords for surmounting it.

Military medals are awarded in proportion to the degree of disaster overcome. So disasters, welcomed because they provide a relief from Parental oppression, an escape from the test, an undeserved deservingness, and an acceptable passivity, may permit the ultimate flaunt. They provide an opportunity to admit to godlike manipulation in their creation *and* to display godlike daring in their management. After Jack Knights sank his Soling in the 1976 British trials, he substituted for the daily bulletins, which had previously appeared in his window to announce his prowess, the single word "Sunk." Within an hour the next bulletin appeared, "Soling crew for hire—own spinnaker!" And as the craft was salvaged, there appeared, "Reopening shortly under entirely the same old management!"

43 / Surrender

If a man does not keep pace with his companions, perhaps it is because he hears a different drummer.

—HENRY DAVID THOREAU

IN THE SPRING OF 1976 I EXCITEDLY LOOKED FORWARD TO THE U.S. Olympic Soling trials. I had bought and rigged a new boat and obtained an excellent crew for the occasion. We won our first race (in the East Coast pre-trials) and felt that we were particularly fast in the light stuff. I organized a cottage near Association Island, and we did all the necessary last-minute things. In practice sessions we were as fast as anyone we met—faster, in light air. We did well in the first four races but had a variety of minor catastrophes that kept us around third or fourth. In the fifth race we took the lead and increased it to about a hundred yards a quarter way up the second beat. There we fell into a huge hole and watched them go by on all sides. We fought our way back to fourth, and finished sixth, but that was the high point of our series.

When the wind disappeared and they abandoned the sixth race, we were a strong third just astern of John Kolius—and I had been thinking, "If this race finishes, Kolius will be unbeatable, they'll call the series, and we will finish third." The fact that I was happy with that prospect meant that I had given up any hope of winning; I was interested in settling for what I had. By the start of the actual sixth race, I was merely concerned to hold my position in the fleet. And during the seventh, after I had lost both Dave Curtis and Bill Buchan, my thoughts constantly turned to whether or not I could hang on to sixth place. I had started the series delighted to be involved, envisioning the prospect of victory and participation in the Olympics, but now I was preoccupied with losing and with a desperate need to salvage whatever status remained. Relaxed, courageous, and enthusiastic at the beginning, I had become tense, fearful, and depressed before the end. I was no longer interested in the fun of racing, only in getting it over with. I wanted to avoid any more competition than was absolutely required of me.

One of Paul Henderson's famous sayings is, Let's not get going so fast we don't have an out! In top-level competition, regression is rarely so overt. It more commonly takes the form of acceptance: "Well, we're behind and that's the way it is." "It looks like they're going to get that new wind first." "We've made another lousy start." "We're here and they're over there. We'll see what happens."

Craig Morton, before he and the Denver Broncos were beaten by the Dallas Cowboys in the 1978 Super Bowl, said, "I anticipate we're going to play a good Super Bowl. It won't be a burden on us if we lose." In other words: "We surrender now; we accept our defeat; don't worry about us, we won't be bad (aggressive, argumentative, domineering)." The Super Bowl Syndrome itself is regressive surrender. "Look how well we've done already. We don't have to prove anything more," is the implication. "We accept the present situation; we will not assert our right to any more. We know you deserve to win more than we do. We know our place in the pecking order."

A common surrender technique, practiced almost exclusively by those in the lead, is to avoid awareness of the competition. Once in the lead they would prefer the game to end as soon as possible, but they know both that they don't deserve to be ahead and that they should not have such feelings. The tension between the desire to retain the lead and the need to relinquish it becomes unbearable. In an attempt to reduce awareness of the tension (which they semiconsciously recognize), they avoid looking astern, at their opponents. They hide from the recognition that they are leading and that by not looking astern they give their opponents a break, surrendering to them.

To keep fear temporarily out of awareness, we can protect ourselves—by denial, intellectualization, magical thinking. Or we can succumb. In surrender one faces the immediate threat and denies its significance. "So I fail, so what?" Once achieved (or while it is occurring) surrender may be easily justified. The rationalization is, of course, that it doesn't matter, that the game wasn't worth playing anyway. Surrender is not being game, not playing the game; it is insulting to all those who continue to play. Surrender is a retention of power despite defeat: "You can't beat me! I decided not to compete. And besides, you are the defective one; you believe in this foolish game."

A boat overtaking from astern on the run often has a kind of cat-and-mouse effect. The helmsman of the boat ahead, preoccupied with the inevitability of the attack, awaits the pounce with bated breath. And thus preoccupied, he fails to steer or trim or use the wind well and soon finds that his paralysis has had the expected (and intended) result. He makes his sacrifice, "lets" his opponent by, and breathing a sigh of relief, returns to racing and sailing his boat. The tension is gone; he has reassured himself that he doesn't retain what he doesn't deserve, and he has shown his opponent that he is a nice guy who won't flaunt his prowess, who deserves approval. That he has lost another race will only dawn upon him belatedly. Just now he is very pleased with himself—besides, "We'll get him back later with ease!"

Excessive concentration upon one's own activity is equally detrimental, as was pointed out in an earlier chapter. Once you've decided what to do, let it happen. Don't supervise your muscles! In oscillating winds I often find myself so caught up in the numbers my compass-reading crew is calling out, so involved in detecting every little shift, that I fail to remember that I'm trying to get to the mark ahead of the other boats. In the 1976 Atlantic Coast Championship I had excellent starts, drove into the lead in race after race, but kept tacking away from the fleet. I concentrated upon the compass—so as to give the others a break, I recognized belatedly. (It is not wise to cover against the shifts, but if the opponent doesn't tack, the leader cannot lose by staying with him.)

Even more detrimental and self-defeating is concentration upon something other than the situation at hand, particularly concentration upon a previous mistake—evaluating, reappraising, justifying. Surrender by this means is fairly overt: "I just tacked too close to Joe, I almost hit that mark, I failed to see that new wind developing. I'll concentrate on my inadequacy, the clear evidence that I don't deserve to be here, until someone passes me. Won't someone please pass me, please punish me, let me atone for my sin?" One competitor banged his boom across my shrouds as he reached down the line at the start of the third race in the 1975 Atlantic Coast Championship, attempted to argue his way through the protest, and was disqualified. The following day, feeling the guilt of the foul and of the argument, he carefully kept to fifth place, behind our fourth, despite the major troubles we had on the heavy-air reach, a condition in which he ordinarily excelled.

Sometimes bravado hides the surrender. The boat you are covering tacks, and you let him go. Or he false-tacks, and you tack and keep going: "He's not that important. I can beat him without covering. (I don't want it to look as if I'm really worried about him.)" Mr. Nice Guy! Big, magnanimous you! Like hell. The fire is getting too hot and you want out of the kitchen. That's what's really involved—surrender. Nowadays, whenever I hear myself say, "Well, let's give him a break," I pull up short and ask myself, "Are you surrendering?" My psyche has been forced to find more subtle techniques for surrender and occasionally without my recognition still succeeds. Its best gambit is, "You've got this great angle and he's on the wrong tack!" That one still works, though I hate to admit it.

Whether deliberate or accidental all forms of surrender represent regression—relinquishing the joy of self-demonstration for the solace of protection and passivity. Regression is viewed in psychiatry as a return to infantile behavior, but this is a misconception in that the infant is often domineering, omnipotent, extremely assertive. What regression does mean is that "life fear" has overcome "death fear," that abandonment has become more threatening than loss of individuality, and the psyche resorts to dependent acceptance. The regressed person seeks approval instead of respect, seeks help instead of control, seeks to submit instead of to conquer.

The need to be safe, accepted, approved (not abandoned) is never far below the surface, so it is not surprising that competitors sometimes try to be Mr. Nice Guy: "Come on in. You don't really have an overlap, but I wouldn't argue with you." When an opponent tacks on their lee bow, they tack away rather than risk a prolonged altercation. They surrender by escaping—both from the threat of the conflict *and* from any implication that they are threatening their opponents. "See how good I am. You wouldn't attack or abandon me, would you? Even though I'm your competitor, you'll still like me, won't you?"

They are saying, in effect, "My Child wants the approval of your Parent." Giving the other guy a break can be a scarcely detectable means of avoiding an undeserved win. (And you can be certain the other guy will never detect your generosity. He *knows* he beat you.) But it is also a way of avoiding responsibility for the loss. Randy Rassmussen says, about team sports, that if you expect to lose, you do no more than your job. You fear doing something wrong and somebody noticing it. In baseball after a bunt, the catcher goes for the safe play, to first, rather than risk the possibly game-winning play to second: "You're looking for a way out of the responsibility."

In individual sports the responsibility feared is that of being beaten, the need is to arrange surrender without being beaten. The rock climber who says he decided to quit because it wouldn't mean anything to continue is surrendering without being beaten. The great Canadian high jumper Debbie Brill, who admits that she couldn't handle the pressure, fared poorly at Munich. "I went through it, but I wasn't part of it," she says now. "I kept watching all those people and wondering, 'What am I doing here?' " She went through the motions; she avoided both the competition and the defeat.

Individuals compete to assert many things, and sometimes to surrender. It is important to understand this and to consider the possibility that on a particular occasion surrender, rather than defeat, occurred. Winning is much easier when you intend to win, much more difficult when you intend not to. Surrender seems so terribly appealing at times: "Why not forget the whole thing? Who cares anyway?" The Child within is crying, "I feel abandoned. I want to be protected from this pain. I don't care about your Adult aspirations or your Parental expectations." It's so easy to forget that you came out to compete, that winning is worth while—and that if you cease to be game, there is no game. When you feel, "It doesn't really matter," just try to remember that you'll be unable to feel that way for long.

44 / Luck

*I'm a great believer in luck. The harder I work,
the more of it I seem to have.*

—F. L. EMERSON

AT THE START OF THE FINAL RACE FOR SOLINGS IN THE 1976 OLYMPICS,
eight boats had a reasonable chance to win the gold medal. And after
the race was over, the top four boats were but 2.0 points apart! When
it gets that close, is the outcome determined by luck?

The purpose of competitive sport is to win, to be first rather than
second, or second rather than third. The final standings do not depend on how far, by how long an interval, or by how many points, the
winning boat is ahead of the second. Poul-Richard Jensen of Denmark
won the series with 46.7 points, and received the gold medal. John
Kolius of the United States was tied for second with Dieter Below, of
East Germany, at 47.4 points. His first in the final race broke that tie,
and he received the silver medal. Below was third and received the
bronze medal. Boris Budnikov of the U.S.S.R. would have won the
series and the gold medal had he remained ahead of Kolius on the final
beat of that final race, but he was passed, lost three points, and
dropped to fourth place, with 48.7 points.

After the sixth race Jensen led the fleet, with 36.7 points, but seven boats were within 14.0 points of him. Below seemed to be in the best position, with 37.4 points and no finish below fifth! Geert Bakker of Holland, Budnikov, Patrick Haegeli of France, Kolius, Willi Kuhweide of Germany, and Glen Dexter of Canada were close behind and within 9.0 points of each other. For the seventh race there was a steady, 12–16 knot, combined southwesterly gradient wind and lake breeze. After two general recalls the fleet got away, with Kolius, Dexter, and Budnikov leading from the middle of the line, and Below controlling Jensen in a crush at the weather end. Below would win the gold regardless of his own finish if he could keep Jensen below fifth and the others below third. At the first mark Kolius was in the lead, with Budnikov second. Dexter, in fifth, hit the jibe mark and fell from contention. Haegeli was ninth, Jensen tenth, and Below, having gambled on holding the Dane back and now only a spectator, was twelfth, just astern of Kuhweide and two places ahead of Bakker.

On the second beat, Budnikov passed Kolius and had the gold in his grasp. But on the same leg Jensen moved up to sixth, with Below seventh and Bakker eighth. A fifth for Jensen would beat Kolius, and a fourth would beat Budnikov even if he remained in the lead. But on the final round Kuhweide overtook Jensen, and Kolius once again took the lead from Budnikov. Coming up to the finish, Kolius was moving away from Budnikov and seemed in no danger. Gastao Brun and David Forbes held third and fourth with ease. The question was whether Kuhweide, in fifth, would hold off Jensen in the final yards. If so, Kolius, by virtue of his first, would break the tie with Below and win the gold medal. And Jensen in sixth would take the bronze, 0.3 points ahead of Budnikov.

The starboard end of the finish line was slightly more downwind. Brun was finishing there when Kuhweide, on starboard, crossed Jensen, a hundred yards from the line. As Jensen tacked to starboard on the port-end lay line, Kuhweide tacked to port. Would he play it safe, tack under Jensen, and go for the port end, or would he bear off, go astern, and shoot for the closer starboard end? Some of the spectators gasped in surprise as he bore off to go astern, but I reckoned he knew which end was favored. Suddenly, he tacked back to starboard and followed Jensen toward the wrong end of the line! Was he confused? Had he ceased to believe that the starboard end was favored *after* he had thrown away any chance to beat Jensen? But panic was hardly to be expected from the tough-minded Kuhweide, who more than any other competitor in the fleet, could have been expected to keep his composure when the chips were down. Regardless of its cause, his behavior snatched the gold from Kolius, handed it to Jensen, *and* dropped Below from the silver to the bronze.

Sailing home almost an hour later, Jensen professed to Bob Fisher that he hadn't realized that they had won the gold medal. He was surprised that a fifth place could have pulled it out and may have wondered at his good luck. But his two second places and his first in the sixth race had not been gifts. He had earned what he had won. Below must have wondered at his "bad luck." Why should Kolius, who in order to tie for the silver had to win the finale *and* have Below finish below fifth, pick this as his only race to win? And why should Kuhweide be the one in a position to pass Jensen through from sixth to fifth?

Before the start of the race, Below had decided, correctly, that Jensen was the man to beat. He had held Jensen back before the start, back to tenth at the end of the first round. He had done what he had intended. He had just not done it well enough. Jensen had passed him on the first beat and pulled progressively away thereafter. And Kuhweide was usually about fifth, and sometimes better. Below had no one and nothing to blame but himself. If he had sailed this race as well as he sailed any other, and come in fifth, he would have then tied Kolius for the gold and beaten Jensen.

After the race Kolius was quite happy with his silver. Rather than resenting the fact that Jensen (or Kuhweide) had snatched the gold away at the last possible second, he was congratulating himself on his "good luck" in moving up to second. He had counted himself out of the series on several previous occasions. But it wasn't luck that brought him a medal. From the start of the series he had been fast enough and good enough to win. Although he realized it belatedly, he was getting stronger with each race. Dexter bemoaned the fact that he had hit the jibe mark and was unable to continue between Kolius and Jensen—but a dozen other boats on a dozen other occasions must have dropped from their position between the two. Dexter did not determine the outcome. Nor did Haegeli or Bakker; each had had two disastrous races previously, one of which was to be counted. It wasn't luck that kept them from winning. And it certainly wasn't luck that caused Kuhweide to bear off astern of Jensen and tack on his quarter.

One final element might have been considered luck—bad for Budnikov, good for Jensen and Kolius and Below. Budnikov had been disqualified from the fourth race, in which he finished first. He would have won the gold medal without sailing the final race if he had retained that first. But it wasn't bad luck that caused him to tack too close to Dave Forbes as they approached the weather mark. It was daring and foolhardiness and perhaps too great a concern for the outcome. He got what he deserved, as did most of the rest of the fleet.

"Blame luck?" asks Casey Stengel. "Bad luck, your ass. You'll have bad luck all your life [if you believe that]. You make your own luck."

By and large, competitors behave as they can be expected to. They want to win, and do their best to do so. Their behavior is not a matter of luck. Nor is the behavior of the weather. Where the wind blows and with what velocity, when and how far it shifts, are decided by natural, determinable causes. That a boat down to leeward picks up the new breeze first is not luck. It is the logical consequence of the simultaneous breakthrough of a flow from aloft at many different sites. That the wind which was previously blowing there is now blowing here may not have been predictable, but the almost random distribution in light air should have been expected. That in a strong northwesterly a boat from the far right comes all the way across the course in a veer which persists for seven minutes is not luck. In strong northwesterlies such prolonged shifts may occur several times a day.

One of the things that does matter is boat speed. After the 1977 America's Cup races Ted Turner had this to say: "Last time seven or eight of us were in the ill-fated *Mariner-Valiant* campaign, and we wanted to come back to show that we weren't the bunch of hacks we seemed to be then. All it takes is a little boat speed to make anybody look like a hero." Being smart also matters, not just doing what the others do because they are doing it. C. A. Marchaj says, "Please understand, gentlemen, the majority is usually wrong." And being mentally tough matters, being able to perform deliberately and efficiently under stress. With boat speed, intelligence, and tough-mindedness you make your own luck.

Paul Elvstrom says, "The advice that I would give to a keen young skipper starting international racing is that he must always remember, however hard it is to accept, that the winner almost never wins through luck; there is always a reason for it." In his book *Elvstrom Speaks on Yacht Racing*, he describes how he watched Henning Jensen win a race, despite a late start, by sailing around the fleet becalmed ahead. "Oh. You were lucky!" Jensen became very angry and said, "Lucky?" "Oh, excuse me," said Elvstrom, "I meant that you were lucky that there was such a big cup for that race." That taught Elvstrom, he says, that it is never nice to say anyone is lucky to win a race, "because you are only lucky if you do something you can't foresee. . . . If there is something you can see, you must see it."

There is no such thing as luck, good or bad. You win because you performed better than the others. You lose because you performed less well than the others. (It is a useful intellectualization, however, to recognize that their doing better is a consequence of their "good luck"—and that yours is about to improve.)

45 / Gamesmanship

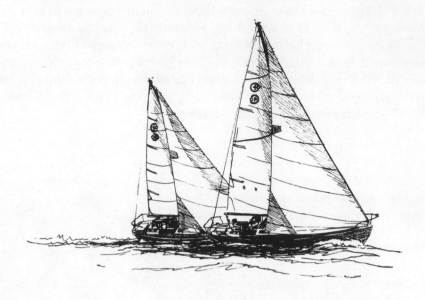

*Let us be thankful for fools. But for them the rest
of us could not succeed.*

—MARK TWAIN

BEFORE THE FINAL RACE OF THE 1973 GREAT LAKES CHAMPIONSHIP, WE
led Hans Fogh by 6.0 points. Before we left the dock, Hans came over
to me, held out his hand, and said, "Congratulations, I think you have
won the championship." I, of course, said, "Thank you," and appreciated his kindness. But then I thought, "Is he trying to set me up?" I
remembered the story of the tennis player who was being beaten and
came to his opponent to ask, "Where was your wrist on that shot?" He
hoped that the opponent would become so preoccupied with wondering where his wrist was that he would play poorly thereafter. On the
way to the start all I could think of was Hans's congratulations. I
realized that this preoccupation was taking my mind off the race and
the preparations I should be making. Although I saw that he was up at
the weather end, I elected to start down to leeward. We arrived at the
weather mark fourth, Hans was sixth, and so we stayed until the
leeward mark. We had a glorious tacking duel for half of the second

beat; after the first four boats were over the horizon, we let him go (or he escaped). In any case the series was over, and we had won.

Now, knowing Hans as well as I do, I doubt that he had any ulterior motive in his congratulations. I believe he was genuinely pleased for me and wanted to tell me so. But regardless of his intention, I subsequently recognized how nearly effective a distraction his congratulations had been. At the very least, he had me preoccupied with the question of what he meant, and close to wondering whether I deserved to be ahead and whether such a nice, competent guy as Hans didn't deserve the victory more than I did. I was well into the race before I was fully alert to my own performance.

Gamesmanship may be employed to distract the opponent (interfering with his realistic appraisal), to embarrass him (diminishing his self-appraisal), to make him anxious (disturbing his control of impulsivity), to make him feel unworthy (disturbing his control of guilt), to make him suspicious (undermining his trust), or to preoccupy him with a combination of these effects. Every element of ego function that is involved in competitive success can be manipulated by an opponent. Although not fully understood by its practitioners, gamesmanship—the art of this manipulation—is nevertheless effective. Every opponent has his Achilles' heel. The gamesman tries to discover what it is and to exploit that particular vulnerability. He plays an ulterior game consciously, deliberately. Gamesmanship is thus distinguished from the playing of unconscious ulterior "games." But both have the same adverse effect—upon the victim *and* the player.

Victor Korchnoi, after losing three straight games in a world chess championship, returned to the playing hall accompanied by a pair of turbaned and tangerine-robed mystic figures. His opponent, Anatoly Karpov, was sufficiently distracted by the presence of Korchnoi's spiritual guides to lose one game and settle for a draw in five of the next six. John Kolius has a piece of string tied to a stick, his "magic twanger," that he takes out and plays to the distraction of nearby sailors when the race gets tight. I remember attempting to distract the boys on the West Coast when I took my 14 out there to race in 1968. I had cut away the transom, leaving only about three inches of freeboard (except for the rudderpost) so as to facilitate drainage after a capsize. But when asked about this arrangement, I told the locals that I was surprised that they raced with "all that dead air trapped in the boat!" I also had a piece of shock cord (and still do) bridging the angle from mainsail leech to boom end to keep the spinnaker sheet from fouling. The West Coast boys seemed surprised to learn that everybody in the East had a similar "de-turbulizer," which increased the "end-plate effect" of the boom by diminishing the "wing-tip eddies." Whether anyone's performance was altered I cannot say, but there was a great deal of distraction ashore.

Far more effective than distraction is embarrassment— diminishing a competitor's self-appraisal. This is particularly likely to occur if he fails when he is trying his hardest. Vince Lombardi's philosophy was to go at the opponents' strength. When it became evident that Tony Dorsett was inclined to fumble, opposing teams went for the ball whenever he carried it. He fumbled in twelve of the seventeen games of the 1977 season, his embarrassment undoubtedly contributing to his problem. Emil Zatopek is said to have embarrassed a competitor into overextending himself. In an Olympic marathon, while sharing the lead, he commented that neither of them was running as fast as he should!

Stewart Morris is reputed to have carried in his stern tank a soggy sandwich that he would take out and pretend to munch while planing past a competitor to windward. Shorty Trimingham once reached over his transom, as he planed his International 14 past me in Bermuda, and threw off a great mass of seaweed. I discovered only later that he had carried the seaweed with him for the whole race, hoping for the opportunity to so use it! Paul Elvstrom tells the story of how he used a broken boom to his advantage while racing against Harald Eriksen in Finns. At the leeward mark he thanked Harald, who had been close to his transom for both of the reaches, "for staying there because my boom is broken and that's the reason I'm so slow!" This form of gamesmanship is effective because it makes the agent seem supernatural. How is it possible for him to go that fast, sail that well, with a broken boom, with all that seaweed on his rudder, while eating a sandwich?

Undermining the competitor's control of impulsivity, making him "nervous," may be damaging. The "secret weapons," the new sails ostentatiously exposed in their bags, are intended to worry the opponent. How can anyone compete against such an advantage? Tense and anxious, the opponent makes a mistake, fails to recognize a changed condition. In the seventh inning of the seventh game, after he had already won two games of the World Series, Grover Cleveland Alexander was brought in to strike out Tony Lazzeri. He walked slowly from the bullpen to the mound and then, practicing, whistled four successive fast balls across the plate. Lazzeri struck out.

Guilt is preoccupying and may make us act in a manner adverse to our long-term interests. Most competitors are already concerned with deservingness; to make them more concerned is to make them more easily conquered. Bucky Dent appeared injured when he left the field in the single play-off game of the 1978 season. Moments later he hit the home run that beat the Red Sox 3–2 and propelled the Yankees into the World Series. Ilie Nastase limps, and groans with a variety of aches and pains, before and during his matches. Although it is difficult to believe that any competitor would feel sorry for him, he at least distracts his opponents, causes them to be "other-oriented," more concerned with Nastase's play than with their own. Jim Palmer, the ace pitcher of the Baltimore Orioles, advises other pitchers to "act as if you feel lucky you struck him out. He'll be off guard the next time."

If the competitor can be made to feel that you should be pitied and supported and that his recent victory over you was unfair and undeserved, he may find himself impelled to atone for his sins. He is made to feel that he "owes" you one—and the next time you meet he will give you a break. Acting as if the game were meaningless also adds to the competitor's feeling of guilt. He "knows" he "shouldn't" be *so* concerned about a mere game. He feels guilty, and again, instead of flaunting his prowess he gives you a break.

André Nelis of Belgium was Paul Elvstrom's major rival in the Melbourne Olympics, and in one of the first races Nelis led him to the leeward mark. Elvstrom decided to drive straight through and over him, instead of making two tacks and going around—and did so! It was also at Melbourne, in a gale, that Paul made four jibes near the launching ramps, without mussing his hair, and while carrying on a conversation with Bjorg Schwartz! Before a race of the 1974 Soling Midwinters, Buddy Melges called out to Hans Fogh, one of his most dangerous rivals, "Will KC-119 please clear the line so that the Solings can start?" These taunts tell the opponents either that their competence is inferior (diminishing their self-appraisal) or that their aggressiveness is inferior (enhancing their guilt for daring to compete). Those on the receiving end know that they could not and would not behave similarly.

Competitors often do clever things during a contest. These may be impressive and engender respect (though they should not be intimidating), but they do not represent gamesmanship. They are not intended to adversely affect an opponent's psyche—only his performance. When an opponent ahead on the same tack (to windward or to leeward) appears to be in danger of overstanding, one's own tack should be continued until he tacks or the lay line is reached. There's no sense in tipping him off that the lay line is near. If the opponent is going for the wrong mark, one should maintain a course that convinces him it is the right mark, as long as this can be done without significantly compromising one's own position. The best story in this category is that of Peter Bordes, who was leading on a reach in a race of the Thistle Nationals when he recognized that the next mark was actually at 90° to his course and to that of the fleet astern. He let go his main halyard, jumped about the boat, and screamed wildly, until the fleet had sailed past, then rehoisted his main and roared off to the correct mark—in the lead once more!

The gamesman is a believer in the significance of psychology in determining the course and outcome of competition. He uses psychology to affect his opponent adversely, to weaken his ego functions, to make him more susceptible to his inclinations to impulsivity or guilt, to force him to use his own defenses. The gamesman intellectualizes his activity: "Isn't it interesting that I understand this game and my opponents so well? Look how powerful I am." Intellectualization separates the gamesman from the tension of the game itself, protects him from the anxiety inherent in the competition. But like all defenses it obscures appraisal and preoccupies awareness. The gamesman's game may suffer as much as that of his victim.

To practice gamesmanship is to substitute another game for the one being played. If gamesmen do poorly in the actual game, they may still satisfy themselves by dwelling upon their prowess in gamesmanship. For many, the defense works well, but of course these are people who are not competing, who are not game, and who are neither acquiring nor demonstrating competence. Some of those who practice gamesmanship are merely adding a flourish to their usual showing off. For them it provides an even more daring, even more exciting, exposure.

46 / Success Phobia

*Who is more foolish; the child afraid of the dark
or the man afraid of the light?*
—MAURICE FREEHILL

IT IS NOT CORRECT TO SUPPOSE THAT ALL COMPETITORS WISH TO WIN OR even that the majority are primarily motivated to do so. The wish to perform, to demonstrate skill, to become competent, is of primary significance to most. And competence once acquired must be demonstrated. (Once you've got it, it's very difficult not to flaunt it!) Winning follows but is incidental for many. For others, it is important—but not necessarily desired. It often represents a counterphobic effort to deny that winning is threatening; that is, it may actually represent a reaction to a need to lose. In addition, many competitors are overtly dedicated to *not* winning. These are of several types. (1) The majority are merely dedicated to maintaining what they regard as their deserved position in the pecking order. (2) Some are so fearful of losing that they dare not risk the kind of action which would lead to winning. (3) Others find winning so threatening that once they experience it they avoid it. (4) A few need to lose, and actively seek to do so.

But although a great many competitors do not intend to win, they do not exhibit a passive willingness to accept losing. If they experienced such a willingness, they would give up competition, or would not have entered competition in the first place. They do have the desire to compete and in many instances are required by their Parents to win. Hence, dedicated losers are found in the ranks of the most determined competitors and even in the ranks of frequent winners, characteristically those who are dramatically inconsistent.

The techniques used to avoid winning or achieve losing run the gamut of human behavior. As winning takes the co-ordination of many attributes and activities, so losing can be achieved by the subversion of any of them. It is important for most dedicated losers to disguise their intent so that it will go unrecognized by their competitors and by themselves. Since the need to comply with or to reject some Parentally determined standard of social acceptability usually underlies the need to lose, it is not surprising that the loser wants to hide a socially unacceptable wish. And the disguise works well. Few competitors recognize that this is a common behavior pattern, that the opponents they beat are often so dedicated to losing. And fewer still recognize the trait in themselves.

Bill Rodgers describes his marathon-racing behavior as "yin and yang": "I have a feeling after a bad race that my next one will be good. Of course, after a couple of good ones, I get the feeling I'm going to bomb out." He recognizes the problem but probably not the explanation. My young friend Wally Greene went 1–DSQ–1–DSQ–3–DSQ–1 and couldn't lose the Sears Cup if he finished the eighth race. He led all the way but missed a mark and was scored DNF. I wonder whether Chris Law's winning of the Finn Gold Cup (with ease) in early 1976 required him to lose (so completely) the subsequent Olympic trials to David Howlett. And whether Howlett's subsequent debacle in the Olympics may have represented a need to atone for beating Law in the trials.

When at CORK I accused Glen Foster of arriving early to prepare his boat and himself for the first time in his life, he was angered. He obviously never recognized during his 14 days that he had always appeared at the last moment and often without some essential piece of equipment. I remember asking him, after a special shroud fitting had pulled out and cost him the Spring Warner Trophy, whether he wasn't going to replace the identical fitting on the opposite side. He didn't—until it let go in the midst of the next regatta. David Thorpe's habitual missing of the first race, which, together with his success in subsequent races, prompted a competitor to hope that no one would give him a watch, was never recognized as a means to avoid winning—but it was an extremely successful technique.

Lack of attention to a competitor astern, a moment of indecision on the starting line, failure to recognize that the vang is still on (or off), are scarcely detectable—and only moderately successful—means of avoiding a win. One *can* win despite them. Many resort to more effective and therefore more obvious techniques, which cry out for recognition. Being disqualified works extremely well. In the old days one could always run into a mark. I wonder how many fewer marks have been hit since it was decided that this was a remediable offense—and how many more close crossings on port have been attempted. Unless the helmsman of the starboard-tack boat is determined to disqualify his opponent, most port/starboard disqualifications must be considered suicidal in origin. It is after all pretty obvious when a bearing is unchanging. Other reasonably direct techniques follow the announcement that winning doesn't matter, isn't important, and is socially unacceptable—which is usually a way of saying, "I intend to lose and I don't want you to condemn me for it."

The usual reason for a deliberate avoidance of winning is that the individual has a greater need to maintain some lower position—and the result is the pecking order. Each competitor has an idea of where he *should* finish and works mightily to ensure that he does so on each occasion. This, of course, is a major reason why the top competitors finish on top so regularly and manage to work their way back through the fleet so rapidly when they do get behind. The greats of yesteryear are often maintained in their top rankings long after they should be because of the concern of their young competitors not to usurp their "rightful" positions. The fact that the pecking order works to keep most competitors astern indicates that most perceive their deserved position as behind. In other words, they appraise themselves as defective in comparison with others; they belittle themselves.

Belittling is a common attribute which may not be recognized as a form of success phobia. However, it certainly results in failure and it certainly is deliberate. Many competitors talk down to themselves: "You dummy, you blew it again—just as I knew you would!" Self-deprecation is at least semiconscious. They expect to fail, and feel it was a fluke when they succeed. Dave Stockton, asked before the Masters Golf Tournament whom he feared most, showed he knew the truth when he replied, "Me!"

The source of belittling is, of course, the belittling, disrespectful, parent. As a pediatrician, I am impressed by how disrespectful of their children American parents tend to be. Children are frequently treated like pets or servants or even slaves. Their parents only infrequently demonstrate a respect for their individuality, privacy, creativeness, or need for self-determination. Perfectionism (never being satisfied with the child's efforts) and impressed overresponsibility (asking the child to demonstrate a degree of maturity, or to limit his self-interest, beyond a level appropriate to his age) are almost as disrespectful.

Cultural attitudes contribute to belittling as well. Emphasis is placed not upon what is accomplished but upon what is publicly recognized, not upon the demonstration of competence but upon winning. The child notes the adults about him fighting not for competence but for recognition, for approval. He hears the moralizing that belittles him unless he is "good" and the prejudice that belittles him unless he is "right." It is not surprising that with both his parents and his society telling him he will be approved only if he is good, right, and victorious, he belittles himself when he is bad, wrong, or defeated, and comes to believe, when he fails so often, that he is defective and deserves to fail.

Self-belittlers have a great need for approval, for acceptance; they fear to offend others, to do anything which would antagonize their competitors. They fear to usurp the places of those (Parent representatives?) whom they assume to be superior. Their internalized Parents constantly remind them that they should "behave," mind their manners, be content with what they deserve. Whenever they receive anything they don't deserve—when they get ahead temporarily, or even win—they are made to feel guilty and therefore depressed. They soon learn that to avoid further pain and feelings of alienation they must keep their "place."

In the society of competitors, the self-belittler finds only reinforcement for his self-deprecation. He hungers for love and acceptance; he needs compliments, admiration, support. He needs to reinforce his sense of self-worth by treating himself with more respect, as a friend rather than as an enemy. Yet if he attempts to displace existing winners, he perceives that he is resented. Only if he finishes where he "belongs" does he see himself as accepted, liked at least if not loved. But as a loser he gains no admiration, no respect, and he develops no additional respect for himself. He is held in bondage—to the pecking order and to his own disrespect.

Some individuals avoid winning because they fear to risk losing. They dare not place themselves in a position where losing will be recognizable. They use various defenses—denial, rationalization, escape, displacement—to arrange never to be beaten. When they lose it is because the wind was shifty, the course too long, the current inconsistent with expectations—because something outside their control occurred. They never allow themselves to become involved in head-to-head conflicts, which would result in obvious victory or defeat. Carl Van Duyne showed what I now recognize to be remarkable insight when, after he had been disqualified in the first two races of the 1968 Olympic Finn races, I suggested that he feared to win. No, he told me, he feared too much to lose. Similarly, the 1978 Red Sox may have found the fear of failure to be intolerable. Rather than postpone the inevitable disaster, they folded in August, and though they subsequently demonstrated that they were clearly as capable as Carl Van Duyne of winning, they did lose, by the slimmest possible margin, tying for the seasonal lead and losing the play-off game.

Other competitors are afraid of winning itself. Some fear the restrictions imposed by the need to keep on winning. Some are concerned that their winning will not be accepted by others. Some fear loss of approval due to resentment of their victory; they fear to be alienated from the crowd. Many fear loss of approval because their internalized Parents tell them that demonstrating superiority, beating others, is unacceptable. For them, defeating an opponent is depressing rather than elating. Losing may be used not only to avoid guilt but as a means of punishment, a means of atonement, for previous aggressiveness. This is one of the major reasons for alternating wins and losses; aggressiveness results in winning, and winning through aggressiveness makes a loss in the next contest essential

A few competitors actually need to lose. But because their losing is partially counterphobic and often associated with a concurrent need to win, they often win. Consequently, they too are among the individuals who tend to win and lose alternately. The two major reasons for needing to lose are to hurt someone, usually a parent (or coach), and to reassure someone, usually a parent, that winning is not intended.

Parents (or coaches) who place excessive emphasis upon a particular competitive activity and become personally involved in the child's sport may find that their interest is resented. The child begins to feel that he is used by the parent to fulfill the parental interests. He may feel cheated of a sense of accomplishment when he does well (it is the parent who does well) and excessively responsible when he does poorly. He may become so resentful that he cuts off his nose to spite his face—he loses. He may then feel elation when he loses and is able to partially atone for his sin (failure to comply with parental demands) through postfailure depression.

Losing may represent surrender to a fear of retaliation. The child equates winning with obtaining the forbidden advantage of the mother's exclusive attention and guiltily fears that the father will retaliate if, in fact, the mother is won. The fear of the "father's" retaliation, which may be accompanied by a need to avoid direct confrontations during competition, necessitates losing. Failure to win avoids the anxiety imposed by the fear of retaliation; losing is felt to reassure the "father" that winning was never intended.

The range of reasons for losing is wide, and the techniques of losing are manifold. Competitors who feel undeserving may never make an effort sufficient to develop competence, and may never win. They appear satisfied with their mediocre standing, and none of their competitors objects to their satisfaction. By contrast, those with a more intense need to avoid winning or achieve losing must deny the need. Therefore, periodically they dare to win, and they force themselves to develop competence so that they have something to lose.

Part Six

Competence

47 / Courage

*A hero is no braver than anyone else; he is only
brave five minutes longer.*

—RALPH WALDO EMERSON

PORT TACK WAS LIFTED AT THE START OF THE FOURTH RACE OF THE 1976
Fall Soling Bowl. We tacked to port and led three others away from
the starboard end of the line. A look astern indicated that if the expected veer appeared, we would have a huge lead over the boats which
had held starboard tack from the line. The veer appeared, we tacked,
and the lead was as expected. Our three original neighbors continued
on port. The wind began to back; our advantage over the boats to the
left began to deteriorate. We could now make a big gain over the three
port-tackers, who were returning from the right corner on starboard.
We tacked and appeared to have the expected advantage. Now, well
in the lead, I began to think about protecting the advantage. The three
to the right were well under control. I decided that I really had to get
back in front of that mob in the left corner. I tacked to starboard in a
minimal veer—which continued and lifted the three inside me. I
didn't look as good as I had expected against the boats on the left, and
the three on the right were gaining rapidly. I had made a small mis-

take by tacking to starboard early in the veer. Now I made a big one. I went to port again before the veer had been completed and crossed just astern of the three to the right. Now to the right of the entire fleet when the following back appeared, I lost the leading boat from the far left and rounded the weather mark fifth, with the whole pack close astern.

Now it's easy to say that I shouldn't have sailed on a relatively headed tack twice, that I should have maintained whatever tack would have given me the greatest gain. If I had stuck to starboard tack when I appeared to be making a big gain with respect to boats to the left and stuck to port when I appeared to be making a big gain with respect to boats to the right, as would have been sensible (particularly when in the lead), I would have led to the weather mark with ease. But why did I make such obvious mistakes? At the time, I believed that I was being sensibly conservative, consolidating my gains. In fact, I had lost the courage that had gained me the lead in the first place, and was fearful of losing what I had gained.

Courage comes easily at the start or immediately thereafter, when all is possible and there is nothing to lose. We start as equals; we perceive equal opportunity, look ahead to the possibility of winning, have no awareness of the possibility of losing. The further the race progresses and the more we acquire a position of advantage, the more we become aware that we may lose that advantage. The courageous, confident, assured attitude we had at the start gradually turns into a fearful, diffident, anxious attitude as the finish line approaches. Prior to the race we gleefully await its occurrence; halfway through (if we are doing as well as or better than expected) we wish it were over. We convert play into work, joy into fear. Initially we delight in the uncertainty, the risk, the chance to win. Later in the race we try to eliminate the risk, and concentrate upon retaining what we've gained.

In many circumstances—notably when the wind is steady and moderate to strong—we learn that this is a sensible technique. The remembrance of such occasions tends to justify "conservative" behavior late in a race. But in light air, when a new wind may appear unexpectedly, and in oscillating winds, when the headed tack results in dramatic loss, conservatism is disastrous. There is a fine line, difficult to draw in the heat of battle, between a sensible conservatism and a timidity caused by the fear of losing.

Johnny Miller once said, "Most guys go out there, make a couple of birdies, and think to themselves, 'Gee, I hope I can get in with a 69, *that* would be a good score today.' When I start hitting it close and getting them in the hole, I try to keep doing it. I want to make all I can to make up for the round I may have tomorrow when nothing drops." He means that a competitor cannot afford to be protective. The opposition is pressing; given a break, they'll push ahead. He is also saying that if one is going to play the game, one should play it fully, courageously.

The attainment of competence depends upon courage, and the competent competitor demonstrates courage—courage, creativity, and mastery. Courage is essential. It characterizes those who perform at levels never reached by others, who break records, who create new techniques, new solutions. Courage is a degree of emotional stability that permits one to face reality calmly, to apply rational methods to problem solving, and to act in one's long-term best interests in the presence of fear, threats, and guilt, despite anxiety or depression. All psychological studies demonstrate the major contribution of this trait to success.

Sailing differs from most sports in that a regatta is usually spread over many days; Olympic and world championships are often decided by a series of seven races, on seven successive days. Not only may a change in attitude and behavior occur during the course of a single race but a progressive alteration may be evident from day to day during a series. John Albrechtson, the 1976 gold medalist in the Tempest class, sailed better and better as the Olympics progressed although it was evident to everyone in contact with him that he was becoming more and more tense. He knew that he had the gold medal in his grasp but that having had one bad race (the fifth), he couldn't afford another mistake. It would be so easy to blow it; so many people were depending upon him (it would be Sweden's only gold medal); he might never have another chance. The fear was there, but he didn't let it interfere.

It is easy to participate "playfully" at the beginning of a race and in the early races of a series. And it is easy to be playful, relaxed, at case, when the game has been lost, when one is so far behind in the race or series that the result no longer matters. It takes courage to maintain that playfulness, that enthusiasm, that delight in the risks to come, when one is nearing the end of a race or series in a position equal to or greater than that expected. More than any other Olympic event, the marathon must, as the end nears, tax the ability of the participant to maintain an enthusiasm, a joy in the activity itself. Erich Segal says of the finisher (not just the winner), "He has beaten fear, he has beaten pain, he has conquered the marathon." What temptation there must be for a marathon runner to feel, "I wish this were over, I've done enough, I don't care," and to give up. Not giving up is the conquest of fear. Fear is a tempter, holding out the easy alternative of escape, the opiate that "it doesn't matter."

Courage is the ability to be daring when it does matter. Anyone can be daring when all is lost—and many believe that it is sensible to "take a flyer" when far behind. Anyone can be daring at the start, when as yet there is nothing to lose. Courage permits the same behavior when there is something to lose. The pecking order is in part based upon the willingness of many competitors to settle for a single, transient evidence of enhanced performance. "I led to the weather mark; that's enough ["to satisfy me" or "to demonstrate my potential superiority" or "to reassure me that I'm as good as they"] for this weekend. Now I'll drop back to my accustomed position." This is the attitude that keeps most competitors from moving ahead of the pack. They struggle only when they are behind their expected position. Once in front, they haven't the courage to maintain their lead. They don't dare risk doing the right thing. They stay between the opposition and the next mark and are passed on both sides. Sometimes they sacrifice themselves, symbolically lying down so as to be ridden over.

Daring must be tempered, of course. An excess of daring may be merely another means of surrendering. "I'll tack away [or "jibe away," "bear away"], daring to be different, so as to let you go by without my being aware that you are beating me!" Sometimes it is more courageous to stand fast, particularly when being overtaken.

A few competitors have no fear and are equally at ease when winning or losing. They play the game entirely for its own sake, can enjoy it as much under the tension of a close finish as at the start. These few perform well and often win. They are not distracted. They solve problems realistically, regardless of their significance. But they are not courageous. Courage is the ability to solve problems realistically in the presence of fear. Most of us must rely upon courage. Fear will be present; the risk of performing poorly is real, and cannot and should not be denied. Courage permits us to set aside the fear and carry on. Courage permits the game to remain a game, the play to remain playful, the caliber of performance to continue at its peak, until the finish line is crossed. And makes winning much more likely.

48 / Mastery

The reward of a thing well done is to have done it.
—RALPH WALDO EMERSON

COURAGE LEADS TO MASTERY, AND IT IS MASTERY THAT IS ENJOYABLE. Courage is an awareness that despite fear and guilt one is in control of oneself—of both the Parent and Child, while they contribute to competence and to enjoyment. The awareness of this control is satisfying. (Since courage is of major importance to survival, it is not surprising that experiencing it should be pleasurable.) To the player without control, the game is frightening, and he may use it as a vehicle to deny fear; or he may manipulate it to gain approval, to ward off feelings of inadequacy, to avoid guilt. Courage permits the player to be game, and mastery permits the game to be played joyfully.

Psychiatrist Stephen Rosenblum says of competition, "The experience of competing and winning is a creative activity engaged in by a confident and complete self. It is the pleasure of mastering and creating that leads to its repetition." The attainment of competence is a re-creation of one's self through courage. The enjoyment is in the awareness that one has caused the change, that one has demonstrated the power to create that new self. The joy in striving is due to an awareness of prospective re-creation and the joy in mastery is due to a display of re-creation.

A neophyte climber describes his joy in displaying his competence as follows: "At the top I just kind of went, 'Whew, that was pretty good.' I knew I had made a move or two far more difficult than anything I had ever done before. Reaching the top wasn't exactly an anticlimax, but I didn't feel especially high—until late that evening as I lay in bed. It was a delayed reaction. The next morning when I woke up, I felt so terrific I whooped when I got out of bed. Nothing special happened that day—I can't even remember what I did—but I do know it somehow was the best day I had all year, no exaggeration. The high lasted for a few more days; every time I thought about climbing that rock I broke into a big grin."

To be game is to believe in the game and to be open to the joy of demonstrated mastery. During an event there is an awareness of fear, of desire to achieve, of concern about failure. Success is valued, but one does not enter the game in order to be successful. Rather, one seeks an opportunity to display mastery in the presence of a significant risk of failure. Mark Hayes, while winning the Pensacola Open, said that it was useless "to go out and try to win a tournament. You just kind of got to let it happen." When a competitive event is perceived as a "happening," when delight is taken in the opportunity to play, winning is more likely to "happen." It cannot, it should not, be forced. A continuous disregard for outcome permits the full exercise of intellect and skill to achieve the best in performance.

I am a good sailor and I often win, but after all these years, I should be good and win often. I cannot take too much credit for having lasted this long. Still, I find elation in sailing well. I remember a March day on the Severn, with a 25-knot northwesterly, ice crystallizing on the sails, my crew hiked in the spray, *Light Brigade* strapped down and charging to weather, when, with no competition in sight, I was elated, enjoying my competence. Competition would have provided additional excitement, additional tension, a more structured, more significant opportunity to display my competence. But winning would have provided only relief from the tension of exposing myself to the risk of failure. My own assessment of my competence would still have provided the joy.

One of my long-time competitors recently asked me what I

meant by this nonsense about winning not being important. I told him I never said it wasn't important. (It is, after all, the only way one can satisfy the desire to be assertive and approved, independent and dependent, simultaneously.) Winning is the object of the game. One is supposed to try to win. I merely propose a better, a more satisfying, and a more certain route to winning: seek competence and enjoy striving toward it.

The attainment of competence and therefore success depends upon the acquisition of the ego functions discussed in this book. Central to this attainment is control over one's self. The Child must be controlled so that fearfulness and impulsivity are suppressed while aggressiveness, assertiveness, delight, and spontaneity are released. The Parent must be controlled so that one can take risks without fear of failure. The need to look good should not block utilization of opportunities to be spontaneous, playful, distinctive. An appropriate balance should be maintained between daring and equanimity.

Realism is the key to effective performance. If one can assess internal and external reality, know one's self and one's world, one can learn. To the extent that the truth remains hidden, to whatever extent any truth remains hidden, learning is impaired. Most of what is hidden is concealed deliberately, to protect the ego from pain. To the extent that it is necessary to resort to unreality, progress toward competence is impeded. Incompetence in appraisal leads to incompetence in control. For many, competence is forever out of reach, the way to it barred by an inability to accept reality. The individual with an effective ego is able to distinguish between the consequences of his own behavior and those of the behavior of others, to separate what is modifiable from what must be accepted. The people who rail against the fates or sink into complacent acceptance are unable to make this distinction. Some are intimidated and many are confused by the question of deservingness. Unable to distinguish the game from the real world, they do not recognize the simple truth that in the game everyone is equally deserving.

Jim Brown says, "When you feel like 'the man,' you play like 'the man'!" While being realistic in self-appraisal, one can still maintain a feeling of distinction, a feeling of being special, that permits pressure to be enjoyed and prevents the significance of the event from causing distraction. Despite failure, despite embarrassment, despite the temptation to take the easy way out, to surrender, or to cheat, one can

maintain a positive self-appraisal and act in one's long-term best interests. Defenses, gamesmanship, "game" playing, and so-called positive
thinking are unnecessary.

In control of Child and Parent, capable of realistic appraisal, the
mature ego concentrates on what matters and ignores what doesn't
matter or would interfere. A story is told about Jack Nicklaus preparing to tee off in a strong wind while the tee sign creaked on its hinges.
Everyone in the gallery cringed, anticipating that the creaking would
disturb his concentration. But Nicklaus hit a beautiful drive. He
never heard the noise. Irving Berlin has said that "the toughest thing
about success is that you have to keep on being a success." The competent competitor has no such concern. He feels, with Nicklaus, that
"winning breeds more winning." He ignores the past and the present.
He is not concerned with consistency, reputation, or significance. He
feels no need to concentrate on what he is doing. Instead he is alert to
what will happen next, what he will do next.

Competence is demonstrated, and success is determined, by the
continuous application of optimal solutions—the correct decision, the
correct response, the correct adjustment, again and again. The great
competitors, the truly competent, never let up. They conceive every
game and every action to be significant.

Both the attainment of competence and its demonstration require
that defenses be used but transiently and be recognized as temporary
protection only. Denial and intellectualization may provide short-
term aid in putting the past aside, ignoring adversity, and disregarding mistakes. But magical thinking, surrender, responses made to satisfy extraneous pressures, "game" playing, must be avoided. Defenses
at the very least interfere with learning and may result in deliberate
defeat.

Finally, the competent competitor lives by a code that transcends
mere observance of the rules. He is free from suspicion; he trusts his
teammates and his opponents. He plays no "games."

Now, few competitors, if any, can reach this level of maturity,
can attain complete mastery of themselves and their game. But every
competitor can and should analyze his behavior and recognize where
and when it seems inconsistent with his desire to attain competence.
He should look particularly hard at repetitive failure, which is usually
the manifestation of some extraneous need. He should consider the
feelings and mannerisms that he exhibits while failing. He should
record these experiences to see whether they form a pattern, whether

they correlate with a recognizable circumstance. Once such a circumstance is identified, a reminder can be arranged by which the possible recurrence of the behavior can be anticipated and forestalled.

Finding a solution to psychological problems is never easy. The first and most essential step is to recognize them. Competitors are said to be particularly lacking in insight, but books like this one should help convince them that they should make the effort. Having been recognized, problems should be dealt with one by one. Just as improvement in skill is attained through practice, a step at a time, so psychological improvement should be attempted in an organized fashion: "In *this* event I will attempt to avoid *this* pitfall." Failure is to be expected, but ultimately progress will be recognized. And the reward—in winning, in competence, and in joy—will be far in excess of any achievable by attention to other matters. It will be worth any effort.

A summary of the characteristics of mastery, never fully attainable but the most worthy of goals, follows.

What Is Required for the Development and Demonstration of Competence—the Attainment of Mastery

1. Self-control
    a) Control of the Child—an appropriate balance between release and suppression
        (1) Release of joy, responsiveness, aggressiveness, determination, creativity, and delight in play, challenge, and surprises
        (2) Suppression of impulsivity, hostility, and fears of powerlessness, dependence, and insignificance
    b) Control of the Parent—an appropriate balance between release and suppression
        (1) Release of the ability to derive satisfaction from receiving approval and from being trusting and conscientious
        (2) Suppression of the need to comply, to be approved, to win, and of fears of abandonment, loss of approval, and failure
    c) Courage—an awareness of control
        (1) The ability to perceive realistically and to act decisively in one's long-term best interests despite anxiety or guilt
        (2) The ability to obtain enjoyment from the development and demonstration of competence
2. Realistic appraisal
    a) Recognition of the difference between the game and the real

world, of the fact that in the game deservingness is not relevant

    b) Recognition of one's own motivations and intentions, and of the outcomes desired

    c) Recognition of one's own defenses, gamesmanship, "game" playing, and tendencies toward being intimidated

3. Self-assurance—maintaining a belief in oneself, a feeling of distinction, despite:

    Pressure (the significance of the event)

    Failure

    Embarrassment

    Temptation—to accept, to surrender, to be approved

4. Realistic remembrance, attention, and conception

    a) Remembrance of lessons learned, attention to the immediate future, conception of personal significance

    b) Ignorance of past failure, present distraction, and future significance

5. Trust and respect

    a) Trust and respect for the game and one's conception of it

    b) Avoidance of extraneous personal concern with particular opponents, team members, or officials

6. Appropriate use of defenses

    a) Recognition that defenses provide only transient protection, at the expense of impaired appraisal

    b) Use of denial and intellectualization to cope with adverse conditions, impaired performance, or the temporary success of an opponent

    c) Avoidance of magical thinking, surrender, and "game" playing

Bibliography

Berne, Eric. *Games People Play*. New York: Grove Press, 1964.

Butt, Dorcas Susan. *Psychology of Sport*. New York: Van Nostrand Reinhold, 1976.

Cattell, Raymond B., and Butcher, John H. *The Prediction of Achievement and Creativity*. Indianapolis: Bobbs-Merrill Company, 1968.

Elvstrom, Paul. *Elvstrom Speaks on Yacht Racing*. Chicago, Quadrangle Books, 1970.

Erikson, Erik H. *Childhood and Society*. New York: W. W. Norton & Company, 1964.

Fraiberg, Selma H. *The Magic Years*. New York: Charles Scribner's Sons, 1959.

Gallwey, W. Timothy. *The Inner Game of Tennis*. New York: Random House, 1974

Gardner, John W. *Excellence*. New York: Harper & Brothers, 1961.

Harris, Sydney J. *Winners and Losers*. Niles, Illinois: Argus Communications, 1973.

Hoyt, Garry. *Go for the Gold*. Chicago, Quadrangle Books, 1971.

Illingworth, John H. *Where Seconds Count*. Southampton: Adlard Coles, 1959.

Illingworth, Ronald S. *The Normal Child*. Edinburgh: Churchill Livingstone, 1953.

Lasch, Christopher. *The Culture of Narcissism*. New York: W. W. Norton & Company, 1978.

Lidz, Theodore. *The Person*. New York: Basic Books, 1968.

Lorenz, Konrad. *On Aggression*. New York: Harcourt, Brace & World, 1966.

May, Rollo. *The Courage to Create*. New York: W. W. Norton & Company, 1975.

Michener, James A. *Sports in America*. New York: Random House, 1976.

Neale, Robert E. *In Praise of Play*. New York: Harper & Row, 1969.

Novak, Michael. *The Joy of Sports*. New York: Basic Books, 1976.

Rank, Otto. *Beyond Psychology*. New York: Dover Publications, 1941.

Ringer, Robert J. *Winning Through Intimidation*. New York: Funk & Wagnalls, 1974.

Scott, Peter. *The Eye of the Wind*. London: Hodder & Stoughton, 1961.

Tutko, Thomas, and Tosi, Umberto. *Sports Psyching*. Los Angeles: J. P. Tarcher, 1976.

The Olympian Magazine (published by the United States Olympic Committee, Colorado Springs, Colorado), 1974–1979.

Sports Illustrated, 1969–1979.